REMEMBER
WHO YOU ARE

What **PEDRO GOMEZ** Showed Us About Baseball and Life

A BOOK OF ESSAYS, EDITED BY STEVE KETTMANN

WELLSTONE CENTER
in the Redwoods

Copyright © 2021 by Wellstone Books

Cover art by Mark Ulriksen

Book Design: Alicia Feltman of Lala Design

Picture Editor: Brad Mangin

For updates on book events, coverage, etc.:
www.TheGomezRules.com

Printed in the United States of America

FIRST EDITION ISBN:
978-0-9600615-1-8

Wellstone Books is an imprint of the Wellstone Center in the Redwoods
www.wellstoneredwoods.org
858 Amigo Road, Soquel, CA 95073

Distributed by Publishers Group West

PEDRO GOMEZ

1962-2021

Sandi and Pedro

Dante, Rio, Sierra, Pedro and Sandi

Sierra and Pedro

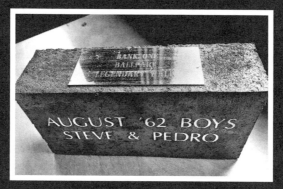

AUGUST '62 BOYS
STEVE & PEDRO

INTRODUCTION

BY STEVE KETTMANN

My first reaction was to be mad at Bob Nightengale for calling on a Sunday evening. My six-year-old daughter, Coco, had just made herself a salad, start to finish, for the first time, gathering the miner's lettuce herself, washing and spinning it, mixing up a dressing of olive oil, lemon and honey. We were at the kitchen table and Coco was raising her fork. Just then Bob texted. And called. And texted again. I tried to ignore him, so I could focus on sharing this little milestone with Coco. A voice inside my head wouldn't let me: The Gomez Rules did not allow it.

Bob and I had in common a great friend named Pedro Gomez, and if another friend of Pedro's called and wanted something, the rules were clear: You picked up. Maybe Bob, a *USA Today* baseball writer, needed my help on something. Maybe it was about Pete Rose or Jose Canseco. I'd worked closely with both on book projects. So I called Bob back and will never stop hearing the catch in his voice as he asked me, "Are you sitting down?" Then Bob told me that Pedro had died, suddenly, at home in Ahwatukee, Arizona, shortly before the Super Bowl. He was fifty-eight.

I immediately called Pedro's wife, Sandi, and we talked in hushed, shocked voices for a while. For me as for so many others who loved Pedro, his death hit first as the story of a husband and father, a man who always talked about "hitting the Lotto" in marrying the love of his life, Sandi, and a proud father who talked constantly about his three children, Rio, Dante and Sierra. The first ripple of pain came with knowing what a void his loss would leave in their lives.

Then came the selfish part of grief, for so many of us, the feeling of having a part of ourselves ripped away. It was as if a vital organ had suddenly been lost that channeled our capacity for joy and enthusiasm for life. Pedro was in love with life and in love with all his friends. He made sure you felt that, every time you connected. That was true if you'd met him once years ago or, like me, been one of his best friends for decades. ("It's your wife!" Sandi would kid Pedro when I called the house yet again in the '90s.)

It's hard to pull many recollections from the deep fog of those first days after the stunning news, but at some point that week my wife, Sarah, and I packed up our 2003 Honda Accord, snapped Coco and Anaïs into their car seats, and set off for an eleven-hour drive to see Sandi and the family in Arizona. Along the way the scenes kept flashing at me. I thought of the time I decided to surprise Sarah for her birthday by taking her to Tegel Aiport in Berlin, where we lived, without telling her we were flying to Venice. Two days into our stay, she ran into Pedro in the lobby of our hotel. He did his best to sell her on the idea he was surprised to see her. Obviously at some level she knew Pedro and I must have cooked this whole scenario up, all of us running into each other in Venice. But when Pedro sold something, he sold it all the way.

"No, what are *you* doing here?" Pedro kept repeating to Sarah in that small lobby, unleashing the full Gomez conviction and a blinding blizzard of charm. We laughed over that one the whole next day, during the requisite gondola ride, Sarah and Sandi and Pedro and me (hey, it was fun, even if Pedro "went Cuban" a little on the mouthy gondolier, as he himself put it with a shrug). Even years later, Pedro still loved to tell that story, laughing before he could start, one more greatest hit in the vast collection.

It's odd to lose a very close friend, to see his death ripple out to millions, and to come to understand that for many of them, this was a deeply painful loss as well. Pedro brought people in baseball together in death as in life. When word spread on Super Bowl Sunday that Pedro had died, a thunder-clap of shock and grief shook nearly everyone in the game, sooner or later. Barry Bonds was among many who sent flowers.

I can tell you that right up until the end, Pedro was doing what he loved. He was, in fact, midsentence, telling a story, when the end came as he stood in his kitchen, not far from where the Super Bowl would be showing on his living-room screen, game time not far off. RIP PEDRO was soon trending on Twitter. *The New York Times* published an obit, memorializing Pedro as "A Pillar of Baseball Coverage for ESPN." Emotional tributes proliferated, not only on ESPN—by in particular

Shelley Smith and Rachel Nichols—but also in newspapers all over the country. (Only later did the autopsy reveal that the cause of death was "sudden cardiac arrest," a detail left out of the first wave of coverage.)

For this book, we reached out to Max Scherzer, whose intensity on the mound Pedro compared to one of his all-time favorites, Dave Stewart, the ultimate embodiment of bringing everything you've got when the moment is biggest. I'd been hearing highlights of Pedro's conversations with Max for years, and knew he'd be eloquent on Pedro. I'll admit I'm a little blown away by the sweetness of his contribution, #7, "Have Fun Every Single Day."

"Pedro saw baseball for what it was," Max writes. "He never forgot how fun it was to go to a game. That was something I immediately gravitated towards. I loved that I could just sit there in front of my locker and talk to Pedro about baseball, and have it be such a delightful conversation because of his insight and his positive personality. Before you knew it you'd look up and see you'd already been talking for an hour."

How would Max try to put into words what Pedro stood for? "Have fun every single day. Whoever you come across, try to find the good in people. And when you find good people, talk to them even more. I feel like that's what Pedro did. He understood who the good eggs were and who the bad eggs were. When you find a good egg, make sure that you always go in depth and you can talk about anything. Building those human relationships is worth more than one story's clickbait."

That open, alert quality of Pedro's pulled him far beyond the limited universe of baseball, and sports more broadly. The story of Pedro in March 1999 returning to Cuba for the first time has now become familiar to many. We were there for a game between the Cuban National Team and the Baltimore Orioles, but Pedro had much more on his mind. Bob Ley, who might have launched ESPN as much as ESPN launched him, writes in his essay that "the most emotional interview" of Pedro's thirty-seven-year career in newspapers and TV must have been on that visit with a former neighbor of his parents in the Havana neighborhood where he'd been conceived. Pedro's parents were finally able to catch an Eastern Airlines flight to Miami to flee Fidel Castro's regime in late July 1962, three months before the Cuban Missile Crisis—and three weeks before Pedro was born. His mother always told him about a strident communist neighbor who ridiculed his parents for their decision to leave. Pedro found that neighbor, Rodolfo Fernandez-Guzman, and talked to him about his parents, thirty-seven years later.

It was an astonishing tour de force of reporting, published in the *Arizona Republic*, and it's widely remembered. Yet I don't think most people are aware of the brave political stance Pedro also took on that first visit. I was there with him—I filed articles for Salon and the *San Francisco Examiner*—and the idea might have come up when Pedro and I were walking the streets of Havana, playing stickball with some kids using wadded-up tape as the ball in a Casa Blanca alleyway, or possibly during a long dinner in a private-home restaurant with a sumptuous view. I don't remember. We talked about it for hours before Pedro decided to write a piece calling on the President of the United States to end the economic embargo of Cuba, a stance he well knew would cost him many friends back home in Miami and lead to countless arguments, Gomez at the center of a circle of worked-up Cuban friends or family members all chopping the air with their hands to make a point as they ganged up on him. (I was there in Miami for some of those later sessions, as a matter of fact, the presence of a longhaired *comunista* from Berkeley, as they saw me, only adding to the list of indictments to be read to their favored son who'd lost his way.)

That Open Letter to Bill Clinton was printed on the cover of the *Arizona Republic's* Arts & Ideas Section, which made Pedro very proud at the time, and we print it in full in this collection at #9. "For so many Cubans living in the United States, it is easy to stand on a platform and declare how the U.S. economic embargo must never be lifted as long as Fidel Castro remains in power," Pedro wrote from Havana just before he and I watched a game in the stands at the Estadio Latinoamericano, maybe a dozen rows back from Fidel. "I am sympathetic to that point of view, having been raised with that idea. All I can say is that after talking to regular everyday Cubans, not the elite from the Communist Party, my feelings have changed dramatically."

After Pedro had made the transition to TV and shown he was a natural, T.J. Quinn and I started working on him to run for Congress. We were serious, very serious. We told him we thought that sooner or later, growing Latin voter registration would help turn Arizona blue. Pedro had met both George W. Bush and John McCain on different occasions and respected both men. He came away from those encounters impressed with the warmth and genuineness of both, but Pedro was a Democrat all the way, as political strategist Paul Begala makes clear in his essay on his lively friendship with Pedro, almost all of it virtual.

Pedro, Paul writes, was a "darn good political strategist" who wrote Paul early in the Trump presidency that someone should dub him "President One Term." "Pedro was prescient, of course," Paul writes. "He was convinced from the start that Trump would be a one-term wonder. Just five months into Trump's first year, Pedro saw the writing on the wall more clearly than most political pros."

Pedro and I were both lucky to have many incredible mentors over the years, including Edvins Beitiks of the *San Francisco Examiner*, a man only Ray Ratto has the flair and fury to summon fully (Ray calls Beitiks a "keenly insightful bag of rumpled laundry" and a "weird oracle"—all true). I knew Pedro was a natural as a mentor to countless young journalists, and knew some of the stories, but only after we'd lost him did I begin to get a sense of the staggering scale of just how many lives he'd influenced in huge ways. Sarina Morales writes in her essay of idolizing Pedro, before they'd ever met, and of him helping her in her career, all the way to anchoring SportsCenter. Alden Gonzalez's essay title says it all: "He Carved a Path for Me."

Pedro's death jolted baseball the way it did, I think, because in his death we all saw a thousand other deaths: our own, of course, for if a man so full of life and love could drop dead just like that, then of course all of us can, but also the death of dreams, the death of those careening and gleeful enthusiasms of youth, the vertiginous feel of unlimited possibility, which baseball can and should evoke, at least in the heart of a true fan.

"He was one who you really looked forward to running into, he had such a smart, wise take on things," Joe Buck told me the week after Pedro died. "He was just gentle in a profession that now for some reason rewards the loudest voice in the room. He was the last guy to say, 'Look at me.' He was one of the true journalistically sound, integrity-filled people who just wanted to do the job."

Pedro knew that if you let it, baseball could take you places, instill in you wonder and joy and most of all, an unforgettable sense of connection with others. He asked only that you be open to the moment, open-eyed and open-hearted, which was why his face twisted into a sucking-on-lemons scowl when he talked about "dead fish," people who were only going through the motions. "He really doesn't care about baseball," Pedro told me in the final weeks of his life about one executive, a pronouncement that made Pedro deeply sad, like Obi-Wan wincing when he felt a weakening of the Force.

I think the outpouring after Pedro's death had to do with more than just charm, more than just likability: Pedro truly did stand for something. He believed that baseball and other sports offered us a chance to be a little more human, a little more passionate, a little more tuned into the spice and variety and sheer crazy wonder of life's randomness. He believed baseball and other sports could bring people together because he lived that for decades. He loved that feeling of standing on the field during a World Series, there at the center of the action, as wired into what was happening as anyone could be.

"I know for me he was the guy you wanted to see ... when you came out on the field in the World Series," AJ Hinch writes in his essay, a thought that inspired the cover art by Mark Ulriksen, who has more than fifty *New Yorker* covers to his credit.

Somewhere along that February 2021 drive to Arizona, as I flashed on different thoughts about Pedro, and turned over in my mind comments people had made comparing him to Anthony Bourdain and other large-hearted people whose deaths hit especially hard, I started gravitating toward a comparison I knew would strike some as unlikely. I started thinking about what Pedro, first and foremost a baseball writer, had in common with the man so many of us consider the greatest baseball writer ever, Roger Angell.

The more I mulled it over, the more it seemed fair to conclude that Roger started something in February 1962 with his first *New Yorker* article on baseball that Pedro, as much as anyone else since, moved forward. From that first dispatch, "The Old Folks Behind Home," Roger found a way to write about baseball that was all his own. He changed the sport, changed what it meant to be a fan by giving so many a vocabulary and palette through which to articulate a nuanced connection to so many facets of the baseball experience.

Pedro, proud son of Cubans, fluidly bilingual, ubiquitous presence on ESPN, gave the game a Latin face; he was suffused with the joy and passion of the Latin version of the game and always made sure it showed. For fans and for countless people in the game, Pedro was the ultimate connector, there to give a manager in a personal crisis a blunt dose of spot-on advice, there to reveal a human detail that reminded people not to obsess about launch angles and numerological metaphors, but to see baseball as a proving ground where character is made, unmade and revealed. Roger and Pedro were both, above all, fans of the game, secure enough in who they were to be utterly comfortable in the role of full-fledged enthusiast, exuberant and passionate fans unafraid of rapture, who also happened to be among the greatest reporters of their generations.

As Roger once explained his pursuit to me, "What I've been doing a lot of times is reporting. It's not exactly like everybody else's reporting. I'm reporting about myself, as a fan as well as a baseball writer." Roger brought the emotional experience of the fan to life with such joy and detail and sweep, for example after Carlton Fisk's memorable Fenway Park home run in Game 6 of the 1975 World Series, he created fans who had more of a connection to the game. That was what Pedro did over more than thirty-five years as a sportswriter and ESPN mainstay. He found a way to unlock secrets and insights about the people in the game that brought alive in fans at home the passion for baseball that burned in Pedro his entire life. All through it, he was never a guy in a role, but a warm personality people felt like they knew, a man whose take on things had to make sense since clearly this was someone who just about everyone liked—and everyone respected.

I remember when Roger and I were nearing completion on *Game Time*, a book of his baseball writing I conceived and edited. I spent the summer of 2002 in New York, flying in from Berlin, to sit with Roger every day and go through the *New Yorker* archives and mull over selections. This was in the Conde Nast Building on Times Square, gleaming and alive with potential. Roger and I were talking about his description of Troy Percival, the Angels' closer, in a section new to the book, not previously published. Elsewhere, Roger had referred to Percival as "pallid and squinting," and in this new section he called him "pale and musing." Roger, deeply committed to nuance, had a rare qualm, and asked me if I thought he had Percival right. I told him I thought so. He stared at me, uneasy. Maybe I'd sounded unconvincing. Then I figured out a way to make him smile.

"Why don't I call Pedro and get his take?" I suggested.

"Could you?" he answered quickly, noticeably relieved.

I could and I did. Pedro offered his take, rich in the credibility of all those years on the field, and Roger felt better. Writing this Introduction, I read back over the passage and was struck at how Roger's words still feel urgent and relevant. "Fans and writers expect a lot of the players— we're looking for the exceptional, every day, and great quotes after—and we're in need of baseball archetypes, as well," Roger wrote in "Penmen." "The eccentric reliever has almost held his own here, while other familiar figures—the wise, white-haired manager; the back-country coach ... and the boy-phenom slugger or strikeout artist—have been slipping from sight, smoothed into nullity by ESPN, Just for Men, the Bible, and tattoos."

Pedro was an *Arizona Republic* columnist at the time, but by the next year when *Game Time* was published, he had joined ESPN, where for eighteen years he waged a war against anyone smoothing baseball personalities into nullity. South Carolina basketball coach Frank Martin, close friends with Pedro back to their days as young dudes working in a Miami bank, explains in the leadoff essay of the collection, "Like a Mike Tyson Left Hook," that Pedro's dream was always to be a writer—and the TV work was an extension of Pedro the writer. Gomez asked only for a seat at the table, a voice to be heard along with so many great ball writers he revered, like Bruce Jenkins, Tim Keown and Dan Shaughnessy, or Ross Newhan, Peter Gammons and Ken Rosenthal, who all contribute essays, and so many others, from Len Koppett and Jerome Holtzman to Thomas Boswell and Claire Smith. Nothing gave Pedro more pleasure than ushering in fresh faces to the ranks of ball writers, showing them the way, as he showed Brian Murphy, who writes about covering the 1999 American League Championship Series with Pedro in essay #13, "Always Grab the Corks."

I'll come right out and say it: I think the world needs more people like Pedro Gomez. I think his love of life and love of getting to know people as they really are offer perspectives and insights that people might find valuable in their own lives, leaving aside what they might think about baseball and other sports. "Pedro sought authenticity the way a wildfire burns toward dry fuel," Tim Keown writes in his essay, "Come On!" "He was a one-man rebellion, chiseling through the hagiography to get to whatever story lay buried inside."

In putting together this essay collection, I've been acutely aware of how lucky I am to be able to reach out and share my grief with so many eloquent and passionate voices, who bring alive so many facets of Pedro, his life and his legacy, in these pages. Not everyone gets to mark the sudden passing of their best friend—or other loved one—by doing a turn as a Dream Team coach and assembling a lineup of All-Stars. Ed Beitiks hammered into both Pedro and me years ago that when it came to honoring the newly dead, you went all out. If not now, then when? In devoting a book to exploring why so many cared about Pedro Gomez, we hope also to make the larger point that we have to honor all our dead, tell their stories, clear space amid the static to reflect and mourn—and learn.

These essays can help people who knew Pedro—and people who did not—find more spark in their lives. They can also try to make up some of what we lost in not being able to mourn Pedro as we would have in non-pandemic times, crowding together to seek solace and maybe inspiration. The essays all, in their own way, carry a suggestion that maybe more people can try to be a little more like Pedro. Or more like who Pedro saw in them.

That was the thought I tried to convey when I stepped up to a microphone suspended over home plate at Salt River Fields in Phoenix for an invitation-only celebration of Pedro's life on the Saturday six days after he died, all of us having been tested for Covid. Other friends had spoken, and the family members would speak next: Dante, Sierra and Rio, and then Pedro's wife, Sandi.

Here are the words I shared that day:

"REMEMBER WHO YOU ARE"

I keep waiting for another text from Pedro. A call. A voicemail to make my day. So many of us feel that—like we've lost a part of ourselves. Our hearts don't just hurt, they feel deflated. What does it take in a person to inspire so many to feel so strongly and with such urgency?

Eleven days ago, Pedro called me when I was live on Zoom for a virtual book event. I couldn't pick up, but after that it was like Pedro had entered the Zoom conversation. Swear to god. A participant who earlier referred to me as "Kettmann," my name, suddenly started calling me "Ketterman." Not once. Several times. It was like he was channeling Pedro. For twenty-five years, Pedro has been calling me "Ketterman," "Kiefelbaum," "Kittiman," and a dozen variations. He would put his hands on his hips and yell at me: "Kettner!"

Pedro showed his love by chopping people he loved down to size, because he knew we needed it. Pedro cared about people, people as they really are. He was a moral compass in a world where that's become exquisitely rare. His phenomenal gift for understanding people, both overall and in the moment, gave him uncanny insights into the little lies we all tell ourselves, the fictions we build up as important in our lives. So, so often, he saw through that to the person we were trying to become, the life we were trying to lead, if only, if only. He was a master of helping us to see a version of ourselves that was a little better, a little truer, and how to get there. He did that for me. He did that for AJ Hinch when he was going through hell. He did it for Ron Washington when he was going through hell. Pedro did it for countless young people looking to him for inspiration and career advice. He did it, I'm guessing, for all of you here today, each and every one of you.

After my Zoom event, eleven days ago, I called Pedro back and we talked about the book we were writing together on baseball managers. I couldn't wait to tell him about a new project.

"What are the two most beautiful words in sports?" I asked him, quoting Gomez to Gomez.

"Game 7," he answered.

And what's even more beautiful? "Overtime in Game 7."

He did that Pedro thing: Oooooo, yeah, I like where you're going. He loved the idea for a book, *Overtime*, about where the country is going with so much up in the air. He poured reverence into the words "Game 7" because he loved the drama and beauty and truth that came through in those little moments that turned games, and turned events, and turned life stories. He loved watching how people reacted under pressure. He loved how the action of the moment showed us who people really are.

We also talked about sportswriters and legacies. Not making this up. Unbelievable. I remember him getting into it and almost shouting— OK, maybe he was already shouting—"But what did you *do*? What will people remember you for?"

Pedro will be remembered by many, I think, as the heart and soul of baseball in this era, the man who loved the game and the people in the game with as much intensity and unwavering commitment and resourcefulness and infectious joy as anyone alive. That's what countless baseball people have told me this last week and that's what the outpouring of tributes reveals.

It reminds me of the death of a great friend Pedro and I shared, Ed Beitiks of the *San Francisco Examiner*. When Ed died, *Examiner* editor Phil Bronstein said at the time, it was like the soul of the paper had gone. Ed, Pedro and I spent an incredible season on the road together, and that year helped turn Pedro into the marvel of a man we all celebrate today. I've heard many people talk about how Pedro embodied a serene confidence, never showing the kind of self-doubt or crippling fear or insecurity that others had. I think it's important to point out that he did have his insecurities, or once did, but came to understand they were beside the point. If you were true to the moment, if you were alert and alive to the pulsing human connection that made Pedro's life so incredibly rich and vital, who had time to give a shit about any sense of insecurity or self-limitation? Just go with it, man.

Pedro and I for years tried to live by a code, a code we called KGB, for Kettmann Gomez Beitiks. Ed was fifty that year the three of us spent together on the road, and Pedro and I, the August '62 boys, JFK babies, as he loved to say, were thirty-two. We'd never known anyone like Beitiks, but then who had? He grew up speaking Latvian in a displaced persons camp in Germany just after World War II, his mother and him relying on each other. When Ed spoke of the A Shau Valley in Vietnam, the images he shared haunted us. Ed was a philosophy major who could review books or compare cheap beer with the same gusto, a writer of peerless originality, precision and sheer overflowing glee, and he lived by a code, which he called the rules. He'd yell at us: "A man does not DO that!" We were an unlikely trio, Pedro the young Latin, me the pony-tailed former Berkeley English major, Ed with his round face and short gray hair the big riddle. People would come up to us in bars and restaurants and ask what our story was, and we'd tell them.

KGB to Pedro and I meant never tuning out that voice in your head, the voice that reminds you who you are. KGB was getting over yourself. KGB was being a fighter, ready to scrap, fearless until you weren't, but KGB was also flying into Chicago a day early to soak up the city, an afternoon in the bleachers at Wrigley, Beitiks bursting out into show tunes to astonish a friendly waitress.

When I published an article in *The New York Times* in August 2000 with the headline "Baseball Must Come Clean on Its Darkest Secret," and said what had to be said about steroids when no one was saying it, that was KGB. When Pedro—famously—used amazing quotes to go after Curt Schilling with a blistering column on the morning of Game 7 during the 2001 World Series, that was KGB, even if I was slow to see it. I was staying at the Gomez house and Sandi and I sat with Pedro just before he filed the piece, both of us telling him, "I don't know about this." The day of Game 7? Really? Pedro knew, and he was right. He earned a handshake from at least one Diamondback player the next day. He'd published the truth.

Pedro and I were still talking about the solemn importance of KGB up to two weeks ago, who was KGB, who wasn't. We always hoped the people who weren't KGB would become a little more that way, a little more soulful, a little more free, a little more willing to treat every moment on this earth as a chance to show us who they are. KGB was key in the '90s for helping Pedro come into his own, but it was only a beginning.

A decade ago, I wrote a tribute to Pedro, trying to sum up all he'd taught me, and read it out loud to him, including the part about what I called The Gomez Rules. When I read it, it was like I was playing Sinatra, he was beaming with pleasure and couldn't stop saying, "Oh man."

HERE'S THAT EXCERPT:

Pedro Gomez was the one who turned me into a sportswriter. I spent two years as a traveling beat writer covering the local NHL team, the San Jose Sharks, for the San Francisco Chronicle, *all the while thinking of myself as "not a sportswriter" and dreaming of an imminent move to Europe to write novels or something. When I switched from hockey to the baseball beat and met Pedro for the first time, I found his whole happy-Cuban thing grating. He just seemed too damn cheerful and too damn perfect, with his unflagging George Clooney smile, his beautiful and amazing Colombian wife, Sandi, a physical therapist, and above all his effortless reporting style. As it happened, Pedro found me grating, too, and made fun of what he saw as my whole angst-filled, pretentious-Berkeley, too-good-to-mix-with-other-sportswriters thing.*

It was like love, the way Pedro and I fell into friendship. Almost by accident we ended up going to dinner in Arizona that first spring training and we couldn't stop talking. That's how the next three years went: Out most every night on the road, we would spend hours talking about baseball, writing and people. We both were fascinated by all the little details of how people really were, when you looked closer, from the heavy-perfume-wearing elevator operator at Tiger Stadium in Detroit with her syrupy voice and motherly concern to the A's bullpen coach known as The Cave Man who toted around a black bag full of sex toys and had endless colorful tales to spin.

Pedro showed me how to be a sports reporter. I don't know if I was too lazy before I met Pedro to do the job right or simply didn't realize what I was missing, but he taught me a moral code for a beat writer:

GOMEZ RULE NO. 1: *Don't only talk to players when they do something wrong or hit the game-winning home run. If for example you notice a third baseman making a subtle but excellent play and happen to get a chance to ask about it, go talk to the guy on the night when everyone is talking to someone else. You do that partly to learn, since usually he'll explain some aspect of the play you weren't quite sure about, but also just to establish a dialogue, so that communication does not only come when you need something from him.*

GOMEZ RULE NO. 2: *Always go talk to the opposing manager, usually before the first game of the series. If you did it regularly, the other managers got to know you a little and usually appreciated the effort you made. We especially loved talking to Joe Torre, Lou Piniella and Phil Garner. Often they would give us scraps of insight that helped us understand the A's. Plus, it was a blast.*

GOMEZ RULE NO. 3: *If you rip someone, always show up the next day, even (especially) if it's your day off. They might want to curse you out. They might want to say you got something wrong—and might even have a point. They might just want to glare at you and make cracks about you from a distance. It doesn't matter. Always show up.*

GOMEZ RULE NO. 4: *Keep your eyes open. Odd as it may sound, sportswriters even then often kept their heads down in the press box, typing away, checking stats, often muttering about their disgruntlement but not often truly focusing on what was happening on the field of play. They just looked up now and then to keep abreast of the basics. That meant they missed a lot. The fun part was the crazy little sequences you might never* write about. Pedro and I both kept our eyes open and talked constantly about what we saw out there.

GOMEZ RULE NO. 5: *Start every relationship you make on the assumption that someone is basically good, basically OK, and let them prove you wrong, rather than the opposite. From umpires to moody journeymen infielders to eccentric coaches, Pedro was consistent. His approach rubbed off.*

GOMEZ RULE NO. 6: *Always have fun out there. Always remember you've got a great job and look for ways to enjoy the hell out of it. This included things like leaving the press box for a few innings to watch the game from the front row at old Tiger Stadium, where it felt like the pop of a fastball getting swallowed up by the catcher's mitt was exploding inside your head.*

I think in one version of that text, I added a Gomez Rule No. 7 about all the other rules besides No. 6 being secondary, but I see now how they all fit together. I see now that as much as I celebrated what Pedro was trying to get across to me and so many others, as astonished as I was by the impact he had on me, I failed to grasp the scale of his influence. It's not that I didn't appreciate Pedro. KGB meant you tried, always, to shake yourself out of complacency, and I never for a second forgot how incredibly lucky I was to have such a great friend as Pedro so tuned in to me, so emotionally alive and so wise, there to help me through writing *Juiced* for Canseco, there as basically co-best man at my wedding, there, always, to give his take on a question I was turning over in my mind, which we'd think through together, adding flavor with our lexicon of favored phrases. "It was a rocket!" and "He showed tremendous stick-to-itiveness and "Nice toss, Golden Richards," and, of course, "Was it over when the Germans bombed Pearl Harbor?"

Pedro thought in movie scenes and in thinking about him I keep flashing back to that John Cusack riff in the movie *The Sure Thing* where he talks about a guy named Nick. "Nick's your buddy. Nick's the kind of guy you can trust, drink a beer with." That's Pedro, our buddy, and it's a little surreal to see this outpouring of love and respect for Pedro, ripples emanating out from a point in the middle, our Pedro, occasionally a goofball, interrupting himself with fits of laughter in the middle of a story he's already told you eighty-three times, but also a truly beautiful soul, a man of courage and commitment so deep, it reached people who could not be reached.

Yesterday morning I called up Rob King, one of Pedro's ESPN bosses. We'd never spoken before, but Pedro had told me all about Rob and what a good guy he is. In short, Rob and I were both part of what I call the Best Friends' Club, the rich and vast network of people Pedro made feel so special, so loved and seen, we were all in a way his best friend, and by extension, all each other's best friends. From Billy in Miami to T.J. in Teaneck to Bruce in Montara, and of course Bob and Charlie and Jose Joe and Willie and so, so many others, we were all connected, lit up on the map in an archipelago of love, of Pedro love.

As T.J. Quinn put it, Pedro's life was a constant celebration of the people around him. And here's Bruce Jenkins on Pedro: "Pure enthusiasm is such a treasure. Not the manufactured kind, summoned out of necessity, but a quality that defines a person right to the core. That's how I'll remember Pedro Gomez."

Rob King and I talked not like strangers, but more like brothers. Before long we were both in tears. I'll admit I wasn't so much pumping him for information as just trying to get through my morning. Rob talked about how there were no hollow interactions with Pedro, not ever, and professional roles didn't matter, heart did, listening did, paying attention did. "In every face-to-face interaction we had," Rob told me, "it was like going to home base, back to what mattered, back to who we have always been, even in this big, beautiful machine."

That led me to share a few thoughts of my own and Rob almost gasped at one point.

"You just reminded me of something," he said.

And he told me about the sign on the wall of his ESPN office, which reads: REMEMBER WHO YOU ARE. He told me how everyone who comes into the office comments on the sign, and how often he talks about it, but he never gets a chance to mention where the words came from. They came from Pedro. Rob's first week at ESPN. Rob is going to write an essay about Pedro for a book we're going to publish, tributes to Pedro from players and managers and writers and broadcasters, and we decided we'd title Rob's essay, "Remember Who You Are."

Half an hour later, I tried to reach Rob again to tell him that's what we're going to call the book in Pedro's honor as well.

"It's perfect," T.J. told me on the phone. It gets it all. The pride in being Cuban. The focus on people. The high standards as a journalist, a friend and a man.

I texted Rob that we'd be using his title for the book, and he wrote back: "Oh my Lord. That's amazing. Thank you for even thinking of that."

Last month marked twenty years since Ed Beitiks died, and of course Pedro and I marked the occasion. We talked about how certain rare individuals, possessing a miraculous mix of qualities, live on among us in ways that are startling and beautiful and also, to be blunt, a little painful. I still hear Ed's voice in my head all the time, talking to me, schooling me, laughing at me, and I know Pedro did as well. A book I wrote was optioned and I was hired to write up a treatment to turn it into a miniseries, and Pedro's reaction was to shout, "Beitiks was right!" and then recite his favorite Ed quote, to me, "You're so Hollywood it makes me sick!"

Pedro and I replayed our greatest hits over and over because they reminded us of who we are and made us, I hope, a little better. For Sandi and Rio and Dante and Sierra, Pedro's presence isn't going anywhere, it's way too strong and vivid for that, and I know so many of you hear his voice in your ear, the way I do. For me, it's Ketterman, don't screw this up! And maybe, just maybe, I can use the rest of my days on this planet to try to live up to KGB. Maybe, just maybe, I can make Pedro proud, and maybe all of you can as well. Just remember who you are.

POSTSCRIPT

Picture editor Brad Mangin and I were thrilled that Terry Francona shared memories of growing up a Roberto Clemente fan (#46, "His Eyes Lit Up"), so we could include pictures of the great Clemente—which are, without doubt, essential to this book. For Pedro, nothing was more sacred than Clemente as a reference point, Clemente the player, attacking the game with what Pedro called "fury," Clemente the trailblazer, "like a god" to all fans of Latin American background, Clemente the first Latin player voted into the Baseball Hall of Fame.

Pedro was six when he fell deeply in love with baseball—in Spanish. This was in Detroit, where his family moved the year after he was born. His grandfather, born in Spain in 1899, worked as a Cuban Winter League umpire in Camaguey, and lived and breathed baseball. He would sit close to the radio, absorbed in Ernie Harwell's game broadcast, despite the

fact that he spoke zero English, having just fled Castro's Cuba in 1967. Young Pedro would ask what had happened and his grandfather would recite every detail, explaining that Kah-LEEN-eh (Al Kaline, Pedro's favorite player) had doubled in Jim Northrup and Willie Horton. Pedro's grandfather understood the language of baseball.

In August 2018, Pedro posted on social media about his *"abuelo from Camaguey,"* Isaac Gonzalez, who "taught me to love baseball." He told the following story: "My grandfather, a huge baseball fan, had just arrived from Cuba in '67. We went to a game. A young couple in front of us was making out and not watching the game. He slapped the guy with his newspaper and told them in Spanish that they weren't here for necking, to watch the game."

His grandfather passed on his passion to young Pedro, whose fandom took deep hold in 1968 when the Tigers won 103 games and prevailed over Bob Gibson and the St. Louis Cardinals in a classic, seven-game World Series. Pedro never stopped hearing the echoes of his grandfather's excited voice, talking about Kah-LEEN-eh and Mickey Es-stanley, and never lost touch with his boyish enthusiasm for connecting with baseball simultaneously in two languages.

In the '90s on the road together, Pedro and I spoke in Spanish often

Pedro's seventh birthday, August 1969: Behind him are his parents, Pedro Esteban Gomez and Marta Elena Gonzalez, his mother's parents, Isaac Gonzalez and Fermina Tellechea Leas; next to him is his little brother, Rick

enough that I picked up a Cuban accent. We'd repeat expressions just for their music and flavor and beauty, like Spanish for unearned runs, at least in Pedro's world, which was *carreras sucias*. Dirty runs. Pedro could talk for an hour about how much more evocative *sucia* was in that context than "unearned." He especially loved talking about the Spanish (OK, Spanglish) for "rally killer," which according to Pedro was *mata rally*. The verb *matar* in Spanish means "to kill," yes, but it is also used for "massacre." I still hear Pedro's voice saying, "You didn't just kill the rally, you *massacred* it!"

Baseball in Spanish transported Pedro even more than baseball in English, and it all connected with his conviction that Clemente played with "fury," a simmering intensity that gave him an electric presence as a player. For Pedro and for me, there was no greater compliment than talking about going Clemente-in-the-corner. That meant going all out with a kind of mad intensity that fused into the poetic. Brad Mangin's amazing work in putting together the pictures in this book helps us to see so much more, including Clemente's fierce gaze. Brad went Clemente-in-the-corner on this book. So did the wide range of voices collected here, from brilliant writers' writers to more plainspoken baseball men. I think it says a hell of a lot about Pedro and what he meant to people that he could inspire so many to open up and share such heartfelt glimpses.

Pedro Gomez, age eleven

TABLE OF CONTENTS

Introduction BY STEVE KETTMANN

1. *Like A Mike Tyson Left Hook,* BY FRANK MARTIN 1

2. *The Day the Music Died,* BY DAVE SHEININ 7

3. *'Come On!'* BY TIM KEOWN 15

4. *When You Went Deep on Baseball,* BY BRUCE JENKINS 21

5. *A Bridge,* BY RACHEL NICHOLS................................27

6. *Be Where Your Feet Are,* BY MARK KREIDLER.....................33

7. *Have Fun Every Single Day,* BY MAX SCHERZER 41

8. *The Art of the Interview,* BY BOB LEY..................... 47

9. *An Open Letter to President Bill Clinton: March 1999,*
   BY PEDRO GOMEZ...................................55

10. *'Know and Understand Cuba'* BY PETER GAMMONS 59

11. *Speechless,* BY HOWARD BRYANT................................ 65

12. *Does Baseball Matter?* BY MIKE BARNICLE............................... 71

13. *Always Grab the Corks,* BY BRIAN MURPHY 79

14. *At the Front of the Circle,* BY CHELSEA JANES............................87

15. *A Man You Could Trust,* BY DUSTY BAKER 95

16. *Remember Who You Are,* BY ROB KING..............................101

17. *He Was My Biggest Fan,* BY RIO GOMEZ 105

18. *Countenance,* BY ROSS NEWHAN 111

19. *He Watched Out for Us,* BY JON DANIELS 115

20. *Can You Believe We Get to Do This?* BY KEN ROSENTHAL............ 119

TABLE OF CONTENTS (CONT.)

21. *Where's Pedro?* BY BUSTER OLNEY.................................125

22. *Our Colleague, Our Friend,* BY SHELLEY M. SMITH.................131

23. *How Do You Want to Be Remembered?* BY T.J. QUINN.................135

24. *Pedro Gomez Day,* BY SCOTT BORAS.................141

25. *The Heart and Soul of Baseball,* BY SANDY ALDERSON.................147

26. *A Brotherhood,* BY DAN SHAUGHNESSY.................151

27. *How a Professional Works,* BY MIKE SWANSON.................157

28. *Remember KGB,* BY ROBIN CARR.................163

29. *The Night We Traded Jose,* BY TONY LA RUSSA.................169

30. *Let Enthusiasm Rule,* BY JASON LA CANFORA.................177

31. *Tell the Story Without Pandering to It,* BY RAY RATTO.................183

32. *He Listened,* BY RON WASHINGTON.................189

33. *Our Colombia Connection,* BY CHUCK CULPEPPER.................195

34. *With the Angels,* BY TRACY RINGOLSBY.................201

35. *He Made the Room Better,* BY BUD BLACK.................205

36. *The Walls Came Down,* BY TIM KURKJIAN.................209

37. *The Music Never Stopped,* BY JACK CURRY.................217

38. *Definitely a Stones Guy,* BY MICHAEL ZAGARIS.................231

39. *Show Me Who Your Friends Are,* BY PAUL BEGALA.................241

40. *'Gotta Love the Shooters,'* BY BRAD MANGIN.................247

41. *Those Yearly Glimpses of the Gomez Family,* BY JEREMY SCHAAP.....257

TABLE OF CONTENTS (CONT.)

42. *The Big Question,* by JEFF PASSAN 263

43. *Don't Be Afraid to Go Out On a Limb,* by BOB MELVIN 269

44. *What It Was Really Like on the Road,* by SCOTT OSTLER 273

45. *The Gomez Glide,* by GEORGE A. KING III 277

46. *His Eyes Lit Up,* by TERRY FRANCONA 283

47. *A Unifying Force,* by DERRICK GOOLD 289

48. *Making Time for Empathy,* by ALEX COFFEY 295

49. *Let Me Tell You 'Bout Some Friends I Know,* by SEAN MCADAM 301

50. *Like a Good Bench Coach,* by BRIAN SNITKER............................ 309

51. *A Natural Teacher,* by BRETT KURLAND 315

52. *He Carved a Path for Me,* by ALDEN GONZALEZ 321

53. *He Was My Idol,* by SARINA MORALES 325

54. *A Beacon,* by MARCOS BRETÓN... 331

55. *Voice to the Voiceless,* by JOHN D'ANNA 339

56. *Cubanidad,* by STEVE FAINARU... 347

57. *Yo Soy de la Misma Tierra* by ORLANDO "EL DUQUE" HERNANDEZ....353

58. *Do Right by People,* by DANTE GOMEZ.................................357

59. *You Should Call Frank,* by BUD GERACIE 365

60. *A Bright Light,* by DENNIS ECKERSLEY.................................373

61. *Deep Down a Tigers Fan,* by AJ HINCH 379

62. *All Friends Are Best Friends,* by KEITH OLBERMANN 387

Frank and his brother-in-law with Pedro in Miami

LIKE A MIKE TYSON LEFT HOOK

BY FRANK MARTIN

My phone started buzzing around 10 that night. I was thinking it was my assistant coaches telling me I needed to call someone or do something. That I could get to later. I was actually trying to enjoy my family for a couple minutes before my kids went to bed. Eventually I went to my phone and opened it and saw that all the text messages were from old friends. I opened the first one.

"Did you read about Pedro?" it said.

Uh-oh.

Then I opened another text.

"Pedro Gomez Passes Away." I was floored. I felt like I'd been on the wrong end of a Mike Tyson left hook. Every ounce of enthusiasm and energy in my body just went away. You saw a lot of fighters, Tyson hit them with that left hook right in the body, and it took their fight away. That's what that moment did for me.

Pedro had one of the kindest hearts of anyone I've ever come across. I've never been a journalist, but as an NCAA basketball coach I'm in the world of interacting with people and trying to get people to allow me to understand them so I can help them. Pedro had a unique quality. He helped you put your guard down, so you could be who you are in front of him and be at peace. You got the feeling the people he interacted with as a reporter for newspapers and then ESPN trusted him the same way I did, and that's powerful. In today's day and age, not too many people let their guard down when there's somebody that is going to report a story about them. We all live in a world of phoniness where we're trying to portray this persona publicly but we're someone different privately. Pedro's stories were genuine.

The one thing I'm going to miss most is when the phone would ring and I'd see his name and answer it, and he would say, "Frankie Mar-TINE!" My family calls me Frankie from when I was a kid, short for Francisco, and the proper enunciation of my name in Spanish is not "Martin," it's "Mar-TINE!" Every time I'd answer the phone and he'd call out "Frankie Mar-TINE!" it would just make me feel good.

I first met Pedro in a Miami bank in August 1983. His authenticity and spirit grabbed me right away. Within fifteen minutes of meeting him I felt like he'd already been my best friend for years. I was seventeen then and he was about to turn twenty-one. We were both the proud sons of families that had fled Castro's Cuba. For Cubans in Miami, it was difficult at that time to line up loans to buy homes, so a bank was created for them: Ocean Bank of Miami, which opened its doors at the corner of LeJeune Road and N.W. 7th Street in January 1983. The building wasn't ready, so we worked in a trailer.

My first day working in that trailer, my boss sat me down at a new desk and there was another young guy about ten feet away, his desk facing mine. As the day went on he introduced himself—"Pedro Gomez," the big smile, the outstretched hand—and we jumped right into a conversation about sports. I'm a huge Cincinnati Reds fans, because of Tony Perez. If you were a Cuban kid in Miami, you loved Tony Perez. We talked about the Reds and then Pedro immediately went from Tony Perez to the Detroit Tigers, the team that he idolized as a kid.

From there it was on to nicknames. Chris Berman was at the height of coming up with nicknames then, whether it be Bert Be Home Blyleven or Dave Parallel Parker, and within minutes of meeting Pedro, he and I were quoting Berman nicknames back and forth at each other. I'm the complete opposite of Pedro. When I first meet somebody, I'm very quiet and very reserved. At that age, I was actually more introverted any time you put me in a space with people I didn't know. None of that mattered with Pedro. All I could think was: *I've got to get to know this guy. I love this guy's spirit. This guy makes me feel better about myself.*

Our bosses weren't as happy. Pedro worked on the bookkeeping side and I was on the proof side. The work I did, checking what the tellers had done, went on to him and he double-checked my work. We'd be sitting there, talking baseball or Chris Berman, and our bosses would have to come over.

"Can you two guys actually pay attention to your work, instead of talking about sports all the time?" they asked us.

That shut us up for a while, but not long. I don't know if we were any good at our jobs, but we were really good at talking. Neither one of us saw a future working in a bank, even if, for Pedro, that was the career his father had followed going back to Cuba when he worked in a bank in Havana.

All I cared about was sports. I was still trying to chase the dream of playing in college. I wanted to walk on as a basketball player at Miami-Dade. My mom couldn't afford to pay for school and I wasn't a scholarship-level athlete, so I figured I'd work full time for a year while I went to school part time and worked on my game. That's how I ended up in the bank trailer one desk over from Pedro.

His dream was to be a writer. There are videos of the Ocean Bank softball team driving to a tournament, with Pedro—who we all called "Tex" then, since he'd lived in Texas—narrating the action like a play-by-play announcer, but his dream was to be a sportswriter. He was taking courses at Miami-Dade South Community College and a professor there named Peter Townsend encouraged him to study journalism and pursue a career in sportswriting. Pedro wrote at his ESPN bio page, "I remember his line vividly: 'Pedro, if you go this route, your career will outlast every athlete you ever cover.'"

Townsend recalls Pedro vividly, of course. Who doesn't? "He caught on to everything very quickly, and I remember he would ask very good questions," he says now. "I did one great thing for Pedro. He was sure people weren't going to accept a Hispanic sportswriter. He thought he would have a greater chance for success changing his byline to 'Tex Gomez,' instead of 'Pedro Gomez.' I told him, 'Always stay true to yourself. People can spot a phony.'"

In 1984 Pedro went from writing articles for the *Downtowner,* the student paper, to covering high school sports for the *South Dade News Leader,* working for a guy named Walter Villa. Armando Salguero, now a well known *Miami Herald* sportswriter, hired Pedro to cover preps for the *Miami News*. "I saw Pedro at a football game in south Dade we were both covering and he came up and introduced himself, and I liked his energy," Armando remembers. "Very enthusiastic."

The guy that opened the door for Pedro's career the most was my neighbor growing up in Little Havana, Leo Suarez. He was a lot like Pedro. He had a joy for life. I'm not into telling people how to do their jobs. What attracted me to Leo, he loved to tell a story with his writing, and it wasn't a story about making people look bad, it was a story about telling the truth of a person's journey. And that was how he ran his sports page at the *Miami News*. Leo had a magic spirit about him where he could identify guys.

"Our sports editor, the late Leo Suarez, saw a lot of himself in Pedro," James Bennett wrote in a tribute to Pedro after his death. "Leo, who died in 1995 at age thirty-seven, covered the Miami Dolphins as a dominant beat reporter before becoming sports editor. Leo's hard-driving success inspired Pedro to follow in his footsteps. Pedro even did a spot-on impression of Leo's high-pitched voice."

Pedro's joy was in writing. He wanted to be great at writing. When he put that aside to become more of a reporter, it kind of hurt him a little bit, because he didn't get to write, because that's what brought him joy.

One thing that made Pedro and me somewhat unique was we were both willing to get up and leave Miami to pursue our careers. That doesn't happen in the Cuban culture very often, at least not in the Cuban culture we came from, where our parents were from Cuba in the 1950s. He spread his wings and he left before me, moving to California in 1988 to take a job with the *San Diego Union,* and then I spread my wings and left in the summer of 2000, first working as a coach at Northwestern, then Cincinnati, and moving to Kansas State, where I became head coach in 2007. That willingness that Pedro and I each had continued to bridge us closer together, but we never stopped talking about Miami and Cuba.

He called me before he visited Cuba in March 1999 when the Baltimore Orioles played the Cuban National Team. Fidel Castro would be attending the game. Pedro was so excited, but to a certain extent it was troubling for him. I battled it too. My grandmother made me promise on her death bed that I would not go back until Castro was out of power, until people in Cuba could live out from under the oppression they'd been under. My grandmother made me and my uncle promise that. I've never been to Cuba. I know Pedro was also troubled by that. Like: *I can't go back and act like everything is OK. This is the country that my family loved that was taken from us.* Pedro never forgot who he was. Never. Not one time.

I miss my guy, man. In life we come across people we don't like. We come across people who don't really do much one way or the other. And we come across people who impact you powerfully. Pedro was someone who touched your spirit every day. The joy he spread to other people, the joy he lived life with, today that needs to be spread even more.

Phoenix Muni, February 2011, Billy Beane and Pedro

THE DAY THE MUSIC DIED

BY DAVE SHEININ

It was an October night on the East Side of Manhattan. An Italian joint called Il Vagabondo on East 62nd Street. This would have been 1998, maybe 1999, back when we were young and an expense account still meant something. There was a big table of baseball writers. There was wine. There was pasta. There were stories being told—or maybe being retold, but that I, newly attached to the baseball beat, was hearing for the first time. And there was, at a table nearby, a woman celebrating her birthday, waitstaff gathered around singing, cake, candles, the whole deal.

Across the table, Pedro Gomez caught my eye. Head tilted, eyes gleaming, he had a look on his face that said, "You gotta do this."

We all have crossroads in our lives, at the intersection of time and opportunity, where one choice leads you down one path, and the other, unchosen one—had you taken it—might have changed everything. In reality, I didn't really have much of a choice here. I was under the influence of both Chianti Classico and the irresistible charm of Pedro Gomez. Either one might have done the trick—but against both, I was powerless. This, without question, was the night my fate was sealed, the night my professional legacy, such as it is, was cemented. From that moment on, whenever baseball people got together, I was the guy who sang and played piano. You know, Pedro's friend. And I'm good with that.

It was Pedro who did this, who hung that star around my neck before anyone else knew about the musical side of me. He was part-superfan and part-agent—in that he both delighted in hearing me belt it out and excelled at lining up opportunities for me to do so. (On the other hand, I can't say he was a great agent, in the textbook definition, because somehow I never wound up getting paid for this stuff—well, with the exception of one night in Anaheim, which we will get to later.) Pedro knew about my music proclivities before anyone else, and he knew there was a memorable night to be had whenever he could place me within the vicinity of a small crowd, a free flow of alcohol and a musical set-up—a stage, a band, maybe a hotel-lobby piano, or in a pinch, an acoustic guitar. Microphones were optional. And sometimes I could make do with just the crowd and the alcohol—such as that night in New York at the Italian restaurant.

You can probably see where this is going. Pedro made the introductions: "Ma'am, this gentleman here is an opera singer, and he would really love to sing you an aria for your birthday." Never mind that I was not really an opera singer—nor for that matter a gentleman (I had only studied at both)—and what I was about to do would have never happened had I been sober. But nonetheless I stood up, right there, in this popular Italian restaurant in New York City—let me repeat that: at a popular ITALIAN RESTAURANT in NEW YORK CITY—and fortified by the wine and my youthful hubris and the encouragement of my friend Pedro Gomez, I cleared my throat and belted a show-stopping Italian number for the startled birthday girl. I'm told it was "O Sole Mio." All I remember is that it was well received, at both tables, plus all the other ones within earshot. There may have been tears in the eyes of the Italian waiters watching from their stations. It may have resulted in the arrival of additional bottles of wine that we didn't have to pay for. It often happens that way. And I'm good with that.

It was music that connected me with Pedro from the first day we met. This would have been June 1989, when I drove across the lower section of the country in a Chevy Cavalier without a working gas gauge or speedometer—owing to a digital dashboard that would no longer light up—

for a summer internship at *The San Diego Union*. I had with me a suitcase, a guitar, an address and a name: Pedro Gomez. The sports department had put out a call for a volunteer to house the intern until I could find an apartment, and it was Pedro who raised his hand. He seemed really cool: Cuban dude, great hair. He said I could crash on the futon in his living room. But it wasn't until I got a good look at his CD collection—R.E.M., The Cure, XTC, et al.—that I knew we would be friends.

A quick word about that *San Diego Union* sports staff, circa 1989: I would put that staff, in terms of its talent and the careers we all went on to have, against any similar-sized staff in the country from that era. Pedro, just twenty-six years old, was covering preps. Buster Olney, later of *The New York Times* and ESPN, was there. Jim Trotter (NFL Network/ NFL.com) was there. Ed Graney (now a columnist in Las Vegas) was there. Mark Kreidler was writing takeouts and columns. Kevin Kernan covered the Padres. Tom Krasovic. Chris Jenkins. Mark Zeigler. Bill Center. Jerry Magee. Barry Lorge. Just a massive amount of talent on one smallish sports staff.

At some point, early on that summer, a bunch of us wound up at a jazz and blues club in a strip mall out east of town, a joint called Pal Joey's. There was an old jazz man named Fro Brigham just starting up his weekly gig—trumpet player, raspy baritone voice, beret perched on his head, little bit of a Satchmo vibe. At some point, I must have let on to the guys about my musical background—music major at Vanderbilt, studying as an opera singer, etc. I don't remember for sure, but I suspect it was Pedro who let the band know there was a singer in the audience who would love to sit in with them. It was, of course, very much NOT true to say that I—a knuckleheaded, twenty-year-old college kid who thought he wanted to be a sportswriter, or possibly an opera singer— wished to sit in with an experienced, talented, PROFESSIONAL jazz bandleader and his equally talented five-piece outfit. But Pedro, though having known me for only a matter of days, had an innate understanding of the most effective way to coax me into this situation, so I was good and lubed up when I stepped up on the stage. I think we did "The Thrill Is Gone" and "Since I Fell For You," but all I remember for certain is that my showstopper—and even now, thirty-some years later, I cringe as I type this—was "Bad To the Bone." Oof. Yeah, that happened. I may have juiced it with some operatic flourishes at the end. But the thing is, people loved it. The sports department lads. The audience. And especially Fro. He invited me back the next week, and the week after that, and it became a weekly sit-in gig for me the rest of that summer.

I eventually moved off Pedro's futon when I found myself a room to sublet in an apartment with three UC San Diego coeds. But Pedro and I would be fast friends forever. In the mid-1990s, we wound up at *The Miami Herald* together, which allowed him to see me perform in an actual opera, in my side-gig in the chorus of the Greater Miami Opera, and allowed me to visit Pedro and Sandi shortly after the arrival of their firstborn, Rio. Somewhere, I still have the picture of me holding baby Rio—a memory Pedro and I, as the years passed, would bring up with awe and wonder as Rio grew into a strapping lefty and blossoming professional pitcher.

"You held him in your arms when he was a baby!" Pedro would half-scream, half-laugh as he showed me the latest picture of the modern-day Rio. "Can you believe it?" It happened pretty much exactly like that the very last time I saw him.

By the late 1990s, we were both covering baseball, and over the next couple of decades he became known as the consummate baseball reporter and one of the most popular and universally respected figures in the sport. I became known as the guy who sings and plays piano. You know, Pedro's friend. And I'm good with that. It was great to be Pedro's friend. He was a force of nature, the type of warm personality that drew people in and opened them up. When I was around Pedro, I eventually knew everybody else around Pedro. "Hey [random player, agent, GM, etc.]. Do you know Dave Sheinin?" And Pedro knew everybody. My experience wasn't alone. This is how it went with anyone who knew him. We were all satellites in Pedro's orbit.

It was in those early years that I became a serial assaulter of Marriott lobby pianos, often late at night or early in the morning after last call, many times at Pedro's instigation. I believe he was there the December night in 2000 at the winter meetings when Tommy Lasorda wandered by as I was doing my thing and joined me for a couple of Louis Prima numbers. By the early 2000s I wore like a badge of honor the fact I had been kicked off Marriott lobby pianos by hotel security in nearly every big league city. It was sometimes messy.

Other times it was glorious. Such as the night of October 26, 2002, when, blessed with those wonderful West Coast deadlines during the San Francisco Giants/Anaheim Angels World Series, a bunch of us, including Pedro, wound up at the Anaheim Hilton. The Anaheim Hilton happened to be the Giants' team hotel, though that's not why we were there. We were there because it had a piano in the lobby with the ideal setup: close to the bar, surrounded by chairs and sofas, minimal security.

I was well into my set when someone first noticed a solitary figure sitting and drinking at a cocktail table facing the piano. It was Dusty Baker. Let me back up: October 26 happened to have been the night of Game 6 of the 2002 World Series, and it was mere hours after what was one of the most crushing losses of Baker's career. The Giants, nine outs from winning the World Series, blew a five-run lead in the seventh and eighth innings and lost. The next night, Game 7, they would lose again, and Dusty's best shot at a championship would be gone.

Pedro, of course, was the first to go over to say hello to Dusty that night, mostly just to check in on him, to ask how he was doing. Whatever Pedro said, he managed to coax a smile out of Dusty. It would be some time later that I got to know Dusty myself—but at that moment, I was happy enough to be the guy who sang and played the piano. You know, Pedro's friend. Dusty stayed and listened and hung out for a while, then stood to leave. Someone had placed an empty rocks glass on the piano and stuffed a couple of ones in it—a makeshift tip-jar—and as Dusty passed by, he nodded in my direction and dropped a fifty in the glass. That was different. It sat there all night, and at the end we gave it to the nice cocktail server who had been supplying us with drinks.

There were so many epic nights—some of them involving a piano, other times just a great night out on the town—that they all bleed together in my mind into a chaotic, boozy haze of memory, with Pedro's big, smiling face at the center of it all. Here at home, my piano, a six-foot Yamaha grand, sits in the front room, angled into the room's far corner, surrounded by barstools. When I sit at the bench and place my hands on the keys, I'm facing the door and the large window looking out to the sidewalk. It's set up in that way to be an open invitation to neighbors who might be passing by. Pedro would love it here.

But tonight my hands are stones and my voice a scratchy whisper. I think of all the tunes that have been my go-tos, my crowd-pleasers through the years, and tonight I just don't have it in me to play them. All

I see is Pedro, elbows leaning on the piano, drink in his hand, shit-eating grin on his face. "Love Train." "Thunder Road." "Let It Be." "Build Me Up Buttercup." "Like a Rolling Stone." "Piano Man." "I Will Survive." I don't think I'll ever play them again without thinking of him.

And "American Pie." Yeah, especially that one. Everyone always sang along to that one. I prided myself on nailing every verse, no matter how many drinks were in me. But I never spent much time thinking about the lyrics, and tonight they are devastating... *February made me shiver... Bad news on the doorstep... I can't remember if I cried... The lovers cried and the poets dreamed.... The Father, Son and the Holy Ghost... They caught the last train for the coast.*

I'll tell you this much about February 7, 2021: For me, as long as I'm on this earth, that will forever be the day the music died.

Tim with boxer Floyd Mayweather

'COME ON!'

BY TIM KEOWN

Technology has spawned the age of self-creation. Myths are propagated, attributes are enhanced, flaws disappear. Photos and videos project an unreachable level of happiness and fulfillment. A public image is crafted by artificial means and curated through repetition. *Check out this post: look how happy/dedicated/generous/sorry this person is.* Fame—and worth—comes to be judged by an arbitrary number of followers or likes or engagements with the similarly famous. A person's essence is distilled to a series of public-relations snapshots. Perfection arrives in synthetic form, and authenticity dies a slow death.

Reality bends toward the process, and truth becomes what is perceived rather than experienced. Packaging, over time, is indistinguishable from product. Along the way, as we've macheted our way through the thicket of superficiality and false humility, the search for authenticity has become a subversive act. To seek authenticity is to risk being branded a cynic.

This is all offered up in the cause of presenting an enduring image of Pedro Gomez: he is standing somewhere—a press box, a dugout, around a batting cage—talking about a ballplayer. After a recitation of attributes or statistics is proffered, Pedro's body leans forward at the waist, his pleading arms shoot out to his sides, his voice rises. "Yeah, I know," he says, an amiable frustration overtaking him. "But what's he *really* like?" He never waits for an answer before providing his own: "That's what I need to find out."

Pedro sought authenticity the way a wildfire burns toward dry fuel. He was a one-man rebellion, chiseling through the hagiography to get to whatever story lay buried inside. There were enough stenographers out there; Pedro sought to *understand*, in both of his languages. If he felt a ballplayer or a manager was spinning him, Pedro would take a step back and plead with those arms again. "Come *on!*" he'd say, refusing to hear another word. It was an authentic appeal to authenticity, and, suitably disarmed, the ballplayer or manager would laugh and proceed to tell Pedro what he was there to discover.

He was a man who lived out loud in a world that was inexorably retreating into its own self-reflection. We are wired neurologically to connect with other humans, to argue vociferously and agree politely and challenge incessantly. Pedro knew you can demand authenticity only if you project it.

Another image: In a hotel room with a group of Bay Area sportswriters during baseball's postseason, could have been Atlanta or Minnesota or Cleveland, 1991 or 1995 or 1997. There's an old Home Run Derby playing through the VHS machine my *San Francisco Chronicle* colleague Bruce Jenkins lugs everywhere he goes. Eight different conversations collide in the air, with the most demonstrative—and pressing—involving Pedro asking Jenkins how he manages to watch a baseball game and immediately string together a harmonious melody of words while the rest of the press box sweats and swears and heads out for a smoke.

"How do you *do* that?" Pedro demands, to which Jenkins offers a self-effacing shrug and a quick laugh. "No—*really*," Pedro says. His curiosity is matched only by his stubbornness. He's a guy carrying a torch into a mine shaft, determined to find something beneath the surface. He's a dog refusing to yield the bone. Jenkins says something about a plumber not being able to explain how he unclogs the pipes, and, suddenly, there's Pedro again: the step back, the pleading arms, the "Come *on!*"

He was fascinated by writing. It didn't come easily for him, and he wanted to know how the mind assembled words and funneled them onto the page. He loved the propulsion of putting one word after another, the writer always one step ahead, laying stepping stones to take the reader toward the intended destination. His admiration, and here's that word again, was authentic, and remarkably devoid of envy. (Admiration untethered from ego: perhaps the rarest and most honorable trait.) Pedro knew he couldn't write like Jenkins, few can, but he also knew there might be something hiding deep inside that remarkable mind that might inch him ever closer toward becoming the writer he wanted to be.

Jenkins and I worked together during several World Series in the 1990s, him the front man, me the guy they allow to stand in the back and smack the tambourine against his leg as long as he stays sober enough to drive the bus to the next gig. Neither of us cared who wrote the column or the game story on any particular night, and we never met after the fifth inning to discuss what angle we'd be taking to make sure there was no overlap in our work. (An industry standard, by the way, that invariably called for further meetings in the seventh, eighth and ninth as circumstances dictated.) In short, we didn't care about title or hierarchy, and back then, in the heady newspaper days of the early to mid-'90s, caring about hierarchy was bloodsport. Writers on the same paper came to blows during the World Series over who got the seat in the press box and who was relegated to the upper-deck auxiliary section. Jenkins and I didn't care; we just wanted to watch the game and tell someone about it.

This, not surprisingly, fascinated Pedro. It became a game within the game. In those hotel rooms, in the pre-internet era, he would ask to read what we'd written that night. We'd dutifully hand over our laptops and Pedro would ask, "So, which one's the gamer and which one's the column?"

We'd shrug. Doesn't matter.

Pedro, again with the pleading arms: "What do you mean *It doesn't matter*? Of course it matters. How can you say it doesn't matter?"

It didn't matter because it didn't change who we were or how we were going to write. When you picked up the paper the next morning, you couldn't tell whether Jenkins and I both wrote columns or both wrote game stories. We just attempted to present our unvarnished—for the sake of argument, and at the risk of repetition: *authentic*—account of that night's game. Pedro acted like it was the most revolutionary thing he'd ever encountered.

Pedro became known as a television personality, but everything he accomplished in that medium was borne of his work as a print journalist, and his insistence on doing it as well as he possibly could. It all came from the same place: The eye for a good story, exhibited dramatically in his emotional visits to Cuba, where he stood on a rocky beach and fulfilled a promise by spreading the ashes of his father and brother into the swirling Caribbean waters; the incisive questioning during his epic Bonds assignment; the ability to respond to a breaking story and be conversant on the intricacies of the topic the second the red light illuminated. I'm convinced none of it happens without his devotion to the written word.

(Random note relating to Pedro's work from Cuba: The word *courage* originates from the Latin root *cor*, meaning heart, and the literal meaning of the word dates back to the concept of telling the story of who you are with your whole heart.)

One final image: a hotel bar somewhere, years after Pedro's Odysseus-like pursuit of Barry Bonds' journey to break Major League Baseball's career home-run record. We both had baseball-playing sons, and Pedro was telling me about Rio, a left-handed pitcher who was at the time planning to pitch for an Arizona junior college.

Pedro was proud of Rio and frustrated at the recruiting process, probably in equal measure. At the big-league level, the game had chipped away at its own authenticity; players were assessed by spreadsheets that compiled numbers developed by academics. Character, and characters, were in short supply. The world was being run by people who couldn't look up from their screens long enough to hear the story of how Dave Stewart routinely turned Roger Clemens into a quivering mass of insecurities. Pitchers had to be six-foot-four and throw 95 mph, but as a major-league pitching coach once told me, "All these guys can throw a fastball on the hands at 90-plus. They just can't tell you why they're doing it."

Pedro wondered if this mentality was seeping into amateur baseball. Rio's fastball then topped out in the mid-'80s, if I'm remembering correctly, and Pedro—again with the pleading arms—couldn't understand why a radar gun was given the credibility once reserved for the observations and institutional memories of flesh-and-blood scouts.

"I'm telling you," he said of Rio, "he just gets people out. Shouldn't that still count for something?"

He and I both knew the truth: modern-day baseball has nearly eradicated the guy who "just gets people out" if he doesn't fit the profile. As always, Pedro had questions. Can a series of numbers tell you whether a kid's heart rate slows in a tough spot, whether he's able to take something off when the situation would seem to call for maximum effort? And why does a pitcher who "fits the profile" get every chance to prove he can't succeed while one that doesn't might get one chance to prove he can?

I could tell this was bigger than a father advocating for his son. To a man with Cuban roots who grew up in Miami, baseball is raucous and messy. Stories of the game are sustenance, and opinions are delivered like slam poetry. It's a game of myth and exaggeration, the stories passed down, gathering layers of embellishment with each retelling. Does that game still exist? And if so, for how long? This isn't just generational throat-clearing; the game is played by remarkable athletes who are taught that a home run and a double every ten at bats is better than a single every three. And the maddening part is, they might be right. Numbers have taken over decision-making, and everyone in the game is cautious and buttoned-up, territorial about their proprietary information. (The next passionate, *authentic* conversation about spin rates and launch angles will be the first.) The entire industry is the catcher with his mitt covering his mouth, eyes darting in all directions, fearing the unseen lip-readers.

Pedro questioned all of that, in exactly the same way he questioned everything else: passionately, pleadingly, genuinely, with a blend of enthusiasm and charisma that managed to touch the soul of whatever topic he found himself entertaining at the moment. There are stories out there, so many stories, and sometimes you just need to cut through the bullshit and find out.

WHEN YOU WENT
DEEP ON BASEBALL

BY BRUCE JENKINS

Pure enthusiasm is such a treasure. Not the manufactured kind, summoned out of necessity, but a quality that defines a person, right to the core. That's how I'll remember Pedro Gomez, always with a particular scene in mind.

I had arranged to meet him one spring-training eve at the Italian Grotto, in the heart of Old Town Scottsdale. From my seat at the bar I spotted him on the street, actively engaged with a bunch of strangers. Once inside, he couldn't move more than two or three feet at a time. Too many folks calling his name. I knew I'd have a moment to turn around and order a fresh drink, for there was something distinct about a Pedro arrival. It took place in stages.

I'd been to spring training in Arizona so many times by the early 2000s, I looked most forward not to the games, but to those nights at the Grotto with Pedro, his ESPN producer Charlie Moynihan, ace photographers Michael Zagaris, Jean Fruth and Brad Mangin, assorted writers, and other shining lights of the baseball industry. So much talent in that room. Such complete absence of ego. We'd be the regaled guests of Garry Horowitz, the tough-talking New Yorker who owned the place and always had a choice table available—even if he had to oust a few tourist types to make it happen.

As if Pedro ever needed help taking the conversational lead in social settings, he left behind his television persona to unveil a booming, authoritative voice. "You didn't have to get a text from him, like 'I'm here,'" Moynihan said on a "Baseball Tonight" podcast after Pedro's death. "You always knew when he was coming around the corner. He had one level, and it was loud."

Charlie said that with the utmost respect, for no one ever turned away from one of Pedro's grand proclamations. He would often repeat them, just for emphasis. Later in the evening, once Pedro had gone home to his Ahwatukee, we'd find ourselves imitating the great man, laughing hilariously along the way. Two or three nights later, the whole delightful scene would unfold again with a slightly different cast, reaching that festive peak as long as Pedro was there.

What would we talk about? It was never "I did this killer interview" or "Then I wrote." It would be all about impressions: of an animated manager, a telling postgame comment, a pitcher looking disturbingly anxious, a weak throw's window into arm trouble, a nasty curveball struck with patience into the opposite field. We'd address questions for the ages: the purest right-handed batting stroke in history, or your choice of a starting pitcher if your life was at stake. I always had a little cocktail napkin and pen in my shirt pocket, just so I could write down some of the observations coming forth. (If you stole an idea from Pedro Gomez or other sage members of the Grotto crew, you'd reached thievery's penthouse.)

Something that deeply impressed me about Pedro: There are implacable, hard-edged writers who stride confidently into a crisis, and there are more gentle types, eminently skilled but most comfortable in harmony. He was *both* of those people, every day. A kinder soul has not walked the earth, nor anyone more caring or considerate. But Pedro had a powerful thirst for challenges.

You've likely heard that he was always the one asking the most difficult questions, actually preferring to work a clubhouse full of beaten, bitter athletes while the winning team celebrated across the way. Good lord, you talk about a challenging assignment: If someone told me I'd be required to cover Barry Bonds—just him, nobody else, and without missing a day, for nearly three years—I think I'd go into the plumbing business. It would be so much cleaner.

In the hands of a fawning admirer, maybe Bonds wouldn't be such a bad beat. He was always a major story, and your work would regularly appear on ESPN. But Pedro didn't much care for his subject. He hated the way Bonds treated people, how he'd become a pariah in his own clubhouse even as he chased down home-run history. Pedro wasn't hearing of any Hall of Fame candidate who ventured into the sinister world of steroids, and he never wavered in leaving Bonds *off* his ballot.

So I look back on those perpetual crowds of journalists around Bonds and, inevitably, Pedro asking the one question others would avoid. This perfect gentleman, Pedro, this prince of vitality and cheer, stepping right into the fight.

There were times when beat writers and columnists scoffed at ESPN's Bonds-Gomez obsession. Bonds himself grew profoundly tired of the exercise, and the two men had some fierce exchanges. But again, here's Pedro: When it was all over, Bonds respected the hell out of him. And one day, not long after the home-run feats were accomplished and Pedro had moved on to other tasks, he walked into the press box at the Giants' ballpark and got a standing ovation from his fellow journalists. Charlie Moynihan told that story on the podcast, and he was in tears before he could finish.

I first got to know Pedro when he covered the Oakland A's for the *San Jose Mercury News*, and we had many conversations about the business. He loved being a writer, nailing down an important story in words—the right ones, and not too many. One night, somewhere out on the road, he told me he'd been approached by ESPN to do some television work.

"Pedro, you are *perfect* for that," I said. "You're confident, you strike a pleasant appearance, you know your stuff, and you have a beautiful speaking voice."

"I don't know about any of that," he said. "I'm not sure I'm cut out for it."

"I'm telling you right now," I insisted. "You'll be one of the best."

We all know how that one turned out—hell, it was obvious to everyone but Pedro—but in the larger view, I can't recall more than a handful of people who were absolutely first-rate as writers *and* broadcasters. If you add an additional, crucial element—not a trace of arrogance or superiority, a trait all too common in television—you've really narrowed the field. That is one glorious trifecta.

It was always a great day for me if Pedro was in the press box. So often it's the province of jaded folks who resent drawn-out games (I hear them now: "End it!") and have become so addicted to the digital world, they spend most of their time looking down, at their keyboard or cell phone. They grasp the game's general themes, but they don't watch. They don't *see* it. I think we're all guilty of that to some extent, given the demands of deadline writing, but when something really special unfolds on the field, I want to jump out of my seat and go talk to someone about it. I've done that many times at Giants games, hurrying up the stairs between innings to get some quick impressions from Mike Krukow and Duane Kuiper, and Pedro was always a source of inspiration, clarity, a powerfully strong opinion. I could only hope the seat alongside him was empty.

When you went deep on baseball with Pedro, it was always about the people, not the numbers. It's a lesson every young writer should embrace, but an increasingly unlikely prospect in the age of analytics. It's ever so trendy these days to speak of "spin rate" and "exit velo," with a hearty touch of BABIP, but such nonsense never came up with Pedro. He wanted to talk about who stood up to the moment, who came up small, maybe something he'd noticed in batting practice, or just the essence of style: Omar Vizquel bare-handing a ground ball, Tony Gwynn drilling a line drive into open spaces, Luis Tiant turning the art of pitching into dance, or a man of diminutive stature—say, Pedro Martinez or Ron Guidry—throwing harder and with greater purpose than muscle-bound teammates.

It's not often that I'm *happy* to have spent fifty years in the business—it's kind of a disturbing stat—but around Pedro, experience served me well. I was twenty years old when the Detroit Tigers reached the 1968 World Series, and that was Pedro's team, his father having moved there from Miami to work in the auto industry. Pedro could talk all night about Bill Freehan, Willie Horton and Mickey Lolich, and I'd fall into the moment with crystal-clear memories of that epic confrontation with the St. Louis Cardinals.

We shared a love of Tiger Stadium that bordered on religious devotion; after many visits to the stately old yard, I was convinced it was the greatest ever built. He loved knowing that I'd occasionally vacate the press box, located too high above the playing field, to find a field-level seat, or that I once became so obsessed with the first row of second-level seats between the foul lines—without question the best view ever offered a baseball fan in modern times—I actually purchased a ticket so I could cover an A's-Tigers game from there. A Pedro Gomez thing, it was.

Here's another: Pedro's grandfather had a favorite Detroit Tiger above all, the great Al Kaline. And when the grandfather spoke, his Cuban heritage shining through, it was pronounced *Ahl Kah-LEEN-eh*. You wouldn't think this would come up too often in Pedro's day-to-day conversations, but we talked so often of the Tigers, the Sixties and that fabulous era, it became a staple. There were many times, in texts and emails, when one of us signed off just that way: *Ahl Kah-LEEN-eh*.

We struggle now through the aftermath. In lieu of flowers, the family asked any interested parties to donate to the Pedro Gomez Foundation at the Cronkite School of Journalism. That's one of the best schools in the country, on the campus of Arizona State University, and I was reminded that a family friend, Rob Werner, wants to be a broadcaster and recently completed his studies there. When I reached out to Rob, wondering if he'd ever had a connection with Pedro, this was his reply:

"He was incredibly kind to me, and during my sophomore year he invited me over to his home. He spent at least two hours hosting me and telling me he liked what I had done. He said he believed the most surefire way I could succeed was simply by being the kindest and most genuine person I could. We stayed in touch, and he was always so generous with his time. He actually came to speak to my class about a year later. He told everyone how the two of us were friends, and it was so cool to be acknowledged by him in that setting."

I can't begin to imagine the level of grief felt by Pedro's wonderful wife, Sandi, and their three children, Rio, Dante and Sierra. Pedro was a devoted father above all, and one sensed that immediately upon visiting their home outside Phoenix. The siblings certainly were aware of their dad's monumental stature in the business, but sometimes kids get so wrapped up in their own generation, their separate world, they may not fully grasp what their parents have accomplished over the years—at least not until they're well into adulthood. Reading the tributes in this book, learning elsewhere of the words that were spoken and the tears that were shed, they might fully realize the effect that Pedro had on people. That goes for all of us in the shadows of loss.

A BRIDGE

BY RACHEL NICHOLS

I'm sure it has to do with how he grew up. Living in Detroit, going to school with American kids but then coming home to his Cuban family, Pedro was constantly crossing from one world to another, over and back again, not just bridging the gap but learning how to become the bridge himself.

Of course, I didn't know any of that when we met. All I knew on that day more than seventeen years ago was that I was trying to find my way at a new job at ESPN, and so was he. We were both newspaper writers trying to shift to TV, hired within a few months of each other. The company lumped us together for all sorts of orientations and seminars and meetings, which meant that even though we lived on opposite sides of the country, we were constantly comparing notes, trying to find our way through together.

David Brofsky was the executive in charge of both of us, and while David couldn't have been more welcoming to me, Pedro was the one he'd wanted to work with for years. Back in 1998, he'd heard Pedro on an overnight radio show, a random listen on a night he couldn't sleep. He was so impressed he called Pedro the next day and invited him to fly to Connecticut to audition for ESPN. "His response was classic," Brofsky remembers. "'You want me to go *where* to do *what*?' He did the audition, and honestly it was not very good. But there was something about him that I really, really liked."

Pedro didn't get the job, but Brofsky never lost track of him. Five years later, ESPN finally hired him. "He may have been the easiest reporter I ever had to work with," Brofsky says. "He got along with everyone, and he absolutely loved his job."

That last part—"he absolutely loved his job"—I mean, if you watched Pedro on television for more than five seconds, you felt that joy. Pedro used to say he never worked a day in his life because he had so much fun covering baseball, but of course the truth is that he worked his ass off every day, all the time, through long days and even longer nights, even when it was hard.

And it was hard a lot, for both of us. We'd spent years training to be one thing—writers—and suddenly had to try to be something else. Personalities? Salesmen? Being a TV reporter is about a jumble of all kinds of stuff all at once. You are trying to inform but also entertain. You are trying to connect with millions of people, even though you can't see them or hear them or even know for sure what they're interested in.

Once again, Pedro had to be a bridge, between the ink-stained world in which he'd spent decades and this new TV world that we both so badly wanted to figure out. So many of our conversations back then were about being in both places at once, one foot in our old lives with our old sources, with the sports we'd known and loved for so long, and another foot in this new jungle, which was full of both possibility and hazard.

Pedro was lucky at least to have a secret weapon alongside him in Arizona as he learned to adapt: one of ESPN's best field producers, Charlie Moynihan. On paper, they didn't seem too alike—Pedro was the bilingual son of immigrants, an optimist whose smile could light up a whole county. Charlie was a hard-boiled, acerbic Northeasterner who also spoke two languages: English in a slight Boston accent, and English in a thick Boston accent, depending on what stage of the night you found him.

Yet Charlie and Pedro became instant brothers, carpooling to work together even when they didn't have to, or sometimes going to the ballpark on their off days, just to sit in left field and drink beers and break down pitch counts for fun.

And when they *were* working, well—Charlie knew just how to help make Pedro comfortable. He didn't coddle him; instead he'd yell "Don't fuck it up!" at Pedro right before the camera flicked on, and Pedro would laugh, and then go on to deliver some fantastic reporting nugget no one else had.

There was another producer we worked with a lot back then, Marc Weiner, who is now at MLB Network. Marc would say that when he was with Pedro, "It was like Pedro was running for Mayor, except he wasn't." That's because Pedro stopped to chat with nearly every person he saw, from the security guards to the ushers to the groundskeepers. One foot in their world, one foot in his. And it wasn't just superficial pleasantries. Marc remembers that by the end of the first day he and Pedro worked together, "He knew all about my family, my favorite teams, my love for Bruce Springsteen and probably some other details that I didn't even want him to know."

Pedro was so tuned into other people all the time, even when learning how to do a whole new job, and he was just as tuned into other people when the degree of difficulty on that job was ratcheted up even higher. Thanks to revelations of Barry Bonds' association with the steroid lab Balco, ESPN tasked Pedro with following Bonds pretty much everywhere, peppering him with questions that Bonds didn't want to answer, earning the wrath of Giants fans who at the time believed Bonds when he continually proclaimed his innocence.

It would have been too much for most people in the business, flat out. And yet there was Pedro, able to shift easily from one of the most intense situations in sports, a hard-boiled crusader for truth inside a crucible of accusations and lies, to being the relaxed charmer who so delighted his family and friends. I remember overlapping with him and Charlie on a road trip one night in San Francisco, during one of the most intense stretches of the Bonds debacle. I wandered into a place called Shanghai Kelly's to find Pedro holding court with half the bar, as if he were in town covering a parade.

Back to being the bridge again, and again—and again. Over the years, I would watch him connect people, connect ideas, connect worlds, like no one else could. He was a fixture in the sport of baseball but loved basketball too. He'd notice the smallest details of an NBA game and ask you about them, and oh boy, the ABA. If you were friends with Pedro, you'd sometimes get a no-context photo on your phone, him daring you to name a random member of the Virginia Squires.

Did you notice that after Pedro died, a bunch of clips started circulating from his 2016 trip to Cuba with the Rays? That's because Pedro did such a stirring job connecting an American audience to what it was really like in a country that so few have visited. Only Pedro could take a sports fan sitting on his couch in Huntsville, Alabama, and make him feel like he was sitting at a café table in Havana. Only Pedro could take an intensely private moment, like sprinkling his father's and brother's ashes in his homeland, and turn it into a catharsis for sons all over the world who had lost their fathers.

I miss a million things about Pedro Gomez already, and so does everyone who ever met him. From our earliest days together at ESPN, he joined so many of us together, sometimes without us even knowing it, and the way forward suddenly feels so much tougher—and much more disjointed—without him.

Mark and his son Ryan

San Diego Union sports department: Pedro, Tom Krasovic, Mark

BE WHERE YOUR FEET ARE

BY MARK KREIDLER

When I lit out for California in the mid-1980s, I had some things with me, just what would fit in the truck. A plan was not among them. All I knew was that it was time to leave. I was a writer, a journalist, and in my first few years out of school I had become convinced that nothing was going to happen for me where I was—that if I wanted to be part of a more interesting life, I needed to go to a place where life was more interesting. Looking back, it is easy to spot the fault lines in that logic. But I was twenty-four, and what's a heaven for?

So I took a job transfer and packed up. More specifically, I took one of the all-time great transfers in the history of transfers. I went from a windowless basement office of The Associated Press in Oklahoma City to the AP bureau in San Diego, located in a glorious building in the heart of Mission Valley that housed the city's two newspapers, the morning *Union* and the afternoon *Tribune*. When you went to the top floor, where the food and coffee were, you could stand outside and look directly west to the Pacific, and some days you could smell the salt air, too, because the water was only a couple of miles away. It was intoxicating.

I took an apartment in Pacific Beach, because no kid from Oklahoma was going to drive to the West Coast and then stick himself somewhere inland. Overpaying at will, I skimped on groceries in exchange for waking up where the water was. I lost weight but gained a perspective.

And I had, indeed, gone to a place where more seemed to happen. Reporters for the AP in those days were expected to wear all hats, and about three weeks after I arrived in San Diego, a man named James Oliver Huberty walked into a McDonald's restaurant in San Ysidro, near the Mexico border, and opened fire. Nineteen people died; I reported for hours from the scene. Not long after, I began to contemplate a career change.

I didn't have to go far, because in one of those great lightning strikes of life, I had unwittingly gotten myself transferred to a city in which the local paper and a couple of editors had decided to try something audacious. The editors, Barry Lorge and Bob Wright, East Coasters both, set up shop at the *San Diego Union* and apparently wanted to see how much young talent they could collect in one place, their sports department.

The answer was a lot. I was a throw-in when hired, loose change amid the couch-cushions of ability and production. The department was already running through top-shelf pros like Michael Bass (later to become Jeff Zucker's top executive at NBC and CNN) and Brian Brown and Bruce Schoenfeld and Peter Richmond. Over the next couple of years, it was Buster Olney and Jim Trotter and Mark Zeigler, Ed Graney and Ric Bucher and Chris Clarey. Kevin Kernan. Dave Sheinin. We had a loaded lineup every season. Everybody batted fourth.

It was a heady time in the business. Newspapers were flush with cash, and editors lived in mortal fear of somehow not spending all of their fat budgets. We were thus dispersed across the country and around the world, sometimes kept on the road for extra days to soak up the last of the allowance so that the department could ask for that much and more in the coming year. The *Union* became a sports section of regional and then national ambition. I covered the Padres, who were terrible, and then moved to long features, then columns. We got on planes and went to where the stories were, kind of the way I had dreamed it might be when I left home. There was no end.

What I am saying is that by 1988, when Pedro Gomez walked

through our doors, it's possible that we felt pretty confident we were already humming along. And maybe we were. But we didn't have a Pedro. It turns out they only made the one.

Pedro was a connector, pure and simple. Sportswriters are funny, cynical people, non-joiners who hoard topics and sources as if they were precious bits of sustenance. Pedro was a funny, uncynical person who believed that the universe, or at least his corner of it, was better with more of everything—more people, more friends, more food, more sources, more games, more ideas, more sharing. He came to San Diego from the *Miami News,* started at the *Union* by covering every low-level prep contest known to man, and never took his foot off the gas. He earned every single thing he got. He worked his tail off for every promotion. And everywhere he went, he connected his friends with his other friends, his pro contacts with his other pro contacts. He did this effortlessly and organically, as though no alternative existed in the world. It was a world that constantly expanded. His world.

I will tell you that we became friends immediately—I mean, we did—but I am only describing everyone who met Pedro. Pedro *was* immediate; his ability to remain firmly in the here and now served him unbelievably well over the next three decades. A long time later in our lives, when my son Ryan got serious about baseball, Ryan began to carry with him a consistent thought: "Be where your feet are." It was a reminder, for a player, to control the moment in front of him, which after all was the only one available. Pedro had been doing that for years before anyone tried to claim it as a thing.

Pedro was three years younger than I, yet the first time I watched him work a baseball clubhouse, I felt myself being taken to school by a person ahead of his time. You will rightfully hear about his passion, and there is no reason you shouldn't; he was all that. But Pedro's great gift was his abiding interest in whatever was happening right this second. Baseball writers sometimes talk about working a clubhouse counter-clockwise—that is, going in the opposite direction of their competitors. Pedro didn't care about any of that. He was too busy going full-bore into a conversation to notice who else even happened to be hanging around. And he had this great sort of reporter's tic—a professional thing, but really it was more about who Pedro was—of starting to walk away, then suddenly remembering something else he wanted to say to the player he'd just interviewed. It wasn't another question; it was something Pedro had just thought of that he wanted to share. He'd turn on his heel and hustle back over to the locker, just for that quick minute. It's how relationships got built.

He was also, and I'll just leave this here, a classic sportswriter, all jumbled up on the inside. He could be legendarily direct (if you only ever saw him doing quick on-field TV hits, you perhaps wouldn't know this), yet it genuinely bothered him when a player snapped back or complained they'd been badly treated by his line of inquiry. He could ask Barry Bonds point-blank questions about Bonds' obvious cheating, and he could deliver his subsequent report on air to ESPN, complete with Bonds' non-answers or his chiding bullshit, but it saddened Pedro. The whole thing left him enervated. "It's just so bad for the sport," he told me at one point. Pedro was good for baseball, or perhaps more directly, he truly and actually loved it. You can see the conflict.

We stayed in each other's lives as we both married, he to Sandi and I to Colleen, and both of us wound up in Northern California for a time, Pedro covering the Oakland A's while I wrote a column from Sacramento. We worked together at the *Bee* for a couple of years before he moved to Arizona. He was the greatest traveling companion I had, and he showed me Miami, and we both agreed that I would not show him Oklahoma. It seemed a fair trade.

When our sons were born, we certainly had no idea how they would bring us closer. Rio Gomez and Patric Kreidler are nearly the same age, as are Dante Gomez and Ryan Kreidler. Pedro and Sandi then had a daughter, Sierra. Colleen and I failed to match, and Pedro declared victory.

All of which brings me to a story. For years, Pedro and I joked about our sons squaring off in a high-level baseball duel, someplace, somehow. We were both in on the joke: We were sportswriters. The history of sportswriters producing elite-level baseball players is, not to put too fine a point on it, scary thin. But, you know, guys talk. Eventually, Rio went off to junior college, and Pat turned down lower-division offers to play ball because he wanted a big-school experience. I figured that ended that.

Instead, Rio found his way to the University of Arizona as a left-handed pitcher, and Pat's younger brother took a baseball scholarship at

UCLA. And on March 19, 2017, a sunny, mild Sunday at Jackie Robinson Stadium in Los Angeles, the senior, Rio Gomez, took the mound for the Wildcats against the freshman, Ryan Kreidler, and the Bruins.

It was delicious on every level, but the real emotional multiplier was the fact that Pedro was actually there to see it. I wish I could cash in on every agonized text he had sent me through the years, as his work took him away from Arizona at the precise moments when he wanted to watch his kids play ball or do some other activity. His life was a life on the road, sometimes on short or no notice. He'd get the call and go. To be at UCLA in person that day was, for him, an utter gift.

Not that he took it that way, of course. Pedro was an almost prototypical baseball dad, completely incapable of functional behavior while his kid pitched. ("He was a nervous wreck every time," Rio told me, chuckling, as we talked about his dad a few weeks after Pedro passed.) This has nothing to do with covering baseball itself, and there is no training in sportswriting to prepare one for it. It must be endured. Pedro was a sufferer when it came to Rio being on the mound, a suffering that he loved deeply. It's hard to explain if you haven't been through it, and it was one of the things that bound us more deeply as friends.

Despite Colleen and I pretty much loving Pedro unreservedly, we kept to our respective team corners as the game began, because that's what you do. But when Rio struggled just a bit in the first inning, Pedro popped out of his seat on the Arizona side and hit the concourse to do some worry-walking. It wasn't long before he settled in next to us—to say hi, he said. We knew better. He was trying to change Rio's luck.

Thus commenced our beautiful afternoon together, our all-time keeper. Pedro sat between Colleen and me, talking about everything and nothing, flinching at every ball and strike call as Rio delivered his pitches; and as if God flipped a switch upon seeing this favorable alignment of old friends, Rio suddenly started dealing. He'd given up a run in that first inning, but now he was in command. Over the next five innings, he gave up one hit and struck out five. It was easily his finest performance of the young season, maybe of his career at UA. And of course Pedro could not move from that seat. Only the purest baseball neophyte would have even considered it.

By the seventh, Rio had faced Ryan twice, walking him and coaxing a fly ball to center field. Arizona led, 4-1. On one level, Pedro couldn't

Ryan Kreidler signs with the Detroit Tigers

believe Rio was sent out there to pitch a seventh inning in March, but he was so thrilled at watching his son perform that it barely registered. Rio gave up a double but was working with two outs as Ryan came to bat. He got the count to 2-2, then threw a pitch middle in.

It's difficult to write over what happened next, because so many people have seen the video. Suffice it to say, the lives of a bunch of baseball parents were suddenly on display. You see Colleen and me jump to our feet, I with my phone in hand, while Pedro between us watches the trajectory of the ball for a second before slumping back in his seat. He and I have watched a lot of ball, a lot of ball. You can tell when one gets hit with enough pop to leave the yard.

Anyway, that's the video people see. It surfaced and went viral very quickly on the night Pedro died, Super Bowl Sunday, and it is charming and funny and telling. Our mutual friend Roxy Bernstein is doing the PAC-12 Network broadcast, another thing to savor about the whole deal. But it isn't the only video. I was recording that moment, too. And when I turn up the volume on my phone, which I have only done a thousand times with that video, I can hear the extended seconds of white noise from the UCLA crowd—and then the unmistakable voice of my friend Pedro, bellowing in my direction in order to make sure my phone picks up his words: "DAMN you, Ryan Kreidler!" And then the laughter. Pedro brought back to earth. Loving the game again. Or maybe it hit him that Rio was still in line to get the win. (Baseball dad.)

When Rio was drafted that summer by the Red Sox, it was a singular moment in Pedro's life. When Ryan was selected by the Tigers in 2019, we began dreaming again, two old sportswriters having a little vision. There was a springtime flash in 2020, before the pandemic shut everything down, when we thought the two might meet in Fort Myers. It could still happen for them, the pitcher and the hitter. And if it does, I suppose I'll try to play both roles, although I think we've established that there is only one Pedro. Perhaps he went on to another place where interesting things happen. The thing is, with Pedro, interesting was wherever he was. Be where your feet are.

HAVE FUN EVERY
SINGLE DAY

BY MAX SCHERZER

One of the cool things about becoming a major-leaguer is all of a sudden you start having conversations with reporters you've been watching on TV for years. I grew up on SportsCenter, like just about everybody in baseball, I guess, and I always watched Pedro when he came on the air. Hearing him talk baseball felt like having a conversation with a friend. Then I was drafted by the Arizona Diamondbacks, and Pedro lived in the Phoenix area, so I got to know him early in my career. We'd have conversations away from the camera and I got to see up close how genuine he was, how much he just loved covering baseball.

To me, Pedro saw baseball for what it was. He never forgot how fun it was to go to a game. That was something I immediately gravitated towards. I loved that I could just sit there in front of my locker and talk to Pedro about baseball, and have it be such a delightful conversation because of his insight and his positive personality. Before you knew it you'd look up and see you'd already been talking for an hour. Pedro was very observant and loved the nuances. We could laugh about all the little things that go into baseball, like not talking into a mitt when the catcher or manager comes out to the mound.

In 2019 he tweeted: "Love how Max Scherzer doesn't feel the need to cover his mouth when he's talking on the mound." And: "Everyone with a glove over their month. Ugh-ly look, especially pitching coaches and even translators with a hand over their mouth as they speak."

I understood Pedro had a job to do and was always going to do it. If he had to report something negative, he was not going to flinch, but his whole focus was on the positive and how much fun baseball is, not always looking for the negative headlines that everybody tries to generate. I always knew he believed in me. When I was younger, the head snap at the end of my pitching motion was much more pronounced. Teams thought my mechanics were too violent. Much was said about it, put it that way. I got tired of hearing about it. Pedro and I had long talks about that. He heard me out. He listened.

"I'm just getting through the ball," I'd tell him back then. "I'm just throwing the ball with everything I've got. I don't see how my head has anything to do with this. Yeah, my head snap might be more pronounced than anybody, it might go against the conventional kind of wisdom, but that doesn't mean my arm slot is in a bad spot. It's actually quite the opposite. Everything is where it needs to be."

We conferred over it in detail, point by point, and Pedro was kind of dumbfounded about how teams had reacted to my mechanics. He was open-minded enough to say: *Forget the conventional wisdom.* Having that kind of conversation meant a lot to me. You never go long in baseball without somebody having negative things to say about you, and you always want to be open to constructive criticism, but there's a time and place for that. Sometimes you just want someone to listen to your side, to hear you out—someone like Pedro who was confident enough to call it like he saw it. He agreed with me on my mechanics. He reaffirmed that what I was doing was correct and helped me to trust myself.

"Whatever you're doing," he told me in private, laughing, "keep doing it, because it's working."

It was almost like Pedro could see into the future. From the time I was a rookie he could see me on the hill in the World Series or winning the Cy Young Award. He talked about it like he *knew* it would all happen. He always thought big things about my future.

My first All-Star Game was in 2013, and that year the game—and all the parties—were in New York. I remember having a couple beers with Pedro at the bar during one of the All-Star parties. For some reason, they had dollars flying around and Pedro grabbed a dollar bill and stuffed it into my pants. We laughed about that one for years and it became an inside joke that kind of evolved, the idea being that if I was being interviewed by Pedro, something good must have happened. It got to the point where I'd see him before a playoff series and one of us would say, "If you want to do an interview with me, it's going to cost you a dollar!"

Pedro opened up so much for me. Being of Cuban descent, he provided so much perspective and showed me a whole different cultural outlook. I always joked with him that I never imagined at fourteen years old, growing up outside of St. Louis, I'd be listening to Latin music all the time and just having a great time with it. Pedro had an affinity for all the different cultures that come into baseball, whether someone was from South Korea or Japan, Oklahoma or Arkansas, Venezuela or the D.R. He loved how many different cultures there are in baseball and how that showed through in all the different flavors of baseball and how it's played. He appreciated that at the major-league level, it's the best players from basically every single culture all brought together. He saw how the game could grow because of that.

He really loved being able to relate to everybody and digress and find out about all cultures. I think that's why players were drawn to him. The teams that embrace their diversity and bring out the different cultures really tend to do well because you get a perspective that you never had before in your life. When you get a new perspective, you play the game in a fresh way, with a new energy. I know that's been my experience and I feel like that was Pedro's experience as well. That's what made him so relatable and so easy to talk to, and that's why he'll be missed so much.

Pedro understood the X factor, which is the human element of the game. As baseball continued to push towards more analytics over the years, and the human element was trivialized by front offices, he really didn't like the way the game was going. That was something we definitely talked about. We saw it from the same light. If you have everybody pulling together, pulling for each other, that can add up to more than what the numbers say. He always recognized that it takes leadership inside the clubhouse. If you have good glue guys in your clubhouse, that's what makes a winning team.

Over the years my relationship with Pedro developed to where we could talk about anything, about how everything influences baseball and how baseball kind of influences everything else. That's why his passing is so devastating to me—he really stood out as one of the reporters I admired the most in the game.

To me, Pedro was all about: Have fun every single day. Whoever you come across, try to find the good in people. And when you find good people, talk to them even more. I feel like that's what Pedro did. He understood who the good eggs were and who the bad eggs were. When you find a good egg, make sure that you always go in depth and you can talk about anything. Building those human relationships is worth more than one story's clickbait. That can apply to everyone. Anybody can take a piece of that and put it into their own lives.

Rio, Bob, Dante, Pedro in Key West

THE ART OF THE
INTERVIEW

BY BOB LEY

Oh, to have been a fly on the wall for what was his most emotional interview. His hair was mostly dark back then, not his well-known latter-day distinguished salt and pepper, when Pedro Gomez followed his father's handwritten map to the neighborhood, and eventually to the actual house where his family lived in Havana before fleeing Cuba in late July 1962. The Cuban Missile Crisis, which nearly erupted into nuclear war, was less than three months off.

On that July day, family legend had it, the fervent Communist living upstairs from the Gomez family had scornfully lectured Pedro's eight-month-pregnant mother, Marta Elena, about leaving Castro's paradise. "By the time that baby inside of you is in kindergarten," his mother recalled the neighbor proclaiming, "the world will be living under communism."

Now, in 1999, on his first visit to his family's country, Pedro saw firsthand the sclerotic shell of Castro's nation hobbled by decades of economic embargoes. A new century was beckoning, though it was hard to see on the block where his parents used to live. Reporter that he was, Pedro located the strident neighbor at the center of his mother's emotional recollections of their sudden departure.

Pedro's account in the *Arizona Republic* is remarkable; finding this man, giving him the time and space to provide context to a conversation that had been an animating force in his mother's life for decades. The neighbor, Rodolfo Fernandez-Guzman, was eighty-four by then, and his memory of that long-ago conversation was not nearly as confrontational as Pedro's mother's. And Pedro quoted him, at length, as he recounted his version of that seminal moment in the life of the Gomez family.

At its core, an interview is a conversation. A give and take, ebb and flow, an exercise in listening (an all too rare occurrence), and, to achieve the best results, establishing a relationship on at least a professional level, between journalist and subject.

By the time Pedro sat with Guzman, he was accomplished at all of this. But imagine the focus demanded even of an experienced professional. Consider his prevailing emotions, his senses all attuned to their max, while speaking to a man whose admonition to Pedro's mother, thirty-seven years earlier, was so powerful that when young Pedro finally did begin kindergarten in the United States, his mother cried in relief and vindication.

The story of his first Cuban homecoming is so poetically perfect, and it lives because of Pedro's interview with Guzman.

Who could resist the opportunity to speak to this man? The answer is, no one.

Baseball's world of information and intel is founded on relationships, the conversations that take place every day, not just when the immediate headline calls for it: at the batting cage, in the dugout, in the hotel bar. Pedro's advice to those new on the beat: always talk to the visiting manager. Pedro's career in television was marked by his unflagging willingness to be "that guy," the reporter in the losing clubhouse, because to be there in October required empathy, relationships and a mastery of how to ask the toughest question in the most unthreatening way. All of that, Petey had in spades.

His first long-form feature for ESPN in the spring of 2003 was on Arizona Diamondbacks reliever Byung-Hyun Kim. During the 2001 World Series, Kim's dominance as the D-backs' closer had evaporated, as he blew Game 4. Tino Martinez took Kim deep in the ninth, and Derek

Jeter homered to win the game in the tenth inning. The very next night in the Bronx, Kim gave up a ninth-inning, game-tying, two-run homer to Scott Brosius, and the Yankees went on to win the game in twelve innings and take the Series lead.

Now, history records that indeed the D-backs rallied at home to win the World Series in seven games, but Kim's experience there was central to Pedro's planned piece eighteen months on. Feature producer Shawn Fitzgerald made the phone calls and went through team PR to line up the anticipated interviews for the story, but still, there were some essential subjects missing on a story that could get delicate.

Fitzgerald was standing on the field before the game. He turned around as the time for interviews was approaching. Pedro was gone. And then, suddenly he popped up. Within minutes, Pedro had ducked into the Arizona clubhouse and secured commitments for the right voices for his piece. Only someone who knew the lay of the land, and commanded such respect, especially on such a story, could accomplish that on a few minutes' notice.

At Pedro's memorial service, six days after his passing, the home plate area at Salt River Fields in Scottsdale displayed a dozen enlarged photographs from the various chapters of Pedro's life. Most showed Pedro with his family and close friends. The last several showed him at work, including a shot of Pedro beaming, at his keyboard, in a press box. And the last was a picture of Pedro sitting in the dugout next to Barry Bonds, the two clearly engaged in conversation. The picture was presumably from that fabled period Pedro covered Bonds on a nearly daily basis, from the whispers of the Balco scandal to the edge of the major-league career home run record.

Their relationship was one of the great subtexts of that remarkable period in baseball journalism, and it was a daily source of admiration from Pedro's colleagues. Bonds, a reluctant subject on the best of days. Pedro, the one constant in the media maelstrom that enveloped the Giants slugger, who was there for the long haul, with the chops in the game, and in news, to ask the right questions, the right way.

There were often times Bonds would invoke Pedro's name in the "money sound bite" of the day, and so their relationship would gain even more currency and celebrity. At its core, and I think Pedro believed this, was a mutual respect, as difficult as that may have been to appreciate in the moment. Many of Pedro's colleagues begged him to write the book of those days, of the weeks and months spent around the greatest hitter the modern game has seen while his very accomplishments and veracity were questioned on a daily basis. Pedro always demurred.

Bonds got his record, and essentially a standoff with the U.S. Department of Justice as his one-count conviction for obstruction of justice was overturned on appeal. Pedro moved on to continue to cover the game that was in his blood.

Then, out of the blue, late in the 2016 season, up pops a text from Pedro telling me that while in Miami to work a story, he was on the field before the game when suddenly he encountered the Marlins' batting coach. "Barry Lamar . . . saw me and approached me and asks about my family. My jaw hit my shoes."

The all-time home run champ sent an arrangement of flowers to the Gomez home after Pedro's death. As one person familiar with Barry said, he doesn't have "people" around him. That was something Barry did himself.

That on-field rapprochement with Bonds in 2016 came at the end of a season which began with Pedro's return to Cuba to cover the visit of President Obama and a game between the Tampa Bay Rays and the Cuban National Team. It was the national story of the moment, but for Pedro it was much more than that. Pedro planned to scatter two sets of ashes, to repatriate his father, Pedro Sr., in fact and in spirit, and to introduce his late younger brother Rick to the land of his heritage.

He had some slight trepidation about doing so, and making it public. Pedro planned to have an ESPN camera recording him in the moment as he went to the shoreline on his solemn mission. But he wondered if it would cause some washback that would ripple beyond the normal channels.

Pedro had the full backing of his bosses in the considerable ESPN contingent. Moreover, it was quickly apparent to us that in 2016, the arc of change in Cuba was such that he need not worry. Yes, we traveled with local drivers provided by the government, and we also had an official "fixer" (who was also our "minder") to smooth anything over. But this story was so simply beautiful, no one stood in Pedro's way.

He introduced the piece while standing at our broadcast location directly across the street from El Capitolio, the national Capitol building.

Pedro's story was simple in its eloquence, and powerful in its message, as he poured the ashes into the gurgling waters of the Cuban shoreline, and the camera kept a respectful distance. On the set Pedro tagged the taped piece with a talkback with Scott Van Pelt, to air later in the evening.

"I was hesitant about the segment," Van Pelt recalled. "It was so personal. I thought about the question I wanted to ask Pedro. I said, 'I know what you brought to Cuba. What do you bring home?' And, he said, 'Closure.'"

The moment was emotional for both men.

"When I heard that Pedro had died," said Van Pelt, "I immediately thought of that moment in Havana."

When the taping was over, Pedro walked down from the platform, tears filling his eyes, and we embraced. His trip had accomplished its mission.

But the complexity of being Cuban, so central in Pedro's life, was on infuriating display for both of us within the hour. I was about to begin a SportsCenter report at that same location, and anchor stories about the ball game that day, and the meeting between Presidents Obama and Raúl Castro. As I came on the air live, three men abruptly jumped up onto our set, one directly next to me on camera, each of them throwing pamphlets into the air. I heard them yell something several times, including the word "Castro." I stiff-armed the demonstrator closest to me and verbally threw our report on to the next reporter at another location.

But we were still rolling with the camera covering me and the demonstrators. Suddenly, in a scene seemingly ripped from a spy movie, three unmarked cars screeched to a halt at the curb—within seconds of each other. Out spilled a half-dozen plainclothes Cuban security policemen. The demonstrators were corralled, one of them violently, dragged by his windpipe into a waiting car, and as quickly as the police had arrived, they sped off with the political protestors. We captured it all on camera. But the cops left behind several of their brethren to try and retrieve all the offending pamphlets, as if squirreling them away from the U.S. television network would blunt our subsequent reporting on their printed demands for legal reform, political freedom and internet access.

Pedro saw it all, right in front of him. We were gobsmacked. But he, more than anyone in our group, understood the forces at play, and the contradictions that ruled. That repatriating the remains of Cuban exiles didn't rock the boat, but a loud demand for free speech earned you a violent arrest on live international television. It was something we spoke of so often in the years that followed.

With no small amount of irony, the last time I saw Pedro was in Key West, Florida, my adopted home town, where still, into the third decade of the twenty-first century, Cuban refugees fleeing the Communist nation are regularly pulled from small makeshift boats drifting in the Straits of Florida. Often, two or three times a week the Coast Guard is called upon to rescue a desperate group of Cubans far less fortunate than Pedro's family nearly sixty years ago.

We sat down by the water and had a few drinks. Pedro brought the entire family on this Eastern jaunt, and they had come to the right town in their pursuit of a good time. We talked of family, of friends, of work, and of life. And of our trip to Cuba, which underscored all who Pedro Gomez was, and even now defines his indelible legacy.

Havana, 2016: Pedro with Baseball Commissioner Rob Manfred

AN OPEN LETTER TO PRESIDENT BILL CLINTON: MARCH 1999

BY PEDRO GOMEZ

First published in The Arizona Republic, *Sunday, March 28, 1999, under the headline "It's Time to Drop Cuba Embargo." Reprinted with permission.*

Dear President Clinton,

My name is Pedro Gomez, and I am a first-generation Cuban-American, born just three weeks after my parents arrived in the United States in 1962. Because of my upbringing, it is not easy for me to say this publicly, but you must do everything in your power to halt the U.S. embargo against Cuba. It simply makes no sense whatsoever anymore.

You see, I am making my first-ever visit to the land of my roots. Cuba is no longer just an idea to me. It will forever have a heartbeat now. After gazing into the eyes of the Cuban people, I have discovered that I see so much of myself. I wish every Cuban exile living in the United States had the opportunity to return and peer into the souls of the people here. For it is they who give Cuba its strength and make this such a beautiful country.

For years, I thought of Rodolfo Fernandez-Guzman as an evil man. He is the man who lived in the home above my parents', the one who pleaded with them to keep me in Cuba, where I might one day become a good communist. Just the idea of him was wretched. I met Guzman a few days ago, and although I had my preconceived notions of him, they were nowhere near what I saw. He was a charming gentleman of eighty-four years with a quick mind who greatly reminded me of my maternal grandfather, to whom I was extremely close. He was no monster, just someone who thinks differently.

For so many Cubans living in the United States, it is easy to stand on a platform and declare how the U.S. economic embargo must never be lifted as long as Fidel Castro remains in power. I am sympathetic to that point of view, having been raised with that idea. All I can say is that after talking to regular everyday Cubans, not the elite from the Communist Party, my feelings have changed dramatically. It is so simple to dictate foreign policy from a living room, but quite another when you actually encounter the pained look in Cubans' eyes and absorb their impoverished lifestyle, which could be eased with the lifting of the embargo. The Cuban people are not the enemy of Cubans living in the United States. The enemy is Castro.

Who is really being affected by this blockade, which was imposed during the Kennedy administration? Certainly not Castro or his top lieutenants. They continue to live their privileged lifestyles, even as Cuba's economy crumbles since the loss of Soviet aid. I'm talking about the person who must scramble each day to earn money so that his family can eat well. The nationalistic pride of the common Cuban people is both inspirational and admirable. I only wish some Americans could realize what utterly fabulous lives we live and stop taking so many of our liberties for granted.

There are several reasons Cuba won't back down from its stance as a socialist country. The first being that the government wields unyielding power over the people, using scare tactics to remain in control. But the second, which I believe is far more important, is the tremendous and unwavering pride that Cubans possess. They will simply not get down on their knees to beg, whether it be Cubans living in Cuba or in the United States.

The one aspect of this trip that has opened my eyes more than anything else is the incredible similarities between Cubans living here and those of us in the United States. Among Latin Americans, Cubans are considered somewhat arrogant. In fact, we are filled with pride—which is sometimes construed as arrogance—at who we are. It is arguably the single greatest gift handed down to each new generation of Cubans, no matter where we call home. When all is said and done, it is that bullheadedness on both sides that perpetuates the trade cutoff.

"By nature, I am not a political person," Abilio Valdes said as he rocked in a chair sipping cool water on his mother's porch. "All I ask is that we be given a chance without the embargo to see what happens. If we drown, like so many believe, then OK, we can say you were right, we were wrong. But if we can manage to survive, then let us be."

It's the type of rhetoric that would get a person stoned on the streets of Miami, where I grew up. I, too, was one who believed the embargo should stand forever. Powerful Cuban-American lobbyists in Washington have spent their careers keeping the embargo in place, refusing to yield to Castro. But after putting faces behind what for so many years were faceless, I cannot in good conscience continue the same way of thinking.

We deal with China and Vietnam and had civil relations with the former Soviet Union. And who knows, maybe our softened stance with the U.S.S.R. led to the crumbling of the Eastern Bloc. People far smarter than me certainly believe so. The embargo has lasted nearly forty years, and what has really changed? Absolutely nothing. The embargo has not come close to putting an end to Cuba's domestic problems, either in terms of economics or human rights. It is time to try a different course.

I have no idea what my father, mother and brother will think of me after they read this. For that matter, many of my friends in Miami may abandon me for what I am saying. I do know, though, that for the most part, they have not had the same opportunity I have had this past week, of walking through the streets of Havana and getting to know the Cubans here.

What makes Cuba so very special is its people. Even as I write this, I can barely contain myself, for now that I have met what I consider my countrymen, I can't help but feel an overwhelming sense of pride to say I am both Cuban and American. In a way, I feel I have been twice blessed.

I am not—I repeat not—a Castro sympathizer. His regime has undoubtedly committed many atrocities. I believe he is a contemptible person who has single-handedly guided a once-thriving country into the gutter. The question now is, what to do to rectify that? A bold man would have the vision to do the right thing, not what a group of powerful people insist he do. I have no idea how family and friends will react to me now. I do know that after visiting Cuba, it's time for a new game plan.

Sincerely,

Pedo Gary

'KNOW AND UNDERSTAND CUBA'

BY PETER GAMMONS

I was a sophomore in Chapel Hill, N.C., like so many not yet in his twenties fascinated by Fidel Castro's face on the cover of *Time Magazine* and his voice every few nights on Cronkite or Huntley-Brinkley. I was raised in a New England town of 2,000, educated in an Anglican church school where one of the courses required being able to answer current-events questions about what appeared in *Time*, *The New Republic* and the Sunday *New York Herald Tribune*. Cuba and the Soviet Union, Castro and Khrushchev, were our worldly issues beyond the Civil Rights Movement (and Roger Maris hitting sixty home runs) that so dominated our consciousness, especially after our Groton School headmaster arranged for Martin Luther King Jr. to spend a half day in January 1963 informally talking with thirty-something members of the senior class, including me. What still sticks with me is how much Dr. King talked to us about the plight of all poor people, not necessarily about black and white, but about the disparity between rich and poor in the country. He was just a fascinating man. I was too terrified to ask a question.

My college friends used to kid me that the reason I was so fascinated by Cuba was the 1959 Little World Series, when the Red Sox top farm club, the Minneapolis Millers, managed by a hero of mine, Gene Mauch, and starring a twenty-year-old phenom named Carl Yastrzemski, played the Havana Sugar Kings. It could be argued that I was taken by that series, reported weekly by the *Sporting News*, but by the time I entered this class the Bay of Pigs, the Kennedy Assassination and a new Miami shaped by the Cuban diaspora were permanent threads of our culture. But the all-Cuban double play turned by the 1960 Washington Senators—Zoilo Versalles to José Valdivielso to Julio Bécquer—had been recreated in stickball games that '60 summer to the backdrop of Sam Cooke's "Chain Gang."

In the fall 1964 semester, the course centered on the Organization of American States, a Kennedy Administration focus, a dramatic turn from an Anglican education focusing on Europe. I knew little about Venezuelan oil or why so many Germans had settled in Brazil, or Argentina, Nicaragua and Mexico, but the professor we had constantly brought subjects home to Cuba and its history before Castro had overthrown Bautista and ousted so much of the underworld playpens from the United States. "Know and understand Cuba," he often reminded us. "Appreciate their culture. We are cultural brothers with Cubans. When you understand the soul of Cuba, you will understand that they are the Jews of Latin America."

I never forgot. I immediately reread *The Old Man and the Sea*. Pedro Martinez helped me ply the man who signed him—the legendary Dodger scout Ralph Avila—with wine fifty years later to try to get him to talk about his role in the failed Bay of Pigs invasion (which he did not discuss, nor has done to his son and grandson currently in baseball). I never covered a player who better represented *duende* than Luis Tiant, and was there at Fenway in 1975 when his parents, thanks to a request from Massachusetts Senator Edward Brooke (delivered to Castro by George McGovern), sat behind the home-plate screen to watch El Tiante pitch. In the winter of 1995, when the Marlins flew Livan Hernandez and Osvaldo Fernandez into Miami and wined and dined them in Little Havana, I was in the party, easy on the Mojitos.

I envisioned the baseball world I have covered since 1968 would be forever changed by the Cuban Invasion. I had listened to Calvin Griffith talk about how his scout Joe Cambria worked out Castro, who wasn't very good, and to Mauch talk about their friendship formed in the 1950s when Mauch played winter ball in Cuba for several winters. What I had pushed to my mind's back shelf was Joan Didion's *Miami*, which laid out the world of the Cubans who were driven out of their homeland to Florida and other U.S. areas, and why they so resented John F. Kennedy and, right up through recent elections, the Democratic Party in general. I didn't remember it when I was doing stories on Jose Canseco for *Sports Illustrated* in 1988, not grasping why a young star who came from an educated and elite family in Cuba declined to talk about his family and their journey to South Florida.

Wrap it up, and take it to July 7, 1995, and the Oakland Coliseum. The Oakland Athletics were playing the Toronto Blue Jays and a Cuban refugee named Ariel Prieto was making his first major-league start. Prieto had fled Cuba and was eligible for the '95 baseball draft. The A's were intending to draft a first baseman from the University of Tennessee named Todd Helton, but thought that Prieto could step right into a major-league rotation and help the A's, who still had Rickey Henderson, Mark McGwire and Dennis Eckersley but were on their way to last place.

Pedro Gomez brought a lot to me that night. He was curious why an ESPN guy would fly to Oakland for this event, which was not exactly national news. He, too, was excited, anticipatory, and introduced me to Latin journalists as my interpreter and drifted into what to me were wonderful tales of Cuban history and their great players. I gushed on Tiant, one of the most dynamic clubhouse leaders of my baseball lifetime, and we bemoaned the injuries that denied Tony Oliva the Hall of Fame.

I remember flashing back to turning Cuban double plays with a stickball bat and tennis balls. I have never forgotten. And, yet, there was an edge to the way Pedro stared back at me as we spoke that I later realized was the flashing yellow light to my excitement.

This was his family's culture of which a college professor in Chapel Hill talked, a culture as revered as that of Israel. There was also that remembrance hanging over each sentence, what happened to so many from that culture as they had to pile out of their homes onto boats headed from their promised land to a new country where prejudice and segregation faced them. I spent fifteen spring trainings in Polk County, Florida, where in the late 1980s towns still had two Elks clubs, white, non-white; I wish Pedro had come into Winter Haven and covered the Red Sox and watched Roger Clemens walk out of spring training to remind me what lay around us was so much more important.

Pedro added to the background of my two weeks in Havana for ESPN prior to the Orioles playing the Cuban National Team on March 28, 1999. One year earlier, Pope John Paul II had become the first Catholic pontiff to visit Cuba, and so much had begun to reopen; my producer, Julie Chrisco Andrews, and I ate at what once were gorgeous homes on El Paseo del Prado, where families finally were allowed to open to serve dinners, like lobster and a bottle of wine for our $30. We went to many playoff games; the La Isla fans had dancing girls on the dugouts. We went to one of their sports academies and I ogled two fifteen-year-olds named Kendrys Morales and Yuli Gurriel, an academy that José Fernández told me many years later he attended and where he perfected his bat flip as a slugging third baseman. I spent the $20 to get to talk to Gregorio Fuentes, the Old Man of *The Old Man and the Sea,* for ten minutes. He was 101.

Lord, their fans loved baseball, and every game was four hours. In the playoffs, the players invited me into the dugout, and made me high-five them. But driving back to the hotel one night, I asked our ABC Network guide about a line outside a dimly lit building. "You would call them spies," she said. "If they line up and tell on their neighbors, they are rewarded with extra food stamps."

I relayed that to Pedro. As we had prepared for Ariel Prieto, his face hinted knowledge of that sort of reminder of what so many of his culture were forced to flee. I thought about that the morning I learned Pedro had died. Like so many in baseball, I remembered the enthusiasm Pedro brought to every day at the ballpark, even when he reported on Barry Bonds day after day. He loved baseball.

In the spring of 2016, Pedro called me for what he said he felt was a substantial favor. His son Rio, whose baseball career was a joy in his life, was in his junior year at the University of Arizona and was going to play summer ball in California. Pedro thought the Cape Cod experience might be good for Rio.

I told him the rosters were set, but I had some close friends who manage in the league. I called former North Carolina coach Mike Roberts, who manages Cotuit. No problem.

Rio came in and pitched well, well enough so that the Red Sox drafted him the following June. I remember a late July night, sitting on a bench in Falmouth with Rio, proud that he was there, proud to know the son of a man who often without realizing had so many times expanded my respect for his birth culture.

At this writing, Rio had pitched himself to Single A, and earned a reputation among Red Sox organization folk as a diligent, reliable pitcher who had at that point made the best of his ability. Coaches loved him. So, too, they said, did his teammates.

I promised Rio on MLB Network the morning after his father died that if he pitched his way to Fenway, I'd be there. His father cared so much that when Rio finished the 2016 Cotuit Ketleers season, he sent me a case of wine. So if and when Rio does make it into a Red Sox uniform, the least I can do is introduce him to El Tiante, and remind him that I covered Pedro Martinez, Roger Clemens and Curt Schilling in Red Sox uniforms and the pitcher I'd pick to start the seventh game of a World Series would be Tiant.

My advice to Rio would be that before he left for Fort Myers in April to watch *The Lost Son of Havana*, the documentary of Tiant's return to the homeland.

Pedro, Vida Blue, Howard

Howard and Rickey

SPEECHLESS

BY HOWARD BRYANT

In the spring of 2003, I waited at the Fairmont Copley Plaza hotel for lunch with David Halberstam, the celebrated writer whose work I held as one of the standards of journalism. I had in tow three of his books I was hoping he'd sign, including *The Teammates*, which he was on the road promoting that year. Along with J. Anthony Lukas, Halberstam was one of the handful of people who inspired me to write for a living.

Two years earlier, the regard I held for Halberstam went from professional admiration from afar to personal indebtedness. Struggling with the structure of what would become my first book, on the suggestion of a friend who vouched for me to him, I sent Halberstam the *Shut Out* manuscript. I never heard back. A year later, I received a voicemail from the great Halberstam himself, asking me to call. In less than an hour, he helped pivot, shape and recast my manuscript, vouched for my ability to complete the work (an ability for which I at the time did not exactly vouch). An argument can be made that with one gracious hour of his life, it was David Halberstam who got my book career started in the right direction.

Up until that day at the Copley Plaza, David and I had never met in person. When he finally arrived, he greeted me profusely apologetic. He had to attend a morning funeral service.

"There's going to come a time in your life when losing people will feel like an everyday occurrence," he told me in that deep, authoritative voice of his.

Fortified by the invincibility of youth, I nodded respectfully and thought to myself, "That's going to be, like, a hundred years from now."

I've got your back is a reassuring, empty promise, one designed for comfort that most people in life never need to fulfill. It is the fire alarm you never have to pull. The comfort the words provide is two-way, to make us feel safer, less alone in the world when our personal avalanches descend and eventually demolish us, and to make us believe we will be strong enough when the people around us are buried by theirs. Looking back, and only then, when the moments have ended and the grief eases, can we truly know who kept us from drowning, and who we were willing to jump in and save.

In the most unambiguous of ways, Pedro Gomez had my back—and never once did he ever advertise that he would. It was only after, with the brush cleared and the damage surveyed, that you noticed him standing there, like the time in 2016 during spring training I wound up in the emergency room after my gallbladder gave way. To whom did the hospital discharge me? Pedro.

Professionally, we first met when I was a young reporter being savaged by future Hall of Famer Tony La Russa, the manager of the Oakland A's at the time, because my newspaper, the *Oakland Tribune,* erred in a headline.

"You *see* the shit I have to put up with?" La Russa said, before zeroing in on my name. "Howard Bryant? Who the *fuck* is Howard Bryant?"

Pedro was working at a rival paper, had never spoken to me, had no reason to involve himself in my fight and risk his own standing with an important person in the sport. Yet, while a roomful of reporters said nothing as La Russa attacked me, Pedro interrupted.

"C'mon, Tony," he cut in. "You know we don't write the headlines. Leave the kid alone. Why are you embarrassing him?"

Sports is a hostile industry, full of ego and insecurity and testosterone. It can be painfully childish, fourth-grade recess. If two reporters were speaking and a Really Important Baseball person who knew one of them stopped by, the known reporter would routinely just carry on a conversation, ignoring the unknown person they were speaking with just forty seconds earlier. Pedro did not need to enhance himself by being professionally discourteous. In an analogous situation with Pedro and then-Seattle manager Lou Piniella, just the three of us in the lobby at the Winter Meetings one year, Pedro merely took a moment in the conversation and said, "Lou, do you know Howard Bryant?" That these anecdotes are proof of some kind of uncommonly decent person is terribly indicting of baseball journalism. Decency in an indecent environment can appear to be a rare gift. Pedro, of course, *was* uncommonly decent, but not for these reasons.

Pedro understood what a hostile business baseball had been because he had experienced the hostility firsthand and, as a true student of the sport, knew that the commonalities between the black and Latino journeys in baseball far outstripped the differences. We were outsiders and the courtesy of manners was not always afforded to the people considered to be usurpers, but his remedy for that was to implore his fellow writers to at least attempt to understand the athletes on their terms. It had always offended me that English-speaking nations are often the most hostile toward bilingualism. Once, in a scrum with Ariel Prieto, the Cuban-born A's pitcher was asked if he felt he was ready to pitch or had to wait a few more days.

"Wait?" Prieto repeated.

"Yes, wait."

"Oh," Prieto replied. "About 230 pounds."

Everybody laughed and not because it was funny. They were making fun of Prieto, not laughing with him, and the cruelty of forcing him to navigate on-the-record news sessions, waiting for him to misunderstand and be ridiculed for it, was fuel for my desire to learn a second language. Pedro was instrumental in introducing me to Latino players and telling them to speak to me in Spanish, that I could be trusted not to ridicule them but to do my part in understanding their positions—in their native words.

On April 12, 2007, I was on the air talking about sports. After the segment, I turned on my phone, which was flooded with messages. My mother died earlier that morning, when my phone was off. A week later, we had the funeral. Two days after that we put her in the ground.

Needing to decompress after the repast, we went to a Chinese restaurant where I received another phone call: David Halberstam had been killed in a car accident in California.

These were the titanic moments. Thirteen years later, in a suddenly relentless tide, during a merciless pandemic, the people that shaped our time with the game—Brock, Gibson, Morgan, Seaver—were being taken in ruthless succession, daily, it felt, without time to process one before another fell. There were not enough nails to batten down the hatches, insufficient amounts of furniture to barricade the door. On the morning of January 21, I woke up to a text message that simply read, "Hank Aaron?" Two weeks later, on February 7, Super Bowl Sunday, I received another phone call, right after halftime. Pedro was gone.

There is a process to being speechless, a phenomenon to which we are so presently aware because of how strongly we fight it. We're not *supposed* to be speechless, as if there is some form of acquired honor or intelligence in talking. In the days following Pedro's death, I did not fight it, did not look for words, but sat instead with the silence, with the comfort of not having anything to say in favor of thinking about the pivotal moments of my life where Pedro Gomez spoke for me—the times he had my back.

People would talk about the *unprecedented* amount of death that surrounded us. They would sound astonished, as if we had been targeted with a special cruelty, but there was nothing unique about what was happening. It is our turn to experience Halberstam's prophecy. *There's going to come a time in your life when losing people will feel like an everyday occurrence.*

Sure, but that's like a hundred years from now.

Today became one hundred years from now—and it happened in less than twenty.

Mike at Fenway with his family

DOES BASEBALL MATTER?

BY MIKE BARNICLE

It was 12:16 a.m. on the night of a broken heart when the ball disappeared into the October night and my eighteen-year-old son Colin shouted above the surrounding noise, "Dad, you better take care of Tim." I turned to my left and there, slumped in his seat, head buried in both hands, tears bigger than hubcaps creasing his cheeks, I saw my ten-year-old little boy Timmy suffering a life wound caused by the single swing of a baseball bat.

It was Friday morning in Yankee Stadium. We were sitting a half-dozen rows behind the Red Sox dugout. It was October 17, 2003 and Aaron Boone, moments before, had taken Tim Wakefield's first pitch in the bottom of the eleventh and hammered it into the left-field stands.

Yankees 6, Red Sox 5. Time to put on the storm windows. Winter had arrived. One more epic defeat at the hands of the dreaded Yankees, somehow more crushing than all those that came before in a long string of hardball heartaches notched by the Olde Towne Team during the half century I'd followed them faithfully and seemingly forever.

And as I held and hugged my little boy in the midst of the tumult, the clamor, the noise and madness of the hometown crowd spilling around us, I was seized by one terrifying thought: *What have I done?*

Had I passed my own lifetime of devotion and disappointment on to my own children? Is this—another hideous Red Sox loss to the Yankees—my lasting gift to my kids? Would they be sentenced like me to years of hauntingly bizarre losses—balls skipping through a first baseman's bowed legs, pop flies on a windy October afternoon in Back Bay dropping into the left-field screen—and on and on and on? Season ticket holders to sadness.

Fast forward several years later to a soft summer afternoon. I am sitting in Fenway Park by the Red Sox dugout. It's about four hours before a night game being televised by ESPN. I am there at that time because I love the sights and sounds of a nearly empty Fenway.

I love to sit and savor the silence of the yard: the field, the few players jogging from right to left field, a handful of them just playing catch, the grounds crew watering the tan of the infield, the batting cage being brought out. It's peaceful and it's beautiful and it's baseball.

Then I felt a tap on my shoulder. Looking up I saw Pedro Gomez standing there.

"I caught a rerun of Ken Burns' *Tenth Inning* a couple nights ago," he told me. "That part where you described being with your son in the Stadium. The night the Yankees beat you guys in the ALCS? That made me cry."

"Really?" I asked.

"Really," Pedro Gomez replied. "It reminded me of being with my own kids. They love baseball because they know I love baseball."

That was Pedro Gomez self-defined: A baseball guy who arrived in your life with a smile, a story and almost always a simple question: How's your family?

Pedro had a huge extended family called baseball. He loved the game and it loved him back. I believe that when Pedro was covering a game, watching a game, he never saw salary when he spoke with a player or reported on what took place.

Didn't matter to him whether the shortstop had a life-altering, guaranteed $25 million multiyear contract or whether he was making the Major League minimum. He saw the players as human beings, individuals with God-given talents that separated them from all others.

He wasn't there to damage anyone. He was there to describe or ask them what they did and what that had meant to the game and to their team.

He knew most players cannot really tell you why or what they did out on the field, whether it was a spectacular turn of a double play, a freakishly athletic catch and throw from deep right field or a game-changing RBI double at a critical point or the pitch hit deep in the zone due to amazing bat speed. He knew that what they just did in the game was actually who they are and their gift was inexplicable.

All part of the never-ending story that is baseball, a continuing tale that goes from inning to inning, season to season, parents to son or daughter told across the years. It is decades of anecdotes mixed with memory to be poured out across time without interruption from a single rain delay or a long winter.

Baseball is patience and conversation. It's a refuge from many of the tools of our culture that have managed to nearly eliminate or certainly trim our national attention span and keep our eyes on the screens of our phones, not on the ball.

How do you explain Mookie Betts in a tweet? How do you describe the heartache of Aaron Boone's eleventh-inning home run in an Instagram? Can you really appreciate Mike Trout's talents in a TikTok clip?

Baseball has indeed suffered as our culture has exploded and accelerated across the last couple of decades. Football, especially the NFL, is nearly perfectly designed for TV and now with 4K hi-def it is rather amazing that so many would prefer attending the game rather than sit at home, practically in the huddle, watching their sixty-inch home entertainment system.

The NBA is leagues ahead of all the other sports in marketing both its product and its players. They have managed an almost impossible task: merging social awareness with a superior athletic product.

All this while major-league baseball seems slow, its stars not shining bright but almost reclusive compared to many other pro athletes in other leagues both global and national. Tom Brady has over eight million followers on Twitter. LeBron James has over forty million. Christian Ronaldo has ninety million. Mike Trout, arguably one of the best baseball players ever, has two and half million.

Perhaps baseball's strongest asset is something many take for granted: its long season. It's an everyday game; 162 days and nights a year someone, somewhere, steps in the batter's box while someone else toes the rubber and the best one-on-one matchup in sport is game on.

Baseball mirrors life. Get up, get ready, go to work. If it's Sunday or Tuesday or Saturday afternoon, baseball is there for you. And if you are inclined to pay attention, it's easy to see—to witness—the small intricacies of the game that make it equally if not more interesting than other sports.

Is the shortstop shading the hitter toward second? Think the runner goes here? Wonder how many hits this left-handed batter would have if he wasn't looking at four guys on the first base side of the diamond. Why don't guys bunt anymore?

The treasure of baseball is time ... Time to think about what you're watching. Time to sit and have a conversation with the fan sitting next to you. Time to appreciate the athleticism and skill of what you witness, to see ballplayers who are not so outsized as to make them appear superhuman.

Watching a Betts or a Baez, a Tatis or a Trout, it is possible that you can go home at the end of a game or a day at the office and play catch. Just like them. That you should hang on to that glove you've had for twenty years. That you can take your son or daughter to the field near your home and hit pop flies to them. Why not?

And maybe that's the way the best game ever created survives the epidemic of impatience that grips our culture; flourishes and grows despite the ugly greed and animosity that seems cemented in the relationship between players and owners.

The antidote to all that has happened to the game in the past couple decades—the PED scandals, the huge salaries, the abuse of revenue-sharing by some small market teams, the increasingly prohibitive cost of a day at the ballyard for a family of four, the absurd start time for October playoff games because TV time is a higher priority than a parent taking a ten-year-old to see their favorite player on their hometown team—might just belong to a generation now coming of age. Baseball after all is for the kid in all of us.

On that long gone afternoon when Pedro Gomez told me that the tale of my then ten-year-old little boy Timmy being crushed by a defeat that came so swiftly in the night with a single swing of a bat brought him to tears, I told him the rest of the story. One with a happy ending.

On the morning of October 20th, 2004, my three boys returned with me to Yankee Stadium for Game 7 of the ALCS. The Red Sox, near death, had come back to win three straight and tie the series.

Johnny Damon led off the top of the first with a single and stole second off Kevin Brown before Mark Bellhorn struck out. Manny Ramirez singled to left and Damon tried to stretch a run out of the hit but got thrown out at the plate. Tim slumped a bit in his seat, his body language uttering "not again," but he gained confidence when David Ortiz took Brown deep for a 2-0 lead.

Derek Lowe set the Yankees down in order in the bottom of the first. Top two brought up Trot Nixon, who grounded out to short. Kevin Millar followed with a single before Brown walked Bill Mueller and Orlando Cabrera to load the bases.

Joe Torre ambled out of the dugout and a disgruntled Kevin Brown's night was over. Javier Vazquez came in. Johnny Damon stepped into the box and swung at Vazquez's first pitch, the ball soaring in a high arc into the short porch that is the right field in Yankee Stadium.

Grand Slam Home Run. Yankees 6, Red Sox 0.

Last year's tears were now little more than a distant memory, replaced by the singular joy of watching a baseball disappear into the seats and listening to the eruption of joy around us as we sat in the same section behind the Red Sox dugout where we were on that distant, despondent October night. As midnight came and the Yankees headed toward winter with a 10-3 loss due to a miraculous and historic Red Sox comeback, my son Timmy was down on the field after the game.

Trot Nixon told him to run the bases. We have a picture of Tim running along the third base line, headed home and crossing the plate. It's an image I often see when I shut my eyes and think about that night and so many others. It's a time and a game we still occasionally talk about today.

And that's just one reason why baseball remains our greatest game. Time, memory and simple conversation let us play and replay it over and over in the never-ending season of our lives. It's why baseball still—and always—matters.

There are no red states or blue states in baseball. The chatter in the stands is almost always stunningly normal and apolitical. It can go from

Johnny Damon with the 2004 World Series trophy

"What are your kids doing?" to "Think he ought to steal here?" There are people with season-ticket packages who regard the other season-ticket holders near them as their summer neighbors; all of them hoping that their ball club will keep the house open through early fall.

Yes, baseball has its problems. Yes, the games are too long and start too late. The relationship between the players' union and management makes that of Israel and Iran look like it's not a problem. But at its core baseball is still the most uniquely American of our games.

ALWAYS GRAB THE CORKS

BY BRIAN MURPHY

I hit the Gomez Lottery. I did Yankee Stadium in October with Pedro Gomez. Covering the NFL from 1994 to 1999, I thought I knew the way. The rush of football game day. The Super Bowl parties in Miami. The royal feeling of writing America's most popular sport. I didn't know the way. Pedro showed me.

More than anything, Pedro taught me to trust my eyes. Covering the NFL, you couldn't do that. After games, coaches would tell us they'd have to watch the film. Baseball was different. You might study the occasional instant replay—what exactly happened there?—but mostly you could tune out the distractions and be alone with the game. You could trust your eyes.

In 1999, I covered the up-and-coming Oakland A's. I owned a box seat to the most fun team I'd ever cover. Jason Giambi would talk to us after games in a hat that read "Drive It Like You Stole It." It was a special deal.

One more special thing: I earned The Tap from Pedro. Even though Pedro had moved on to become a columnist for the *Arizona Republic*, he loved ball writers. He loved new ball writers, because he could help us.

Be friends with us. Look out for us. I had Pedro Gomez calling me amigo.

"You're an A's beat writer now," Pedro said. "You're part of the family. We look out for each other."

The A's didn't make the playoffs in 1999, but my sports editor at the *San Francisco Examiner,* Glenn Schwarz—he was a ball guy. Budget be damned, he was sending his A's and Giants beat writers to cover the League Championship Series. In 1999, that meant John Shea drew Braves-Mets. And it meant I drew Red Sox-Yankees.

It meant I drew my new best ball-writer friend, Pedro Gomez, in baseball's best city, in baseball's most hallowed stadium, in baseball's greatest month.

I can still hear Pedro: "My Irish amigo! Let's go to Yankee Stadium! Meet you in the Grand Hyatt lobby."

I can still see Pedro in his coat and tie, laptop satchel over his shoulder, bright white teeth smiling under those eyebrows, waiting in the lobby. His smile was for Yankees-Red Sox. His smile was for October. His smile was for the excitement of showing his rookie ball-writer pal the way to do it. The Pedro Way.

So the Pedro Way was the No. 4 subway, of course. The Pedro Way was to feel the pregame energy through the jostling crowds of Yankee fans in O'Neill T-shirts and El Duque jerseys, crammed together in the train and spilling out into the Bronx, where we smelled the sausages and onions from street vendors and felt the chill of the night air and saw the brightness of The Stadium lights against a dark Gotham sky.

The Red Sox and Yankees in October strained credulity. We drew the two most storied teams in the game. I had a sensei like Pedro to show me the way in, to take me to the packed press room downstairs, and to make sure all the New York writers and broadcasters—George King, Joel Sherman, Tyler Kepner, Michael Kay, Suzyn Waldman, on and on— knew that the new kid from the *SF Examiner* was OK.

Pre- and postgame press conferences were run by the American League, and their venerable and respected director of public relations, Phyllis Merhige. Phyllis was like the White House press secretary, only more important, because it was The Stadium in October.

"Phyllis, whatever you do, don't take any questions from Murphy from the *SF Examiner,*" Pedro needled, eyes glinting. "This Mick is trouble. Stay away, Phyllis!"

That was all Phyllis needed to hear. She winked and made sure to call on me.

Game 1 was everything. Extra innings. Bob Sheppard on the PA. Eddie Layton on the organ. A controversial blown call against the Red Sox. A walk-off home run by Bernie Williams. Frank Sinatra. Frank Sinatra. Frank Sinatra.

I figured the press conferences with Yankees manager Joe Torre and Red Sox manager Jimy Williams would do the trick for quotes, not knowing clubhouse access in October. Pedro wanted more.

"Make sure you get Rod Beck after the game," Pedro urged, speaking of the ex-Giant who surrendered Williams' blast. "He'll be in the clubhouse for sure. Squeeze in there!"

Ol' Shooter Beck was a stand-up guy, sure enough. I can still feel the crush of bodies around his locker, can still see the beer in his hand, still hear his disappointed, yet patient voice, explaining the one that got away.

That advice? Made my story. An adrenalized write, for sure. Heady stuff. Filed to the *Examiner* around 1 a.m. Eastern.

"Ready to go?" Pedro asked a few laptops over.

"Where to?" I asked, still dazed from the drama, the lights, the scene.

"Dude! Come on! It's New York in October!"

That Pedro grin. I soon learned that an October in New York with Pedro meant the ball game was only the opening act. There was too much life to be lived, too many laughs to be had, too many stories to tell, too much ball to argue. The night, to Pedro, was but an infant.

A stash of Town Cars waited for late ball writers. Pedro knew where to go. I wish I could bottle the feeling of having written postseason baseball from the Bronx, blended with the comfort and warmth of the backseat of a Town Car bearing down on the city, mixed with the adrenaline of knowing that Manhattan's taverns awaited our arrival, their generous 4 a.m. closing times a virtual welcome mat—topped off by Pedro's high-pitched cadence of amazement at the theater as we rode . . . *"Can you believe Rod Beck hung that slider? It was the only batter he faced! . . . What was Rick Reed watching when he blew that call? . . . How great is Yankee Stadium in October? . . ."*

Pedro knew where to go. American Trash, 1st Avenue and E. 77th, a few blocks from the East River. As these things happen, we met the famous New York Jets fan "Fireman Ed," who was glassy-eyed and feeling no pain. Fireman Ed was famous for sitting on the shoulders of a fan and spelling out "J-E-T-S JETS JETS JETS!" Pedro took stock of Fireman Ed, who went about six-foot-two, 230 pounds of muscle. "You sit it on someone's shoulders?" Pedro asked, pint in hand, eyes glinting. "That's my brother," Fireman Ed said, leaning against the bar. "You should see the size of him."

As these things happen, Pedro and I decided the bar needed to hear "The Cowboy Song" by Thin Lizzy, over and over. It was a good choice at 3 a.m. for a couple of ball writers.

Roll me over and turn me around/Let me keep spinning til I hit the ground/Roll me over and let me go ridin' in the rodeo . . .

We felt good. So did Fireman Ed. Thin Lizzy sounded great. Fireman Ed proclaimed his life philosophy. "It's all good," he said, grabbing my shirt. "Because if it isn't . . . what is it?"

Pedro and I cackled, over and over. We had a new mantra.

And Thin Lizzy sings: *Roll me over and set me free/The cowboy's life is the life for me.*

We never said it out loud, but Thin Lizzy might as well have been singing about us. With Pedro, the unwritten rule was: You didn't do New York right unless you stepped on your door-front *USA Today* going back into your hotel room. That meant sleeping until 2 p.m., then rising to do it all again. Game 2 called.

Pedro in the lobby. Coat and tie. Laptop in satchel. The grin. The eyebrows. The wattage of energy undimmed by the previous night's burn. The subway, the pregame, Phyllis Merhige making sure to call on my question.

The ancient rivals did not disappoint. Game 2 was another dandy. Red Sox lead, 2-1, in the bottom of the seventh, but Chuck Knoblauch ties it with an RBI double. Stadium favorite Paul O'Neill plates Knoblauch with a two-out single. The Stadium comes unglued, the notes from O'Neill's walk-up music—The Who's "Baba O'Riley"—still hanging in the night air. Pedro is loving it, slapping my shoulder with the back of his hand. That slap on the back tells me how lucky we are.

Ramiro Mendoza gets out of a bases-loaded, one-out jam in the top of the eighth. Heartbreak for the Red Sox. Mariano Rivera finishes it.

Frank Sinatra. Frank Sinatra. Frank Sinatra. Now I know the deal. We talk to a relieved Torre and an exasperated Williams. Phyllis calls on both of us.

Impossibly, our experience heightened. Games 3, 4 and 5 at Fenway Park. If riding sidesaddle with Pedro in October at Yankee Stadium was a singular experience, October in Boston with the ball writer's ball writer was a heck of a runner-up. Even better, Game 3 featured the return of ex-Red Sox star and new Yankee villain Roger Clemens on the hill for the Bombers. The Red Sox answered with Cy Young winner Pedro Martinez.

We could go into the details of how the Red Sox—and their taunting, howling fans—dismembered Clemens that day, sending him to the showers after two innings, but it would be extraneous. Just close your eyes and picture Fenway Park in late afternoon October light, and hear the singsong of "Rogerrrrrrrrrrr .... Rogerrrrrrrrrrr ... Rogerrrrrrrrrr," a horsehide version of a Gregorian chant.

Red Sox 13, Yankees 1. Pedro couldn't contain his enthusiasm for the theater. Of course he couldn't. Years later, we found a questionnaire he filled out for the Baseball Hall of Fame. Education, background, newspaper experience. A question near the end asked: Most memorable game you've ever covered? "Game 3 of the 1999 ALCS," he wrote, "when the NY Yankees played at Boston with Roger Clemens facing Pedro Martinez. The game was filled with emotion and lived up to all the hype, with Martinez shelling Clemens."

That victory was Boston's death rattle. Game 4 went New York's way, with yet another critical call going against the Red Sox. Fans rained debris on the field. The game was stopped for eight minutes. The call was not changing.

I was disappointed that Game 5 would become an inevitability, that the Yankees would take care of Boston and close it out en route to yet another World Series title. My disappointment was rooted in two things: One, I wouldn't get back to Yankee Stadium. Two, my week with Pedro was coming to an end.

Pedro didn't let it end without more memories.

"Come on, let's go through the stands, get some color," he urged me in the ninth inning of what would become a 6-1 Yankee clincher.

We stood behind a fan who watched the ninth-inning fatality play out, shouting to the oncoming winter: "At least we shelled the fat man!

They cannot win the World Series! Roger Clemens must die a bitter, ringless old man!"

Pedro dug his elbow into my ribs: "You can use that!"

I did.

We snaked through the dank walkways of Fenway to the visitor's clubhouse, where the American League champions were partying on enemy soil. I will never forget certain things about that cramped, smoky, beer-soaked room. George Steinbrenner in a blue blazer and turtleneck, telling Pedro and me that "the Yankees are on top, where they belong." A twenty-five-year-old Derek Jeter taking a long pull on a cigar, heading to his third World Series.

And I will never forget what Pedro said to me before we entered.

"You have to listen to me," he said. "Do you have any friends that are huge Yankee fans? Like, friends who truly care, so that the Yankees actually mean something to them?"

I did. An old pal from high school came to mind. He was born in New York. He moved to the Bay Area in junior high. He was devoted. And he was getting married in two weeks.

"I do," I said.

"So here's what you're going to do," Pedro said. "You are going to go in there and grab Champagne corks from the floor of the clubhouse. You put them in your jacket pocket and do not lose them."

I nodded.

"Then, go back home and find that friend and give him a cork and you tell him it came from the New York Yankees clubhouse, just as they celebrated the pennant."

So in between Steinbrenner and Jeter, late on a Sunday night in October, I grabbed those corks. Two weeks later, at the wedding reception, I cornered the groom at the bar. I told him the story. I had him hold out his hand. The tear in his eye came because Pedro Gomez taught me the way.

Chelsea with her dad, Garth Janes, at a Pittsfield Mets game

AT THE FRONT OF
THE CIRCLE

BY CHELSEA JANES

I remember their voices most. I'll never forget the day I leaned against a dugout rail in Tampa and heard the voices of the Yankees broadcasters I grew up hearing talking, in real life, a few feet away.

It was as if thousands of nights spent falling asleep to far-off games had sent me hurtling into some baseball Oz where I ended up watching batting practice with the wizard. When I started covering baseball and pulled back the curtain, many of those voices remained distant and disembodied. Pedro Gomez's grew clearer.

The first thing I think of when I think of Pedro is his cadence. He was one of several ESPN reporters I can still hear in my head today, signing off as they always did. I hear "Sal Paolantonio, ES...PN," whenever I end up in Philly. Andrea Kremer. John Clayton. Tom Rinaldi. Michele Tafoya. When I think of them, I think of those signoffs, easily mimicked but not easily duplicated.

Those voices, their cadences, punctuated the score of sports to a young kid who, for a solid five-year period, could probably have told you who was due to anchor SportsCenter tomorrow. I watched from afar.

Those voices brought me closer.

Pedro was one of them. I can still hear him signing off from AT&T Park after the latest update about complicated Barry Bonds and his complicated chase for the all-time home run record. I can hear him from Wrigley Field after Steve Bartman deflected a foul ball and made Moises Alou (and an entire, desperate baseball city) lose their minds. "Pedro Gomez, ESPN." He was there and I was there—at least, from my couch—so we were there together.

When I got to baseball Oz as a young beat reporter, older writers introduced me to Pedro. I thought it was enough that he looked me in the eye and introduced himself. I never expected him to learn my name. What stuns me is he never forgot it.

The night of Pedro's death, I texted my co-worker, longtime *Post* writer Barry Svrluga. All I could think to say was "my god." Barry went much further back with Pedro than I did, so he probably had far more memories of meals shared or beers downed. All I could say was "he always knew my name and acted like he cared that he was seeing me."

"That was the thing," Barry wrote back. "He did. He was genuine."

By no coincidence, I always ran into Pedro when the Nationals were in the big games, the ones the ESPN cameras stormed in to see, often changing the game times and interview setup. Beat reporters considered the whole thing an inconvenience: The big TV personalities parachuting in for one game and one moment, then retreating to the safety of Bristol or Los Angeles. But Pedro never acted like he should get anything just for showing up. He talked and he listened.

From the World Series in 2019 to a run-of-the-mill regular series in Chicago, Pedro seemed to inhale clubhouse monotony and exhale enthusiasm. He popped his head into the manager's office and asked about his kids. He shook hands with a grizzled coach and made a joke. He addressed an up-and-coming player by name.

And as for the writer trying desperately not to let him beat her to the news of the day, Pedro always had time to say hello, always knew her name, and was always willing to tell a story or talk baseball like I'd been there all along. As a kid, his was one of the voices that taught me about baseball. As an adult, his was one of the voices that made me feel like I knew enough already.

Pedro treated everyone like they were the one everyone knew from

TV. He treated everyone with effusive respect, though no one I ever met in baseball could be considered his equal. He made me feel like I was an important part of the baseball universe, even if my biggest scoop at the time was probably a Nationals' minor league call-up in mid-June.

His arrival also infused a little terror into my days. He could walk into a clubhouse I had covered day in and day out, pop his head into Dusty Baker's office and chat like old friends, slap Bryce Harper on the back and get the latest on his swing, and even get a friendly handshake from Stephen Strasburg, one of the quieter guys in the game. I was just hoping most of those guys didn't think I was an idiot. He knew all about them, knew their kids' names, knew their situations, and seemed to know how to put them at ease.

In the least trusting room in sports, Pedro was trusted because he always seemed to care. As consistent as he was in his willingness to talk to players at tough moments, he was an outsized presence because of the way he talked to them in the little ones, when no one was watching, when he didn't have to care.

Pedro was also fearless. Like many people, I tend to appreciate most those qualities in others I do not see in myself, and "fearless" was not the first adjective I would have used to describe myself in my first years on the Nationals beat.

I hesitated before asking tough questions. I stutter-stepped before approaching surly players. I danced around awkward questions and made them even more awkward than they had to be, a habit that extends to my social interactions outside the baseball clubhouse, and perhaps can't be helped.

But Pedro didn't flinch. I can't remember the exact circumstances of the one day that stands out most—the day that always comes to mind when I think of Pedro's unique ability to barrel straight through awkwardness and into the truth—but I know it was in the visitors' clubhouse at Wrigley Field.

Recent renovations notwithstanding, the visitors' clubhouse at Wrigley is the smallest and least luxurious in baseball. Players hardly have room to change. Beat reporters hardly have room to exist. After the Nationals played series there, I always found myself uniquely equipped to analyze my colleagues' shoe choices, having spent much of the pregame hours looking down toward the floor.

In a clubhouse that tiny, looking up almost certainly meant seeing something you didn't mean to, or looking at someone at an awkward moment. I usually got my interviews out of the way early, then huddled in a corner out of the way.

Because of the tight corners, Nationals public relations staff would often corral all the reporters in front of a water cooler for postgame interviews. They were always careful to make sure the cameras were shooting straight on, lest someone appear in a shot unintentionally. The quarters were crowded, every question audible to everyone, and—after bad losses, in particular—the mood stifling.

Pedro was there after one particularly devastating Nationals loss in 2016 or 2017. I've narrowed it down to two different games—one in which Ryan Zimmerman left a record fourteen men on base, another in which Ryan Madson allowed a walk-off grand slam (The Nationals found many creative ways to lose to the Cubs in Chicago in those years).

Whatever the circumstances, as beat reporters gathered around the water cooler for despondent interviews, Pedro headed right to the front of the circle. He didn't hesitate before asking the necessary questions or wait for anyone else to do so. He went with a high fastball, right at them, no nonsense.

That day, as on many days during the much-hyped end of Bryce Harper's Nationals tenure, Pedro just asked the question. Players usually answered him. They seemed to know he understood what they were going through, seemed to think he was a worthy interrogator, rarely blew him off. I often left scrums thinking that I wanted to be more like Pedro—more fearless, more effusive and more direct. I often came out of conversations with Pedro with new aspirations, too. The most common takeaway: "I want to enjoy this as much as he does."

Major League Baseball is full of embarrassed optimists masquerading as cynics for the sake of self-preservation. Players, coaches, and especially writers always appear, as prolific Rockies' first baseman Todd Helton once put it, "comfortably miserable."

Baseball writers are often particularly committed to the character, determined to hide the last vestiges of optimism behind a protective coating of sarcasm and eye-rolling. Thanks to its long, grueling seasons and long, grueling games, Major League Baseball culture praises the even-keeled, the dependable, the pragmatic. It treasures the stoic and the hearty. Conventional wisdom suggests survival requires equal parts sarcasm and patience.

Every once in a while, you may look across the press box and spot a twinkle in someone's eye, someone holding back a smile as they ask "Did you see that?!" But look back and the smile is gone, replaced by groans about another slow-working starter or the endless futility of the hometown bullpen.

Pedro Gomez always had the twinkle. He didn't mask passion with indifference so as to fit quietly in the background. He glowed with enthusiasm and molded moods of every room he entered, instead of the other way around. He was confident without arrogance, and emanated a sense of certainty but not infallibility. He was welcoming and warm.

If you could draw up a perfect hitter's mentality, one centered in confidence and enthusiasm and not subject to the many whims of long baseball summers, Pedro probably had it. I have the feeling that may be the perfect mentality for a lot more than just hitting.

I know many of my colleagues talked to Pedro more over the years. They would chat on the phone and swap decades of stories, shoot supportive texts here or there. I didn't know Pedro that way. I knew him as a voice of my childhood that materialized in adulthood, one whose death leaves me confronting the mortality of the voices that taught me the game and acutely aware of the responsibility that comes with succeeding them.

Pedro inspired me to think more about the way my words can welcome a different generation, of the way being open with passion allows others to do the same. He also inspired me to consider, more than I ever had or thought I would, what the next generation will learn about me when they end up leaning against a dugout rail next to me one day. At least I have something to shoot for.

What I found in Pedro was a kind-hearted person who cared so much you could feel it, a person who would introduce a young reporter to a vaunted manager without a second thought—the person across the press box with a twinkle in his eye and his foot in the door, gesturing for you to sneak inside before it closed because you belonged there, too.

I don't watch SportsCenter as much these days. I watch games, toggle on stats sites, and read articles. I try to interpret the baseball world for myself so I can do the same for others, try to write like I care so others will care about what I write. I don't listen to those same baseball voices anymore, at least not like I did.

But I still hear them clearly, like I did on the small TV in my family's kitchen while I scarfed down waffles before middle school each morning, or on the couch watching "Baseball Tonight" before "Sunday Night Baseball," then when I caught a glimpse of coverage in college and beyond. I'm sure I'll hear "Pedro Gomez, ESPN," for decades to come, one of the voices that called me into this game and made sure it didn't disappoint. His was a voice that can't be duplicated, but should be emulated—a voice that not only was unabashed in its own joy, but beckoned everyone to share in it.

Dusty and Darren, 2002

A MAN YOU COULD TRUST

BY DUSTY BAKER

What kind of dude was Pedro Gomez? How would you try to capture what made him unique to someone who never met him? I've been thinking about that since we lost Pedro. My mind's been jumping all over the place, hitting on different times we talked, that smile, the way he made you feel. Funny the things you remember. Like that time Pedro and I ended up at a little dive bar in the Tenderloin District of San Francisco, just hanging.

This was a couple weeks before the start of the 1997 season, my fifth year as Giants manager. Back then they had a big lunch to bring people together from both teams in the Bay, the Giants and the A's, beat writers and team officials. They would kind of play up the rivalry. In 1996 a comedian named Rob Schneider made fun of the A's, and you should've seen the look on Sandy Alderson's face. He got off some one-liner about Schneider. Don't fire on a former Marine if you don't have some ammo in reserve! The next year was more relaxed. We all drove out to Treasure Island and had lunch in a big place with huge windows pointing back toward the city, just a beautiful, sunny, easygoing day.

I was walking around after my official duties were over, just kind of checking the place out, when I saw Pedro sitting off to the side with his running buddy at the time, Steve Kettmann. They were laughing at something, talking nonstop, and working their way to the bottom of what looked like their third round of beers. *Damn*, I was thinking, *these A's writers are different cats than the writers on the Giants beat who I'm around most of the time.*

It was like: How do I *not* go over there and talk to these guys? You gravitate towards certain people. I mean, you gravitate *away* from certain people, too, but right then where I knew I belonged was hanging with them.

I pulled up a chair. We all sat there a minute, kind of looking around. They exchanged a quick look, like they were ready to make their exit but weren't about to leave me sitting there. I nodded knowingly. I knew the look.

"Where you two dudes heading?" I asked.

They glanced back and forth again.

"Tell him," Gomez said.

"Place called the Blue Lamp," Kettmann said.

I nodded.

"In the Tenderloin?" I said. "I know it."

Sounded good to me. I was like: We're off work. Let's just hang and have a good time. Especially back then, I loved to hang. That's good old-fashioned fun. People that have never hung out, you don't have to be doing nothing to hang. You don't have to be getting drunk. You don't have to be doing nothing but just talking, laughing and it's good for your soul, good for your heart, your brain. It's good for everything when you're with good company and you're hanging. People would say, "What'd you do?" And I feel sorry for people that don't understand when you're telling them, "I was just hanging."

Pedro was a guy just about everyone loved hanging with. What made him special is that he was very consistent in his outlook on life. I never saw Pedro down. I'm sure he had problems like everybody else, but he never took his problems with him and especially never laid any of that on his friends. He was always more concerned about you and your family's welfare than he ever was about his. I knew how much he loved his family because he talked about his son Rio all the time. He also loved baseball. A lot of people, they have an air that they may not like their job, and may not like the *people* in their job, but Pedro loved his job and loved his family and genuinely loved life.

I knew Pedro in the early years. The *San Jose Mercury News* had him on high schools when I was hitting coach of the Giants, in the early '90s, but he'd find a way to get up to the ballpark and write some baseball. Pedro and I always had powerful discussions, and you know what? Pedro was hard to convince. He wasn't argumentative, but he wasn't afraid to speak his mind, if you asked him a question. He would let you know if he agreed and he would let you know that he disagreed and it wouldn't change his opinion or outlook of you. He was proud of being Cuban and yeah, we had some powerful discussions about Castro and his parents and just the Cuban situation in America. We had some debates.

Pedro and I talked about life stuff all the time. What really impressed me about him was, you could talk about anything off the field and you weren't worried about it creeping into an article next week or next year or whenever. Pedro was working in an industry full of mistrust, but I never for a second worried that he would betray my trust. And he never did. Pedro was someone you could trust.

I actually felt sorry for Pedro *and* Barry, both of them, during the years Pedro was reporting on Barry for ESPN. Pedro was around every day and Barry is a private person. He got tired of it fast. I don't blame Barry, but Pedro had a job to do. He would stand up to Barry, he never backed down, but I never felt like he was real pushy either. Barry's a tough assignment. Only Pedro, I think, could have pulled that off.

Over time, Barry realized Pedro was just doing his job. He realized he wasn't on a personal witch hunt, or personal vendetta, you know what I mean? When I found out that Barry sent flowers to the family after Pedro's death, I wasn't surprised. Now see, that's Barry. As hard-ass as Barry tries to seem, Barry is a very good soul, but he didn't let people see that side. Before it was all over with, I think Barry and Pedro really genuinely respected each other.

One of the best judges of character I've ever seen was my father, he and my son both, and my dad liked Pedro. Especially when I was with the Giants, and my dad was always around, he and Pedro talked a lot. I could leave those two alone—in the dugout or the clubhouse—and feel comfortable and safe that they were both not only occupying each other's time, but they were having meaningful conversations. My dad was a deep thinker and one of the most honest people that I ever met, and Pedro was in that mold.

You know one thing I think about? Pedro and I talked about catching some music together. We both loved live music. He loved that I wrote a whole book about catching Jimi Hendrix at Monterey, *Kiss the Sky*. Pedro and I were supposed to go see music but never did. One of those things that you say, "Hey, man. Let's go hang and let's just jam." And then you figure, "I'll do it next week or I'll do it next month or next year." Nowadays, because of this, I'm not putting off doing anything anymore, because you never know. Tomorrow's not promised to anybody.

Pedro's death was as big a shocker as I have had. Hank Aaron's death in late January, a couple weeks before Pedro's, hit me hard, but Hank was eighty-six. You're not really surprised, but it still hurts big time. With Pedro, shoot man. What was he? Fifty-eight? I mean, if I'd have died at fifty-eight, my son would have been five years old. I'd have been dead already almost fourteen years. There's so much, so much living that you can do in fourteen years and so much contributing. You try to imagine your family and the hurt because it could be you too. Could be you at any time or any day. So I just think about Pedro's wife, Sandi, and their three kids, Rio and Dante and Sierra, because I know how much he loved them. Rio's got a good head on his shoulders, he's a left-hander in the Red Sox organization, and I'm pulling for him. Big time.

The thing about Pedro was he could be around anybody of any race, any religion and feel comfortable and not be judgmental. He was proud of being a Cuban, and sure, he had an ego, don't we all? But he never wore that on his sleeve. When I think of Pedro, I'll always think of the way he lived "Be who you are."

Rob with his kids at Nationals Park: Amanda, Amani and Eli

Rob and his dad, Colbert King

REMEMBER WHO
YOU ARE

BY ROB KING

In September of 2004, I began my career at ESPN by attending a "Talent Meeting," a semi-annual event which brought anchors, analysts, producers and reporters together from all across the country to learn about strategic priorities, engage in creative brainstorming sessions and emerge with a common sense of purpose. I'd spent the previous fifteen years in the unglamorous theater of newspaper journalism, where our uniforms consisted largely of blue button-downs, pleated khakis and sensible shoes. Which is to say I was unprepared for the precise coifs, seamless tans and casual elegance filling the hotel ballroom that day. In that moment, I suddenly felt like a thirteen-year-old transfer student holding a tray of chocolate milk and mystery meat, searching for a place to sit in an unfamiliar school cafeteria. And just as that thought hit me, Pedro Gomez appeared.

Pedro and Rachel Nichols, journalists whose bylines I'd followed long before they decamped for ESPN, greeted me like family. "Come sit with us," they said, almost in unison. So the three of us found our spots, and within minutes, thanks to their affability and complete lack of pretension, I felt very much at home. As the event progressed, they acted as virtual translators for all the alien jargon suddenly filling my ears. For instance, I'd never previously heard "leverage" used as a verb. The phrase "at the end of the day" found its way into every presentation, as did "net-net."

Of all the things I heard and saw that day and all the interpretations my two new friends whispered my way, I retained only one resonant thought, and it came from Pedro. "ESPN's an amazing place, and there are a ton of amazing people here," he said. "All these things can seem big and overwhelming, and you could spend a lot of time trying to figure out how you fit into all this."

Then he leaned in like Morpheus, shortly after giving Neo the red pill.

"Just remember ... ESPN hired you, for who you are and what you bring to the table. Don't forget that. Remember who *you* are."

About a month later, I designed, printed and hung a small sign bearing that essential credo, which over the course of sixteen-plus years has since moved around varied walls of my varied offices. Whenever a visitor would ask about its message, I'd pass along the gift that Pedro gave me.

Now, in Pedro's profound absence, I must make sure that everyone knows the wisdom on my wall is his. And I also want everyone to know that in Pedro's typical fashion, he delivered wisdom and grace to someone a) he knew only by reputation, b) higher on the organizational chart and c) he might or might not have to ever see again in the normal course of business.

Over the course of Pedro's and my time as colleagues, we had days when he worked in an entirely different part of the operation and days when his team reported up to me. But really, neither Pedro nor I cared about that much. He'd make the surprise appearance in my office whenever he made his way to Bristol, lock eyes with me and lean in, asking about my family, telling me about stories he had coming, and find a way to riff on unfinished ideas. After strategic and tactical meetings with the Bureau Reporting Group, Pedro would invariably hit me up with that One Additional Smart Question, a request for insight that he knew would inform his work and that of his teammates. And on those terrible days spent calling coworkers to inform them of the elimination of their jobs, I could count on a call from Pedro asking me how *I* was doing.

Pedro died as the PGA Tour was hosting the 2021 Phoenix Open at TPC Scottsdale, and I watched a late replay of this year's event recalling the 2015 event. That year, as Marshawn Lynch deadpanned, "I'm just here so I won't get fined" down the road at a Super Bowl XLIX media availability, Pedro and I spent about nine holes following a chip-yipping Tiger Woods. We walked and walked and talked and talked, and I'm not sure we said a single word about golf. The galleries were predictably Woods-swollen and lightly lubricated, so it could easily have been hard to hear one another, hard to have an intimate conversation.

Except he was Pedro, characteristically leaning in to make our interaction meaningful, and I felt like I'd found my home base in a sea of verdant chaos. And Pedro? He might not have said a word about golf, but pretty much every other word was "Rio," the name of his son, a star pitching prospect, uttered with a blinding smile and electrifying pride. When I close my eyes and try to envision him, that's the Pedro Gomez I see.

I count myself among those fortunate to have been befriended by Kobe Bryant, a happiness in no small way due to the connection made by our mutual friend Stephen A. Smith. In the aftermath of the tragic helicopter crash, I noted with interest the extraordinary complement of people who could, as I do, point to all the times they found themselves in text exchanges with Kobe and marvel at his amazing range of contacts and interests. He was really cool, and like I said, I'm pleased and honored to have gotten to know him a little.

By contrast, I see the outpouring of love and incredibly vivid and intimate memories others have for Pedro, and I feel envious. The emails and calls and in-person moments he and I shared apparently constitute less than a scintilla of the emotive and intellectual impact he had on this world. I knew him to be kind and principled and loving and courageous. Yet the wonderful remembrances we share now and forever give Pedro the fathomless dimension he so deserves.

So now I look over my shoulder and regard that sign: "Remember Who You Are."

I'll do my best, Pedro. Some days I'll be better at it than other days. But I'm certain about one thing. I'll always remember who you were, are, and will always be.

HE WAS MY BIGGEST FAN

BY RIO GOMEZ

My dad could be loud, real loud. We'd have friends over to the house and everyone would be shouting at the same time. For me as a kid sometimes it was a little embarrassing. I remember times when I'd be thinking, "Why are we always yelling? Why are we always so loud?" But when I think about it now, I'm thankful my dad was like that. I'm happy we were able to be that kind of family where we could be loud and upset and yelling at each other, because you know what? Five minutes later, we'd be over it. We were like, "OK, I'm upset at you. You're upset at me. We're just going to let it out right now and then we can move forward." There was no way to bottle up feelings inside of us. We were able to just let it all blow over and be best friends again, talking and hanging.

My dad was never afraid of emotion. He didn't hide from anything. He wasn't the kind of dad who only got excited about me playing sports when it was going well. He was always there, for every up and down, especially the downs. There were a lot of downs. People tend to assume if you're a professional baseball player, pitching in the Boston Red Sox farm system, you must have been a star at every level, all-state this, all-region that, always some accolade written next to your name. It was never like that for me. I was never the best player on any of my teams growing up, not in middle school, not in Little League and not in high school. I was never even one of the best ten. I was the guy scraping by year after year just to make a team.

My senior year of high school, I got cut from the varsity baseball team. I'll never forget that day for the rest of my life. I didn't call my parents. I was so shocked this was happening, I didn't tell them anything, I just drove home from tryouts and parked on the street right in front of our house. I sat there and just cried and cried and cried and cried. I was eighteen and all I could think was: *Wow, this is the last time I will ever play baseball.*

I'd been out there awhile when the car door opened and my dad got in and sat down next to me. There were no words of encouragement or motivation. He had no words at all, he just listened. He was there to help me feel it all, and to just let it all out. We sat in that car together for well over an hour, maybe two, and I just bawled my eyes out the whole time, because I couldn't believe that this was how my baseball career was going to end.

Not a single person believed in me then, except my dad. Not even another friend, or another teammate. Nobody. That was February of my senior year and from that day on he just started encouraging me and motivating me. Having my dad behind me like that carried me all the way through to the fall when I enrolled in junior college.

"This is not how your baseball career is going to end," he told me. "There's more to it and you need to figure that out for yourself."

I was a walk-on at Mesa Community College, which meant I had to try out all fall before I found out if I'd made the team. Through all that, I still never got support from friends and other people you rely on. The only person who kept backing me was my dad. I can remember so many times that summer or fall when I was working out on my own, just trying to make the team, and I'd be ready to give up. I'd be thinking: *This is just fool's gold. I'm chasing after nothing.* So many times, my dad was there to talk me off the ledge and to keep me pushing. He'd always tell me that the path to success is a lonely road, and he was right. I don't think I ever felt that more than those six months.

Without my dad, I would never have played junior-college ball.

I would never have gone to the University of Arizona as a walk-on or gone to the College World Series in Omaha, Nebraska, or played in the Cape Cod League. I would never have been drafted by the Red Sox in the thirty-sixth round of the 2017 MLB draft. None of this would ever have happened. It all would have ended at me being eighteen, cut from my varsity high school team. Through it all, my dad kept emphasizing the positive. When I was at Arizona, he told me, "No matter what, you've already reached a level that so few do. You've pitched in the Pac-12 Conference. That's amazing."

He was more nervous than I was every time I pitched. It was hilarious, to tell you the truth. He'd have to get up from his seat and walk around. If he couldn't be there, he'd bug his friends for any information he could get. He was on pins and needles the first time I pitched in a spring-training game in Florida, on March 15, 2018, and hated that he couldn't be there. "He has his first outing in a minor-league game today," he emailed a friend. "As soon as I know, I'll pass along." Sure enough, a couple hours later he followed up: "Today's outing (from someone who was at the game): He just finished. 1-2-3 inning. Looked good. F-9, 4-3, F-8. Faced two lefties, got ahead. Threw 12 or 13 pitches. Went well. Clean inning."

I got left back in extended spring training that year. I didn't break with a minor-league team, and I was really depressed. I kept questioning myself: *Did I make the right decision to try and play professional baseball? Was this worth it? What am I doing with my life?* I was so down, my dad got on a plane to come see me in Florida. He didn't tell me, he just surprised me in Fort Myers. He could tell over the phone that nothing he could say would get me back on track. So he showed up in person and that really turned things around for me again. Any time I had to fight my own self-doubt, he was there to set me right.

We talked after every outing. All of college, all of summer ball, all pro ball, any time I pitched, the first thing I'd do afterward was find a way to talk to my dad. The second I got in the car, the second I just had a moment away, I would call him. Obviously he was following the games, watching if he could or listening on radio or finding play-by-play on the internet. He would know what happened, but we'd go through it pitch by pitch and play by play and break it all down. We'd talk about it all whether it was a good outing or a bad outing. It was basically: *How can*

I illustrate a picture of what was going through my mind at every point during the game?

I'd been talking baseball with my dad my whole life so nothing felt more natural. Because of his work, I had access to insights others wouldn't. When I was in grade school, I talked to Barry Zito during a spring-training game. I was a bat boy for the Giants that day, and Barry sat next to me on the bench for a few innings. I remember once when I was at a tournament in Irvine having a phone conversation with Nomar Garciaparra, who I'd met a couple times, about how to handle pressure in big situations.

One time, I asked my dad about the best grip for a changeup, and he decided to get advice from Greg Maddux, a future Hall of Famer. Here's how he told the story once to a friend: "I spoke to Maddux at spring training in 2008 when he was with the Padres. I had to do an interview with him in Peoria at their facility, and after we were done I asked if I could get some advice for my son Rio, a lefty pitcher who was thirteen at the time. Maddux was known to have the best changeup in the game so why not ask about his grip so that I could show Rio how Maddux holds his? He gladly showed me his grip, which was to tightly hold the ball with his thumb and ring finger and let the other fingers softly drape over the ball. 'Pedro,' he said, 'you find a grip you like and that's the one you use!'"

My dad always had a great feel for what I needed to understand and what I needed to hear at a certain time. He had a knack for getting things across that I probably didn't want to hear in the moment, but needed to be told. Some things you have to learn for yourself, the hard way, but with my dad around I didn't always have to figure everything out through firsthand experience. He could give me a little bit of a heads up, like: *Watch out for this.* Then at the same time, he could just be my dad. So it was the perfect combination of everything I needed. He was there on the darkest days and also on the brightest days, like in Omaha when he was beaming proud and shaking uncontrollably and pacing back and forth and just a nervous wreck. It was great to have him for both ends of the spectrum.

That's what was so great about having a dad with so much knowledge of the game and so much experience. When he told me that the game will always punch you right back in the mouth when you're flying a little too high, I knew he was right. I also knew he was going through what I was going through. He didn't want to put any pressure on me, but of course he'd have loved to see me pitch one day in a big-league game, preferably at Fenway Park. I would have to tell him, "Keep your fantasies to yourself." He did a good job of riding the emotional roller-coaster for me so I wouldn't.

My dad always tried to reiterate that baseball is all about the long game, it's a long season and you're not going to be judged off of one outing, you're not even going to be judged off of one season, but a full body of work. When things were going well, he'd remind me not to ride it too high. When things turned bad, he'd be on me not to ride it too low. He taught me to humble myself before the game, because if I didn't, the game would do that for me.

Ross and David

COUNTENANCE

BY ROSS NEWHAN

I think the word I have been looking for is countenance. Not in the dramatic Biblical context of "the Lord lifting up his countenance on you." I am thinking more earthly. I am thinking of a countenance that Pedro Gomez seemed to exude, drawing new friends, sustaining all friends. The newspaper and media beat demands tough questions that can fray (fry?) relationships but Pedro maintained multilingual respect and admiration. I first fell under Pedro's countenance—that smile, that large greeting of "Ross!"—during the many times we found ourselves in the same baseball press box. My retirement significantly reduced those encounters but a personal link of another kind developed, a true kinship.

◆ ◆ ◆

David Newhan, my son, is in his mid-forties and twelve years removed from his last major-league game in a career in which he played parts of eight big-league seasons. He is neither too old nor too far removed to forget that one of his favorite quotes when interviewed or when speaking to a group was one aimed at his parents. He would laugh and say, "Look at the genes I had to overcome." His mom, Connie Fisher Newhan, and I would bristle but how could we argue? Neither of us were very athletic. Youth sports had not been developed beyond the playground when I was young, and my only athletic exercise during my sixty years in the baseball writing business has been an occasional go at golf, much to the chagrin of the pro who has attempted to provide periodic lessons. Connie was a school district library supervisor during her working years. She grew up a Dodger fan, and my love for her was hastened when I learned that she had written a high school theme paper on Walter Alston, the Dodger manager. At one point she tried her hand (feet?) at adult soccer until learning there is no age limit on slide tackling. While I traveled covering ball, first at the *Long Beach Independent, Press-Telegram,* and then the *Los Angeles Times,* it was Connie who fed, chauffeured and kept David motivated, although he did a good job for himself when initially snubbed by scouts and recruiters. Ultimately, his arrival at the major-league level enabled father and son to claim a unique title. There is no official category, no plaque or trophy awarded, but it is generally acknowledged within the BBWAA that David and I were the first combination of a baseball-writing father with a major-league-playing son.

◆ ◆ ◆

"We're going to be the second," Pedro Gomez would laugh and say to David or me whenever encountering one of us in recent years. It was a nod to the hope that his son Rio, a left-handed pitcher in the Boston Red Sox system, would achieve what David had enabled us to achieve. Hope is eternal but the calendar is a menace. The pandemic of 2020 and 2021 disrupted advancements for minor-league players. As I write, Rio is about to enter the 2021 season at twenty-six, having never pitched above A-ball, the lowest step on the minor-league ladder, and his father's death had to be a body blow. Yet, it is often a mystery who survives the climb and who doesn't. David wasn't selected in the pro draft or recruited by a Division I college out of high school. He believed in himself, went to a community college for a year, was playing for Georgia Tech the next year and was ultimately drafted by the Oakland A's out of Pepperdine, the school from which he graduated. It was a circuitous route but one on which he maintained determination, as he did during the ascent from that lowest A ball step on the professional ladder. He would be asked by reporters at the major-league level if he ever considered giving up, if he ever considered becoming a sportswriter like his dad. He would laugh and say, "No, never. I heard him scream and curse at the computer too many times."

◆ ◆ ◆

I did scream and curse at the computer, and the typewriter before that. I also screamed and cursed when covering extra innings on deadline and labor meetings that were designed to fail and when discovering office editing changes on which I was not consulted. I survived, persevered and lived in concert with baseball for almost fifty years, covering and savoring most of the historic events and special moments over that span. Hank Aaron, Pete Rose, Rickey Henderson, Nolan Ryan, Cal Ripken, Reggie Jackson in Game 6, Bucky Dent in Fenway, Smoltz and Morris in Game 7, Koufax and Drysdale in '65, Gibson in '88, Sparky and the Big Red Machine in the 70s, Tom Lasorda in Dodger moment after Dodger moment, Marvin Miller, Gene Autry, George Steinbrenner, Charlie Finley, the O'Malleys, a series of forgettable commissioners and two special managers who tried their best to provide insights into what I was watching every night: Bill Rigney and Gene Mauch. Through all of that, through all the games and personalities, I suspect that what every baseball writer would say, and what I would say, is that the people they remember most are those with whom they shared a press box. Too many are gone, too many too soon, including Pedro Gomez. Rest in peace my friend. Yours was a special countenance and kinship.

HE WATCHED OUT
FOR US

BY JON DANIELS

Since the Super Bowl, I've been trying to think about when I first met Pedro, but I can't place it. Somehow over the years, we developed a dialogue and a professional friendship that I've come to realize in the past few weeks was his signature. We'd connect at the annual Cactus League media day each February in Phoenix—he'd ask for stories about my kids, and vice versa. He always seemed to have a compliment on how we'd handled something—a player situation, a bit of drama or controversy with a staff member, our support for an employee who needed help—and it was almost always in that category. He loved the people in the game, and appreciated those who shared that sentiment.

On a few occasions, Pedro would reach out randomly during the season to share his thoughts on topics that could be sensitive. He wasn't judgmental. He wanted to see good people treated fairly and be given second chances. In 2015 when we signed Matt Bush, who had spent time in prison for a drunk-driving incident that badly injured another man, Pedro reached out. He asked about what due diligence we'd done on Matt prior to signing him, and specifically if he had taken accountability, shown remorse, and understood the consequences of his actions. Confident Matt had satisfied those requirements, Pedro approved of the move, and asked about what type of support Matt had with the organization and elsewhere to succeed. He wanted the best for people.

When Ron Washington admitted in the spring of 2010 that he had used drugs, he gave one of his first interviews after the incident to Pedro. They had developed a relationship over the years and Ron felt he could trust Pedro to be fair. Pedro asked the hard questions necessary, but treated Ron with the respect he deserved. Afterwards, Pedro came over and told me he appreciated we were standing by Ron through the controversy. He understood we all have flaws, we're not perfect, and second chances are earned by the way you treat people before you're in the spotlight. Ron had treated people well when no one was looking—and so Pedro was going to support him in a time of need.

In August 2017, Hurricane Harvey caused mass devastation in South Texas. On the baseball front, it rendered Minute Maid Park in Houston unplayable. The schedule had the Rangers playing there before the city and facility were ready to host events, so other arrangements had to be made. Unfortunately, especially against the backdrop of the much bigger issues at play for the people suffering from the storm, the two teams and MLB didn't agree on how best to handle it. The series was moved to Tampa Bay. It was an emotional time, with a lot of misinformation out there—about why the decision was made, and who was involved. I caught a lot of flak publicly. Rather than set the record straight—which was irrelevant in the bigger picture—I tried to be quiet and not engage in the rhetoric. Pedro reached out. He asked for some background on the situation so he could better understand it. But really, he was calling to empathize and check in on a friend. He told me to hang in there, and reinforced the decision to lay low and let it pass.

Last June, in the midst of everything the world had going on—baseball shut down for months, the pandemic, political battles, and the social justice movement in the wake of too many deaths of innocent men and women—Pedro texted me to talk. The book *Cult of Glory* had recently come out, describing a dark and controversial period in the history of the Texas Rangers—the law enforcement agency, not the baseball team. Similar to other sports franchises whose names touch on various sensitive/offensive topics, our organization had received some inquiries about whether there were plans to change the team name. Pedro, believing the name of the team had over the years grown to be separate and distinct from the law enforcement agency, had an idea. He shared with me the history of the Golden State Warriors' team name. How the Philadelphia Warriors used to have a Native-American-inspired cartoon character as their logo, one which if it existed today would rightfully draw heavy criticism. However, the team rebranded itself away from that image, and eliminated the cartoon character. "You guys have already done that (rebranding)," Pedro said, "And you don't deserve the scrutiny for association with people you don't share values with." It floored me. With the world seemingly upside down, Pedro took time out of his day to look out for us.

Early in my career, I had the opportunity to learn about the game and business of baseball from one of the all-time successful front office executives, John Hart. In the 1990s, John established himself as one of the top GMs in the game. In a way, John, Pat Gillick, and Sandy Alderson were kind of the patriarchs of the American League at that time. Their teams dominated, and in their own ways, they revolutionized the sport. Pedro had spent a good deal of time covering Sandy when he ran the Oakland A's. He spoke highly of Sandy—believing he had a strong combination of intelligence along with character and a feel for people. And so it led to Pedro asking a lot of questions about what I had learned from John, how we handled internal personnel matters, and how that compared to what he'd seen firsthand with Sandy. He valued innovation and winning on the field, but he seemed to enjoy it more when winning was coupled with treating people right.

Preparing for this essay led me to review years' worth of text messages between Pedro and me. What stood out? His love for his family—he was too happy to share about his kids. His genuine care for his friends—the number of times he'd randomly check in on me, seemingly with an innate understanding of when it might be most needed. And his love of the game—on a visit to the minor leagues in 2019, he singled out four players on our Hickory Crawdads team that he told me to watch for. And so I will. Demarcus Evans, Yerry Rodriguez, Wes Robertson, and Sam Huff. The Pedro Prospect list. I'll miss those texts, but I am extremely grateful for the perspective you've given me on what's important. Love your family and treat people well. Thanks, amigo.

Kenny and Jason Heyward

CAN YOU BELIEVE WE GET TO DO THIS?

BY KEN ROSENTHAL

So you're down on the field, where the 50,000 people in attendance would love to join you, or maybe you're inside a clubhouse, where the average person never will tread. A media pass allows entrance to those places, allows privilege most baseball writers never imagined for themselves, yet often come to take for granted. Pedro Gomez never did.

Pedro loved that world, relished it, reveled in it. Heck, he stood at the top of it, stood right there by the batting cage, on the grass in foul territory, going live on ESPN. Yet, he wasn't some sort of unapproachable, ego-driven overlord, ignoring the everyday Joes who are as much a lifeblood of the sport as the players and managers. Pedro could be going live on ESPN in two minutes, and hold on! There was the bullpen catcher, an old friend from early in his career, or maybe from college or back in Miami, stopping by to say hello.

It's a bit of a magic trick, live television. Guys like me and Pedro, guys who started in newspapers in the late 1980s, never considered becoming talking heads at the outset of our careers.

My dad would say to me, "Hey, maybe you can be the sports guy on the 11 o'clock news, make more money that way than writing."

I would sneer at him in disgust. Reading off a teleprompter for three minutes? No thank you! And then one of our own, Peter Gammons, made the transition from print to TV, creating a world for many of us that we never thought possible. Sometimes while working the postseason for Fox, I'd walk across the field in the hours before the game, and there would be Pedro, preparing to go live on ESPN. I'd stop, not wanting to distract him by walking through his shot or even by taking a detour behind him. We'd catch each other's eye. Pedro would look at me and flash that big smile of his, his eyes sparkling. His look would say it all: *Can you believe we get to do this? Us?!?!*

Seconds later, his "hit" would begin, and of course he would roll through it, making it look easy. The truth is, live TV is not easy, especially for former print guys who had no training in the medium, and who learned *not* to draw attention to themselves while working for newspapers. Fox had to put me in a bow tie to help snap me out of it. Pedro's big, warm personality seemed more suited for on-camera work. But his longtime producer, Charlie Moynihan, said it even took Pedro a while to feel comfortable.

Pedro and Charlie developed a ritual to help settle Pedro's nerves, not that Pedro ever appeared nervous on air. Right before Pedro would go live, Charlie would tell him, "Don't fuck it up." Actually, that would be the last thing Charlie would say. His overall instructions were more expansive, albeit terse. *You're live in thirty seconds. You've got thirty seconds on camera. You're throwing it to sound, tagging it and throwing back to Bristol. Don't fuck it up.*

But really, there was no way Pedro was going to fuck it up. He mastered the mechanics of live television, as much as they can be mastered (weird stuff can happen during those pregame hits, from the audio connection faltering to an errant throw hitting you in the back to some dumb-ass walking in front of the camera). Pedro's greatest strength, though, was the command of his subject matter, the game he lived and breathed. How did he acquire that command? Through all those organic connections he made with people in every corner of the industry. People who came to love him, and trust him and share information with him they would not share with others. In English, *and* in Spanish. Few media members did more to make Latin players relatable to English-speaking fans.

"Whether it was a backup clubhouse attendant, a third-base umpire, a PR director, male or female reporter, a college kid who was in the press box for the first time, he had time for everybody," Moynihan said. "He was organic. He was sincere. He was genuine. He was fearless. All the traits you want in a person, he had 'em all."

What Pedro also knew, almost instinctively, is something I slowly came to understand—that the best part of being a baseball reporter, the relationships you form with all sorts of different people, is the defining element of the job as well. All news reporting requires an ability to relate to people. But on most beats, the contacts are not as varied as they are in baseball. There are players, coaches and managers. Owners, general managers and agents. Scouts, umpires and club employees. People young and old, male and increasingly female, North American, Latin American and Asian, too.

No baseball reporter can do the job well without finding a way to connect with people from all of these groups. But Pedro's essence—his natural inquisitiveness, his radiant warmth, his intense desire to share in the human experience—was his secret. His separator from the rest of us.

AJ Hinch, who got to know Pedro when he was hired as Diamondbacks manager in 2009, tells a story about when the Astros signed infielder Yuli Gurriel out of Cuba in July 2016. Pedro had a particular affinity for Cuban baseball; his parents had fled Cuba for Miami in 1962. He knew that Gurriel's father, Lourdes Sr., was one of the all-time best players from Cuba. He quickly determined that Hinch, as a member of Team USA, had played against the elder Gurriel in the 1993 Intercontinental Cup and 1994 Baseball World Cup. And he couldn't wait to tell Hinch that the Astros' signing of Yuli meant he would now get to manage Lourdes' son.

"I feel like he always covered the sport as people first and 'content' second," Hinch said. "He had a way of understanding you in a depth that few other media members ever attempt, let alone master."

Or as another friend, Brewers bench coach Pat Murphy, put it, "Pedro made it about everyone else. Never about himself."

The Athletic's Jayson Stark, a former colleague of Pedro's at ESPN, bears many of Pedro's attributes—his spirit, his warmth, his boundless passion and curiosity for the game. Yet Jayson, too, expresses wonder at the unique relationships Pedro formed in baseball. From a fellow journalist's perspective, it could be almost intimidating watching Pedro in action.

On a typical night at ESPN headquarters in Bristol, the "Baseball Tonight" crew would be sitting around the green room, talking about an adjustment a player might be making, or a decision that might have backfired on a manager. Pedro would say, almost casually, "I'll call him." Or, "I'll text him." Then Jayson would sit in astonishment as the person got back to Pedro, sometimes within minutes. How is it that Pedro warranted such responses so regularly? Because he was all baseball, and no agenda.

On the set, it was more of the same. The "Baseball Tonight" crew would talk about a player who just did something meaningful in a game, and Pedro would blurt out, "You know, I was talking with him last week." It happened, Jayson said, literally every show. "And you know why it happened?" Jayson asked. "Because he built real connections with hundreds of people, and they paid off every day."

Which isn't to say Pedro was a soft touch, or to use a derogatory term writers sometimes use, "a player's pal." Ask Barry Bonds if Pedro was tough. Ask Curt Schilling about the column Pedro wrote calling him "something of a con man" before his start in Game 7 of the 2001 World Series. That column did not appear on ESPN's website or in some other national outlet. Pedro wrote it for the *Arizona Republic*, the hometown paper for a team on the verge of winning its first World Series title!

Hinch, after getting fired by the Astros and suspended a year by Major League Baseball for his role in the team's sign-stealing scandal, knew his friendship with Pedro would not prevent him from covering the story as doggedly as he would any other. Pedro was close to both Hinch and his former bench coach with the Astros, Alex Cora, who lost his managing job with the Red Sox and also received a yearlong suspension. Didn't matter. Pedro was willing to tackle the unpleasant as well as the pleasant, to ask the questions that needed to be asked, to do his job the way it was supposed to be done.

"He had a great way to balance the human obligation that he created himself, and the professional obligation he needed to cover difficult scenarios," Hinch said. "He separated the personal from the professional. He never crossed over necessarily. But he also never feared either side."

Pedro and I were the same age, began our careers covering baseball at roughly the same time, and approached the job with the same sensibilities. A few years back, a clubhouse incident involving a younger writer generated a good amount of attention. Pedro texted me, unprompted, in a state of exasperation. In our early years, he noted, such an incident would have been considered routine.

"How many times did you get yelled at by a manager or players?" he said. "La Russa and Showalter would do that to me at least twice a year. Who cares? I'd yell back. And players, too. What has happened to beat writers? How soft are they now? I truly believe it has something to do with their lack of people skills from being buried in PlayStation, etc. Not entirely, mind you. But just a generation that doesn't know how to SPEAK to others, just text."

I can't say Pedro was old school—the writers who came before us probably thought *we* were soft—but we came from the same school. That shared experience bonds all ball writers of a certain age. The job at times can be quite difficult. You have to live it to truly understand. And once you did, the way Pedro and I did, the way so many of our colleagues and rivals did, you were bound forever.

We were competitors, me working for Fox, Pedro for ESPN. But do this job long enough, and at some point that tension diminishes. Oh, it helped that Pedro later in his career was more of a television than print presence, so we were not competing for scoops on the internet. But we both knew that when you're down on the field before a postseason game, going live on camera amid the busy din of batting practice and the giddy anticipation of a gathering crowd, the moment is all that matters.

Pedro thrived in that moment, and all of the interactions and connections leading up to that moment. I'm kicking myself that it took his death for me to understand just how much being at the park meant to him, and how much him being at the park meant to all those he touched. He might be in some distant locale, thousands of miles from his wife, Sandi, and three children. But if he was working at a game, reporting on the sport he loved, he was home.

Pedro and Jose Reyes

WHERE'S PEDRO?

BY BUSTER OLNEY

What we discovered afterward, when we began to grieve, was that Pedro bore running gags with just about everybody, connective threads he pulled day after day. With me, it was the perpetuation of a big lie.

"I owe my career to Pedro," I would say to anyone who came within earshot of Pedro and me when we worked together, at ESPN. "I got my big break when Pedro was fired by the *San Diego Union,* and I was hired in his place."

Pedro would protest loudly and indignantly, infusing the drama—*C'mon, that's not what happened at all!*—but I would persist, laughing and thanking him profusely.

It's true that I was hired to fill a job vacated by Pedro, when I jumped from the *Nashville Banner* to cover South Bay high school sports in San Diego—my first opportunity to work in a city with a major-league baseball team. But Pedro left the *Union* of his own volition, because he was wanted by the *San Jose Mercury News.*

The truth is I became somewhat jealous of Pedro, because everybody loved and respected him in San Diego in a way I would've loved. "What's the biggest challenge for this team, Coach Ohnesorgen?" I asked the emperor of the Chula Vista High School football program

"Where's Pedro?" George Ohnesorgen responded, and he was merely the first to react to my presence that way. I heard similar disappointment from the coaches at Sweetwater, Castle Park, Hilltop and Montgomery. They all wanted to know: *Where's Pedro?*

I tried to cover Pedro's old beat while working from Pedro's former desk, with its tan metal tabletop and file cabinet and PC, the seat within point-blank range of the sports editor referred to by the young writers as Cement Head, because once he formed an impression of you, it never changed. Cement Head liked Pedro; everybody liked Pedro, his work and his personality.

He was with the *Union* for a relatively short time, less than a couple years. But Pedro created such a strong impression that it was like he never left. Whether it was the department's administrative assistants, other reporters or Cement Head, everybody wistfully shared funny stories about Pedro, most of which reflected his humor and his outsized personality.

Ed Graney, a fellow writer, was the coach of the department's adult baseball league team, and he and Pedro entertained teammates—and probably opponents—by loudly debating decisions, their voices rising, maybe to the point where those listening fretted about a possible brawl. But Pedro would defuse the moment by loudly calling out his friend's name, and then they would laugh, Ed recalled. On nights when high school games were played, Pedro would return from covering a game, and then he and others would go to the fifth-floor cafeteria well past midnight to play a version of stickball—paper wadded up tightly into a ball and smashed around the empty tables and chairs.

Sometimes, they would go to a bar near Pedro's place in Pacific Beach, and he would inevitably glean the back story on somebody they met. You would never say Pedro was a wallflower, Ed said. The coaches that Pedro covered responded to him because he got to know each of them, because he got to know where they were from, got to know their families, and everything about their assistants. "He connected with them like he connected with us," Ed said, and years later, I would see the same dynamic develop with major-league players, managers and coaches.

Pedro wasn't that way because of the requirements of his job; that was Pedro and his personality. Tom Krasovic took over the Padres beat for the *San Diego Union-Tribune* in 1995, and even under normal circumstances, there is a steep learning curve for anyone covering a team and a league for the first time. But for Kras ("Jerry Seinfeld!" Pedro called him), the challenge was exponentially greater, because he jumped into the assignment near the end of the players' strike of 1994-95, and there was a mad scramble of transactions and exhibitions in a truncated spring training.

The Padres played an exhibition game against the A's at Phoenix Municipal Stadium, with veteran left-hander Fernando Valenzuela making the start against Todd Van Poppel. Kras had not yet learned how different the camp access rules were from guidelines in the regular season, when reporters waited to the end of a game to descend into the clubhouse. During spring training, the starting pitchers would typically do some jogging and get some treatment after finishing their two or three or four innings, and then depart the park in the middle of the game, to beat the crowd. This is what Fernando did, exiting rapidly after giving up eight runs in two innings, and Kras had no idea until after the game that Valenzuela—of particular interest to San Diego readers, because of all of the years he had pitched in Southern California—was long gone. Pedro covered the A's for the *Sacramento Bee* at the time, and Kras mournfully recounted the ugly reality that he had no quotes from the person at the center of that day's story. Pedro heard this and wherever Fernando was—a golf course, or at his condo, by a pool, whatever—Pedro tracked him down, spoke to him in Spanish, on behalf of Kras. The information Pedro gleaned from Fernando was, of course, better than what the pitcher had told the beat writers; through the generosity of a friend, Kras went from having nothing to having quotes exclusively his.

Pedro chided Krasovic for having grown up a fan of the Cincinnati Reds, and while Pedro lived in the Bay Area he made a point of taking days off to host Kras for a series between the Reds and Giants—a set of three games in which Cincinnati was swept and blown out, much to Pedro's delight, with former Michigan quarterback Rick Leach having big moments and seemingly trolling Kras. Pedro badgered Graney for being a Dodger fan, teasing him about how the Dodgers spent so much money in free agency, and extolled the virtue of the Tigers teams for which he rooted as a kid.

I first met the legendary Pedro when he returned to San Diego for visits, but really got to know him best in the years when he covered the Diamondbacks for the *Arizona Republic*; by then, I was at *The New York Times*, the beat writer assigned to the Yankees. During the 2001 World Series, Pedro sat a couple of rows in front of me, and during games, he would step back to compare thoughts about the ongoing games.

He was attuned to the disagreement between aces Curt Schilling and Randy Johnson, and the internal questions about the bullpen decisions by manager Bob Brenly. I was impressed by the blunt honesty of his sources, a treasure cultivated only if the reporter is deeply trusted.

Neither Graney nor Krasovic remembered Pedro ever mentioning an ambition to be on television, because as Ed recalled, there was a separation of church and state when it came to TV and newspapers; you either did one or the other, and Pedro was a newspaper guy. I thought of myself as a writer first—I still do—who manages to find a way through the television medium. Like me, Pedro had no formal training in broadcasting, but he seemed much more at ease, much more comfortable, than I ever felt. As Ed observed, Pedro's sincerity translated on television; he was genuine, the same as he had been when he would argue over baseball with Ed back in San Diego. There were no affectations. I remember covering the Home Run Derby with him, intense nights when a voice in the back of your head might whisper to you about how many more millions of people happened to be tuned in, and how any mistake might turn into a viral moment.

I always felt an extra dollop of anxiety for these types of broadcasts, but in watching Pedro, he always looked completely at ease, utterly comfortable. There was a post-Derby trophy ceremony, in which the sponsor and Major League Baseball officials would be involved on live television, and I remember feeling relief when our ESPN bosses asked Pedro to do it. I was not confident that I would get the sequencing right in the ceremony, and identify the gathered executives correctly, before asking the best questions of the winner. I was confident that Pedro would handle the responsibility deftly, and he did.

Especially when one of the finalists of the Derby spoke Spanish as a first language. I have already mentioned that I was jealous of Pedro—but never more than when I'd watch him seamlessly conduct interviews in two languages, in a sport in which 30 percent of the players speak Spanish as their primary language. On live television, Pedro would ask a question in English, for the benefit of the audience that predominantly understood English, and then pose the question in Spanish, and after getting the answer, immediately translate. For Latin American players—especially young players, some of whom fretted about who they could trust and if they might speak awkwardly in their second language—Pedro was an important ally, something that All-Star shortstop Francisco Lindor mentioned in an ESPN interview after

Pedro's death. For the viewers, he was an impeccable source who could provide information—the perspective of the players—immediately.

When Pedro and I were together, I'd pepper him with questions about specific players from Latin America, knowing that they would open up to him in their primary language in a way that they would not be able to with me, who got a D+ in my last year of college Spanish. I remember a conversation with Pedro about the Americanization of names and how it grated some—for example, longtime Yankees catcher Jorge Posada was referred to by older white teammates as Georgie. Hall of Famer Roberto Clemente—who, in the year before he died, asked in Spanish for his parents' blessing on national television, after the Pirates won the World Series—was often called Bob by peers and broadcasters. As Pedro and I discussed, for some players, that kind of bastardization of a name was viewed as disrespectful to the parents of the players, especially the mother. A lot of players born on the U.S. mainland might not care whether they were called Lefty, Sparky or Jetes, but Pedro told me how some players felt strongly that the name chosen by the mother should be honored, respected and used.

Pedro had a powerful belief in right versus wrong, about conduct. The general perception of Yasiel Puig, in his first months in the big leagues, was that he was a fun, undisciplined player. What Pedro seemed to know before anybody else was how often Puig showed up late and how much his tardiness grated on his teammates, and how clear it was that his questionable habits might eventually lead to his departure from the Dodgers. He was being marketed like a superstar, but Pedro noted the divisiveness he fostered and all the mistakes he made—missing cutoff men, recklessly running the bases and getting thrown out needlessly, and being overmatched by opposing pitchers in big moments because he didn't adjust. I remember bumping into Pedro at Dodger Stadium and talking with him about his pointed reporting, and what really struck me was how passionate Pedro was about the lines of conduct Puig had crossed—in his respect for teammates, in his place of work. In Pedro's eyes Puig was effectively expecting others to treat him differently, under a different standard.

And what distinguished Pedro Gomez, from his first days in San Diego to the days when he became recognized in airports, was that he never expected special treatment. He never thought of himself as a big deal. He was always self-effacing, always connecting, leaving his friends old and new to now ponder the same question, through the saddest prism: *Where's Pedro?*

Shelley and her daughter, Dylan

Pedro with David Ortiz and Miguel Cabrera

OUR COLLEAGUE, OUR FRIEND

BY SHELLEY M. SMITH

Pedro didn't make it to all of our ESPN annual bureau meetings because they always came at the same time as the MLB All-Star Game. We missed him when he wasn't there. He was the person who could light up the room with his smile, his dazzling good looks and his humor. We'd fight to sit next to him when we had the chance. He had that kind of effect on people; he made us happy and always reminded even the most dour among us how blessed we were to be in our jobs, and of our talent and good fortune. He never took anything or any of us for granted. He was kind and warm.

When I was getting ready to go to Cuba with Shaq (and my daughter) on a goodwill tour in July 2016, Pedro was our virtual tour guide, regaling me with stories on where to go, what to eat, what to buy and what to be careful of. Of course, being with Shaq and his security detail, we were perfectly safe and never once had to think about the bad things. Much of that came from Pedro and his knowledge of his home country. It's when I learned that his family fled the Castro regime in 1962 when his mother was eight months pregnant with him—she lied and said she was six months along so she could get on the plane. Pedro was born three weeks after they landed in Miami, spurring him to say (all the time, according to producer Jim Witalka), "I was made in Cuba, born in the U.S."

He was fiercely proud of both statements and for years he had yearned to go back to Cuba and see what made his parents live there and then want so desperately to leave. When President Obama loosened up travel restrictions and MLB agreed to allow the Tampa Bay Rays to play the Cuban nationals in early 2016, Pedro was there again, one of five visits he made to Cuba for work, starting in 1999. He made the 2016 visit emotional by visiting his family's old house again, as he had in 1999, and then scattering some of his father's and brother's ashes along the coast. His father never returned, having vowed to stay away as long as the Castros were in power.

I gained so much respect for Pedro the way he went about covering Barry Bonds' home run chase. He was there every day for close to three years, by the end standing in the back of the throng, but waiting until he got his question in to Bonds, who either ignored him or gave some non-answer answer. That's what good reporters do, and Pedro was among the best. Maybe even THE best in the way he challenged players and was unafraid to ask anyone anything, even if the pitcher had lost the game or a hitter had blown the game. He was fearless.

My favorite stories, though, are about Pedro and his producer, Charlie Moynihan, exchanging barbs as if they were arch enemies. They were the best of friends.

"He's terrible, horrible, shouldn't be on air," Charlie would go on. Every once in a while, as a prank, he'd cancel Pedro's room reservation or change the room numbers. Pedro gave it back to him, once taking a photo at a game of a garden-tool race and sending it to Charlie with the caption, "I found a race you can run in."

The last time I heard from Pedro was the afternoon he died. Our boss wanted to know if Pedro and I could handle the news the next two days for SportsCenter. Pedro's text: "Of course." He said that a lot, never wanting to turn down an assignment if he could help it.

Writing Pedro's obituary for ESPN and then voicing it was the hardest thing I've ever had to do. It took me at least three tries to get the first sentence out through the microphone. I've written (and voiced) dozens of obits. I wrote my mother's in 2018 and my sister's in 2016. But

I didn't have to voice them, they were for various newspapers. I think the sound of my voice reading the words about Pedro scared me in an emotional way I'd never felt before. As I said then and will say now, "He was our colleague. He was our friend."

T.J., Mikey and Pedro in Brooklyn to see Rio pitch

HOW DO YOU WANT
TO BE REMEMBERED?

BY T.J. QUINN

We were in an Atlanta bar around 1 a.m. during the 2001 National League Championship Series when two guys in Diamondbacks jerseys started in on Pedro. He wasn't a national figure yet—he was still a columnist at the *Arizona Republic*. But the eyes, the eyebrows and the smile of Pedro Gomez were instantly recognizable from the thumbnail picture over his columns.

"Why can't you write one positive thing?" one kept repeating. "Why point out the flaws when this team might go to the World Series?"

The idea that Pedro Gomez was a relentless critic could only make sense in the mind of a fan unaccustomed to seeing his team on a national stage. One of the two men turned to make his case to me, as if I would be sympathetic. Being, first, a friend of Pedro's, and second, a reporter for a New York City tabloid, I was not. To Pedro's right was another friend of ours, one of his closest since high school. José Beiro was an FBI agent with a strong instinct for loyalty. While I jawed, José simmered. There was a vague hint that this could go badly very quickly if one of these two idiots crossed a line.

Pedro, on the other hand, had a matador's skill for deflecting the aggrieved whines of liquored-up fans, never backing down but never quite losing his smile, either. He had no taste for conflict unless there was a righteous cause at stake, and deluded fans were not a worthy cause. He was also too nice to tell someone to piss off and leave him alone. But José's stare soon went from noticeable to worrisome, and Pedro decided we needed to get him out of there, but quick. Pedro could take it, but he was worried José would end up mangling them on his behalf.

I had that scene in mind a little more than a week later when the Diamondbacks did indeed reach the World Series. Their opponent was the New York Yankees, who were riding the emotional surge of 9/11—lower Manhattan was still smoldering at the time—and were the betting favorite to win their fourth straight title.

For all the drama of that series, most of it revolved around Curt Schilling, the former Phillies ace who had been traded to Arizona the year before. Schilling had a well-established reputation in the game for being a self-involved horse's ass, but led the National League in both wins and innings pitched that season. It was a season worthy of the title *caballo*, which Pedro recognized.

In Game 4, Schilling pitched a masterful seven innings, leaving after the seventh with a chance for the win. He was then removed for twenty-two-year-old closer Byung-Hyun Kim, and most Diamondbacks fans can recall what happened next: Kim allowed two runs in the ninth, and then he gave up a game-winning home run to Derek Jeter in the tenth. After the game, in the crowded catacombs and clubhouses of Yankee Stadium, there were questions that needed to be answered, mostly about why manager Bob Brenly pulled Schilling and stuck with Kim. It made sense to remove Schilling with a lead, which also kept his pitch count low enough to make him an option for Game 7. There didn't need to be any particular controversy about Schilling. So, of course, Schilling created one.

After the game, he declared that he could have continued. But the truth of the matter was that after the seventh, Schilling had told Brenly, "Don't hang me out there." Pedro knew that and couldn't stand that Schilling was willing to use Brenly to make himself look tough. Word also "leaked" from a team source that Schilling had a sore arm, and Pedro knew the source was Schilling himself. The pitcher had used some gullible member of the press to set himself up for a can't-lose scenario if he were to take the mound again: Win, and he heroically overcame an injury. Lose, and he's a gamer who gave it his all. A dry run for the bloody sock game three years later.

Sure enough, a few nights later, the two teams found themselves headed for Game 7. No Arizona team had ever won a professional championship, which meant that more or less the entire valley was pulling for Schilling to deliver them. In the heart of a fan, at least the kind that recognizes sportswriters in bars, this was a time for myth-making, not dissection. But sometime during the day of Game 6, Pedro Gomez decided that the next day's lead column in the state's largest newspaper needed to take Schilling to account, to let these fans know that their hopes rested on a phony.

Pedro told Diamondbacks pitcher Greg Swindell what he planned to write, and Swindell later said he begged him not to write it. Pedro told his wife, Sandi, and his friend Steve Kettmann. They tried to talk him out of it. The group called me and I said I wasn't really sure what the right move was. I don't know how many nights Pedro had like the one we'd shared in Atlanta, facing the yaps of idiots who thought a reporter's job was to cheer. I do know he was perfectly aware of what he was stepping into with that column. And I know he made decisions based on one principle: *How do you want to be remembered?*

Readers woke up to a column that began with acknowledgment of Schilling's prowess, which was undeniable. Then it quickly got to the point: "The past few days also have offered the country insight into Schilling's little secret, the one baseball insiders have known for years, but one that has rarely surfaced publicly. Schilling is something of a con man, someone more intent on polishing his image through whatever means available."

Thus began a world-class shredding. He called Schilling a "me-first" player, the "consummate table for one." He also said that if Schilling were to win that game, none of it would matter.

There are writers who revel in the fury of their readers, but Pedro was never one of them. I worried that his sense of honor and obligation would leave him with slashed tires or a rock through his window or a punch in the face the next time he went to a bar, which would probably be that night.

I got to the ballpark around the same time he did, a few hours ahead of Schilling's scheduled first pitch. He looked tired. I asked how he was and he gave a half smile and said, "Come listen to this." He dialed into his work voicemail and played some of the messages readers had left him during the day. "You piece of shit wetback motherfucker," one baritone said. Pedro looked up at me. "Wetback?" he said, "I'm Cuban! We flew here!"

What I knew about Pedro as much as I knew anything was that he did not seek attention for attention's sake. I knew that his quip aside, the voicemail and all those like it bothered him deeply. He could never fathom how someone's purported love for a game could lead them to lash out at a man's heritage. Even if that fan did get the nationality wrong.

We shared a few seconds of silence because we knew there was more of this to come. If Schilling lost, Pedro would never hear the end of it from fans. If Schilling won, he would never let Pedro forget it. And who knew how Schilling's teammates would respond, no matter what they might say about him in private? Anyone who recognized Pedro in that stadium the rest of the night was a potential assailant, whether with a word or a half-empty beer or a fist.

"I need to go down there," he said, "don't I?"

"Yeah," I said. "You do."

He wasn't really asking. He was always planning to go. I asked if he wanted me to go with him and he said yes. He collected his notebook and a tape recorder and we headed down to the field for early batting practice.

There wasn't really anyone to interview. The only point to our being there was to be seen. Pedro was offering himself up as a target so that no one could ever say he hid. Because this was the way it's done. If you take a shot at a guy, you show up and you take whatever is coming.

His mission in writing the column wasn't to even a score or generate artificial heat, it was to hold Schilling accountable. And he walked onto that field, strolling the length of foul territory from one dugout to the other, to hold himself accountable. He stayed light and loose as we talked and I kept looking from the fans behind the backstop to the players around the batting cage, waiting to see if anyone suddenly recognized him or was gearing up to say something.

As one hitting group finished, Swindell, who had been shagging fly balls in the outfield, headed for the Diamondbacks' dugout. He crossed the white line, spotted Pedro and then cut sharply in our direction. I tensed. Swindell slowed down, extended a hand, and shook Pedro's firmly. He nodded slowly and definitively with a tight smile of approval on his lips, and then he left without a word. Pedro whipped around to find me.

"Did you see that?" he said.

I beamed back at him.

"Yeah, I saw it."

There were plenty of pats on the back in the press box, and I heard the word "cojones" mentioned more than a few times. But Swindell's approval might have been more important. If Diamondbacks players had rallied around Schilling that day, Pedro would have been crushed, but he would have understood. He knew players and what motivated them, and if he had a fault, it was caring about what they thought. He was not thick-skinned. He was not fearless. But fear never stopped him from doing his job. That's what made him so goddamned brave.

I know he hoped that players would respect what he did, but to have one of them shake his hand, on the field, in uniform, a couple of hours before Game 7, it was more than he hoped for that day. It told him someone in the clubhouse recognized what he had done, that he had spoken up for the ones who did their jobs with honor. For the ones who worked through injuries without leaking it to friendly reporters. The ones who knew part of the job was to be accountable. It told every fan that you could believe what he told you, whether you liked it or not.

And it told every reporter in the business, this is how it's done. This is how you'll want to be remembered.

Billy and Scott with Matt Chapman

José Fernández

PEDRO GOMEZ DAY

BY SCOTT BORAS

When I first got to know Pedro, he reveled in talking about one of his favorite subjects: University of Miami baseball. Pedro was a journalism major at Miami in the early '80s and he would grill me on which Hurricanes would become future stars. The thing I learned quickly was that Pedro was very perceptive. He knew his stuff.

I should have known better when Pedro took an interest in my playing career. Pedro was the kind of reporter who did his research and he loved to ask me about my four years playing minor-league ball. He had praise for my .370-ish on-base percentage. I can promise you OBP was rarely talked about when I played in the mid-1970s.

"In today's game you would be a valued guy," Pedro would tell me, "because you could get on base. They love the on-base."

"What do you think, I'm a lug?" I'd kid him.

He would tease me all the time about my playing skills and I would joke with him about his reporting career. This went on for years. It was just pregame banter at the ballpark and we shared a ton of laughs. There are a lot of people in baseball where, I'm not sure they're passionate about the game. Even players. They play it because they're good at it. They would gladly do something else, if the opportunity was there. You can tell. You know. Pedro and I saw in each other that we were two who wouldn't be anywhere else.

What I do for players, it's not a job, it's a way of life, 24/7. You represent people in all senses of the word. You care for them, their kids, their families, their parents. You protect them. I've never wanted to represent athletes in other sports. I want to focus on the game I love. I'm a believer that to really be good at this, you could only represent one sport because it takes so much time to know the ins and outs of every organization, every thought process, every young general manager or veteran general manager, every owner.

One thing that hit me after the terrible news about Pedro on Super Bowl Sunday was: Who doesn't love Pedro? He was very good at probing as a journalist, but he was also a great listener. He had a real talent for getting the most out of someone in an interview. He became somebody that was accepted and respected, where people would talk to him where they wouldn't talk to others.

He had the sense—and the ability—to disagree with you, but still listen to you and really try to understand your point of view. He never lost interest. He'd keep asking questions. Even if he disagreed with you, he would take time to exhaust every line of questioning and understand the reasoning behind your point of view. He responded to what he knew and didn't know in his questioning. He had the ability to read people, to really probe in an area that was unexpected. His openness was natural and real. He didn't come to you with a known expectancy for what he was looking for.

I talked to him a lot about Barry Bonds when I represented Barry, and he would ask me questions about what Barry was like in a personal setting. I remember telling Pedro stories about Barry when he went to the All-Star Game. I had young sons at the time, and Barry picked them up and took them in his arms. "Hey, come with me," he would say, and my sons would go spend time with Barry in the back of his hotel room.

One year Barry insisted on giving my son Shane his All-Star ring.

"I really appreciate what you did for me," Barry told me, "and I wanted your son to have something from me."

The very next year, we went to the All-Star Game again and he did the same thing for my youngest son, Trent.

When I told Pedro that story, he asked me: "Did that surprise you?"

It did, because an All-Star ring is the type of memento that every player finds most personal. Barry knew that would be a very personal message of gratitude for the work that I did for him.

"It was really touching," I told Pedro. "It brought tears to my eyes."

Pedro was always listening. He never checked out.

"What other things have brought tears into your eyes?" he asked me.

I thought about it a minute.

"One time I was doing an interview with Michael Kay, and he asked me about my mother," I said. "It just brought out a side of me during the interview that really I just didn't expect to feel or discuss when I was doing that."

That was so Pedro. He was interviewing me about Barry, but when conversation veered to talk of my mother, he went with it—and he never let me forget that day. For years, I'd run into him on the infield before a game, and he'd kind of lean in and say: "Hey, can I make you cry today?"

Pedro loved—and lived—the intimacy of the game as much as anyone I can think of. He always talked about feeling lucky to work in baseball, and I think he was most appreciative of his work allowing him to be intimate with the game we both love. That allowed him the access to communicate to outsiders about the inside of the game.

I remember the outpouring after José Fernández died in a boating accident in September 2016. Bob Ley anchored an "Outside the Lines" segment on ESPN about the emotional tribute his Marlins' teammates paid to him, mentioning an "eloquence that was heart-rending," and then kicked it over to Pedro, who was at the game.

"Bob, I've been covering major-league ball for thirty years, and I've never been to a more emotional game than last night here at Marlins Park," he said. "The Marlins' decision to have a very muted in-game experience I think captured the moment and captivated everybody inside the stadium. ... They did nothing but play José Fernández photographs on the big board in center field. It was very quiet, there was not any loud music whatsoever. It really led to everyone understanding that, hey, tonight, there's something a little bit bigger than baseball going on, and the players took that on as well, as you witnessed there by the Mets in a completely unscripted move going out to hug their rivals."

Don Mattingly kneeled on the pitcher's mound and kissed the rubber, explaining to Pedro: "I just felt like I wanted to say goodbye to José one more time."

I still mourn Jose's death. Whenever I go to a game in Miami, I wear a José Fernández button to honor him. Maybe we could do something like that as a remembrance for Pedro Gomez. At some point during the course of the season, whether it be pregame or postgame, we all wear PEDRO GOMEZ DAY buttons. Maybe everyone would contribute to the Pedro Gomez Foundation that day to help young people pursuing careers in journalism. We could make it a National Pedro at the Ballpark Remembrance Day. That would be a way to bring attention to Pedro, his love for the game, his connection to so many people in baseball, and to his legacy.

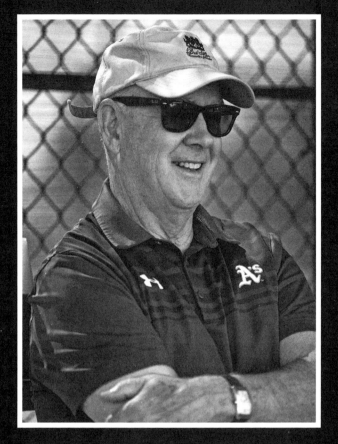

Billy, Sandy and Pedro

THE HEART AND SOUL
OF BASEBALL

BY SANDY ALDERSON

I'm sorry to start this remembrance of Pedro Gomez with a long anecdote, but I think it expresses what I so much admired in Pedro. In 1997, the A's were not very good, finishing last in the American League West. We had been in the World Series three years in a row from 1988 to 1990, but after the 1992 season, when we lost to the Toronto Blue Jays in the League Championship Series, we entered a period of decline. Too many long-term contracts with too many aging players. Because the 1997 team wasn't very good, we were touting the strength of our farm system as a source of hope for the future. We put a lot of effort into promoting our prospects to the media.

Also that year, the Arizona Diamondbacks were one year away from their inaugural season in the National League. As part of their preparation to play in 1998, the Diamondbacks scouted every major-league organization for an expansion draft that would take place for them and the Tampa Bay Devil Rays in November 1997. This draft would allow both teams to select unprotected players from every existing major-league team.

The Diamondbacks assigned a former A's player, Ron Hassey, to scout the A's system. Ron was with the A's for three years—and three World Series. He was behind the plate when Kirk Gibson hit his famous home run off Dennis Eckersley in the 1988 World Series. His assignment was to see every A's team from rookie ball to the major leagues, so Ron would occasionally visit Oakland, where he would chat with our beat writers about the World Series years, but also share his opinions about players in our system. Pedro, then working for the *Sacramento Bee,* was one of those beat writers.

Hassey enjoyed putting a different spin on our farm system, opining that the players were not as good as the organization believed they were. The brightest prospect in the system at that time was Eric Chavez, drafted as a shortstop the year before out of high school in San Diego. In 1997, he was playing his first full season at Visalia in the California League.

Late in the summer, Hassey made his final appearance in Oakland and was critical to the media about Chavez, particularly his defense at third base. Pedro wrote an article that quoted Hassey about Chavez's shortcomings. After all that we had done as an organization to promote our prospects in the media, that article lit a fuse. I confronted Pedro the following day on the concourse above the press level at the Coliseum.

We had at it. I wasn't really mad at Pedro, but I was irate over the situation of a former A's player ripping our best prospect on our turf. Pedro defending his reporting, as he had every right to do. After all, it wasn't his opinion that was expressed in the article. He had a responsibility to report anything newsworthy to his readers. But I went on and on—and Pedro heard me out. (By the way, during his major-league career, Chavez went on to win six Gold Gloves at third base, thanks in part to Ron Washington!)

Pedro and I laughed about that confrontation many times in succeeding years, but it was a credit to Pedro that we even had a relationship thereafter. That was Pedro, passionate about his work as a journalist, but also a forgiving human being who enjoyed what he did, and with whom he did it.

I always felt that Pedro was less interested in the game than he was in the people who were engaged in it for a living. That focus on the human element is something that baseball has lost in the last few years. Analytics have prioritized the physical measurement of a player over the heart of that player or his value as a teammate. As one who was early to recognize value in new ways to assess player performance, my perspective is that the game has gone too far in the direction of efficiency and probability. We need to reconfirm the human element that is so vital in any sport and consider changes that will bring back that aspect of the game.

Human stories were what Pedro really loved, and he wrote them, or conveyed them on camera, with an obvious passion for his subjects. These subjects, whether player, front office employee, equipment manager or groundskeeper, were animating for Pedro, and his joy in these stories and ensuing relationships was palpable. In print and on camera, he embodied the heart and soul of baseball.

This came through in a very personal way when he talked about his son, an excellent player at the University of Arizona and now a rising prospect with the Boston Red Sox. Pedro was so proud of Rio, as he was of his daughter, Sierra, and his other son, Dante. Rio, though, gave Pedro another lens through which to appreciate the game he loved. Pedro expressed that love through his professional work, but Rio created an added dimension to that emotional attachment to the game. No longer an objective reporter of baseball goings-on, Pedro was now the father of a pro player. And he relished that role, as almost any dad would.

I think that Pedro's experiences with Rio informed his work in recent years as he grasped even more fully the challenges the game presented to young players trying to make it to the major leagues. Sadly, Pedro will no longer be able to help Rio, or simply watch him with pride, as he faces those challenges. I can imagine that this is a terrible realization for any son who loses his father way too early. A father-and-son bond, born out of a mutual love of baseball, has been fractured, but not broken. Pedro will always be there for Rio, Sierra and Dante, serving as a spiritual guide and providing lasting memories of a life well lived.

A BROTHERHOOD

BY DAN SHAUGHNESSY

Curt Schilling despised both of us. To his dying day—and it's still painful to type those words—the thing I shared most with Pedro Gomez was our coveted claim as Schill's two least-favorite baseball writers.

Our small club was formed during the 2001 World Series when Pedro called out the Diamondbacks ace on the day of the seventh game of the World Series against the vaunted New York Yankees. These were not normal times. America's soul was ripped open when the Towers fell and the presence of the Yankees in the World Series became a metaphor for American resilience. The Yanks and D-Backs helped heal our country with a spectacular seven-game series, but in my capacity as a *Boston Globe* sports columnist, I was blissfully unaware of Schilling's fraudulence and clubhouse divisiveness until he was called out by *Republic* columnist Pedro Gomez on the day of the most important game in Arizona's franchise history.

It was brave and correct. Arizona players thanked Pedro for telling the truth, then went on to win Game 7 in spectacular fashion. In subsequent years Pedro would be validated by legions of supporters who came to know Schilling's dark side, but on the day of Game 7 in Arizona, Pedro was just a brave local scribe emboldened by the knowledge that he was on the right side of history.

Three years later, Schilling came to the Red Sox intent on breaking the Curse of the Bambino and bullying any media person in his path. It turned out that I was "that guy." I was the Boston Pedro, calling out Schill on his bullshit. Pedro by then was a big deal at ESPN and of course, he backed me. And it's one of the great honors of my professional life.

Covering Major League Baseball for a major media outlet is competitive, fun, challenging, rigorous and often soured with petty jealousy and judgments. When you work in the minefield of the baseball media, you come to understand that not everyone is going to like you. That's OK. But there are always a handful of peers that matter. You want their approval. You want to know that they think you don't suck. Achieving this acceptance from the great Pedro Gomez stands as one of the validating benchmarks of my career.

If you were a thoughtful baseball writer in the twenty-first century, it mattered what Pedro thought of you. He was the best of the best. He loved ball. He understood the game. He held people accountable. He was fluent in Spanish, trusted by the Latino ballplayers, and got the best interviews from players trained not to trust the American media. He spent two years of his life following and challenging Barry Bonds, which should come with its own award.

Schilling loathed Pedro.

And me.

Which I loved.

In the years between 2004-2008, Pedro would come to Fenway as an ESPN big shot and we would tease Schill about which one of us he hated more. I urged Pedro to ask Schill which one of us he would save if he was standing on the edge of a dock with a life preserver and both of us were drowning in the water below. Pedro went to Curt's locker and presented him with the hypothetical. I believe the answer was "None of the above."

Baseball writers are a brotherhood. Sisterhood, too. We think we are special. We strive to be tough, but fair. We don't let the ballplayers off the hook, but we show up the day after we're critical just in case the blowhard pitcher wants a piece of us. Veteran ball writers observe the rules of home and the road. We check with the manager of the other team before the start of every series. We know that you always learn more about your own team by talking to the guys in the other room. We eschew the Pentagon-esque group interviews that have created a modern culture of scribes who never learned how to cultivate sources.

In Boston, we work in the sacred space of Fenway Park where Babe Ruth played and where Ted Williams regularly insulted the knights of the keyboard. Baseball wasn't invented at Fenway, but it may as well have been. The place has been home to major-league baseball for almost 110 years and our town is still a hardball hub where fans know their team and care deeply about the fortunes of the local nine.

What does all this have to do with Pedro, you ask? Everything. Pedro grew up in the BBWAA covering the A's with the *San Jose Mercury News* and *Sacramento Bee*, which made him part of a West Coast brethren that those of us in Boston long admired and embraced. Members of the A's press corps were our cousins in coverage of big-league baseball: knowledgeable, collegial, dedicated to baseball, and never soft. They knew an error when they saw an error, and held players to a standard of excellence and professionalism carved out through the decades at the vaunted Oakland Alameda County Coliseum.

Pedro was raised in this baseball writing culture and it never left him. I'll never erase my text chain with Pedro, which dates back to 2015 and includes our dialogue the night the 2021 Hall of Fame voting was announced.

Our exchanges were almost always about baseball. When I wrote a column in the *Globe* about being the old guy in the press box, uneducated in WAR and still receiving AOL messages bellowing, "You've got mail!" Pedro answered, "Man, I'll be fifty-seven in a few days and everything you wrote applies to me and I'm happy about that. Great read, amigo."

We swapped many messages about Pedro's son Rio, a star left-handed pitcher with a chance to make it all the way to the majors. I am a decade older than Pedro and have a son who got to measure himself against future major-leaguers in his college years. Rio Gomez has a far better shot at the bigs than ACC outfielder Sam Shaughnessy ever did, but I understood the dynamic.

When I was nominated for the BBWAA's Hall of Fame award in 2015, Pedro wrote, "Took me four seconds to put the X by your name." I responded by telling him I hoped we would see Rio in the Cape League at Wareham the following summer. When I won the Spink Award and told Pedro that *Globe*/Red Sox owner John Henry was demanding a recount, Pedro wrote, "Schill calling it, 'Rigged.'"

When Rio was drafted by the Red Sox in the thirty-sixth round in 2017, his proud dad wrote, "A tremendous honor to be drafted. And I'm glad he's going to an organization with so much tradition."

It was the all-time Father's Day gift, something we talked about whenever Pedro came to Fort Myers or Boston. Watching your child progress through college baseball or the lower levels of the professional game gives one a good sense of just how difficult it is to make it to The Show. You develop new appreciation for how hard it is for these guys to get to the major leagues; for how good they really are.

Pedro and I took our Cooperstown voting privilege seriously, and soured on the process as it got increasingly nasty. In 2019, he declared, "One thing I'm doing starting this year is not revealing my ballot. Cannot stand the ugliness on social media, so (expletive) it. Not revealing mine . . . In almost twenty years of voting, I have never voted for ten. It's now where voters don't want the pushback and grief that comes with it so they have shrunk and vote for popular names so they don't get grief. Completely off the rails."

When Schilling—a bubble candidate by any measure—came up short in the Hall balloting year after year, probably hurting himself with his open disdain for the media, Pedro declared, "Once again, Karma remains undefeated . . . Our boy never could avoid stepping on his (expletive). I'd say time, and events, have proven who the sane ones were and who was the nutcase. Advantage Shaughnessy and Gomez."

Appropriately enough, our final missives concerned Schilling and his self-immolation after he missed by a handful of votes in 2021 and asked to be taken off the ballot. Schill's Facebook screed described me as "morally decrepit."

Pedro was crushed.

"He went at you and left me off?" Pedro complained. "I'm slipping."

Not true. Pedro Gomez never slipped. He was the best at what we do and it was an honor to know him.

Mike with his wife, Renee and daughter Rachel

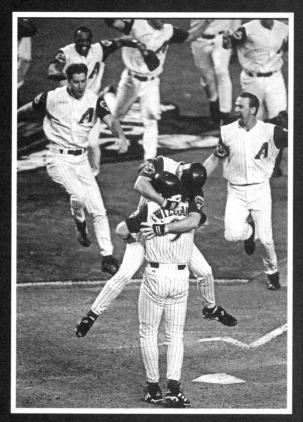

The Diamondbacks just after winning the 2001 World Series

HOW A
PROFESSIONAL
WORKS

BY MIKE SWANSON

Relationships were what Pedro was all about. I saw that from the beginning, when he started doing baseball sidebars and the occasional fill-in gamer in 1989, my sixth season with the San Diego Padres. He was a young up-and-comer from Miami who landed a job with the *San Diego Union* and was able to communicate with any player in the clubhouse thanks to his Latin heritage. Though I was far from the veteran PR person that I am today, Pedro was one of the first I watched who was able to get the most out of any player, using both his ability to communicate and a certain charm and flair that he had for creating a relationship. Full disclosure: At first that didn't sit well with some others in his profession, because Pedro could disarm almost any player in the clubhouse regardless of his ethnicity. But because it was Pedro, competitors who initially bristled later became some of his closest friends. They came to see Pedro never had an agenda. He just wanted to do the job to the absolute best of his ability and never hurt or irritate anyone.

Pedro and I immediately hit it off. Cerveza was one thing we had in common and I quickly introduced him to Bully's East, just a couple miles southwest of the ballpark, "THE" postgame hangout, where our relationship grew, as did Pedro's relationship with so many others in San Diego and so many who miss him today. Pedro left our beat shortly after I moved on from the Padres and while we went our separate ways, we never lost our connection. I remained in the N.L. West with the Rockies and Pedro had made his way up the West Coast to the Bay Area, for the most part covering the A's.

We would reconnect every spring training in Arizona, but then the big reconnection occurred in 1997 when he was brought to Phoenix as the new national baseball writer for the *Arizona Republic* a few weeks after I agreed to become the new PR director for the Diamondbacks. Working in lockstep with Pedro over the next seven years showed me why he'd come so far, so fast and I watched him set the stage for his multimedia transition to television with ESPN.

During his time in Arizona, Pedro was on the national beat, but since the hometown Diamondbacks came out of the expansion draft hot, winning a hundred games in just their second season and a World Series in their fourth, he spent more than his share of time covering the local team. He was able to forge relationships in the clubhouse and sometimes that didn't sit well with others. I've heard it all through the years from some big name managers and players: "Don't trust that guy, he's just trying to stir up crap and ruin our clubhouse." In other words: A total copout. Just because Pedro or another scribe isn't your cup of tea, he must be in there to destroy the team. That attitude generally stems from a control junkie who has realized he cannot control everything in his realm and has a self-imposed paranoia over how things are perceived versus how things really are.

In all of my years knowing Pedro he literally had one issue that I witnessed. Yes, I've heard all the stories about when he was assigned to the Barry Bonds chase and eventual fiasco, but I wasn't privy to any of that. I got to witness the distaste that Pedro and Curt Schilling had for one another. Look, in the role I play, I can't pick sides. All I can do is enable all parties to get their jobs done, whether it's the player doing his job on the field and then being accountable to the media for his performance or working with the media to make sure they have the opportunity to ask questions of said player after he performs. This brings me to the incident that most sticks out in my memory and also will most display the absolute professional that Pedro Gomez was.

Curt Schilling was pitching on this one night in Arizona and after the game when I was trying to pin down a time for him to meet with the media, he said, "If Pedro Gomez comes over to my locker to ask questions, I'm going to stop the interview immediately." He also asked if I had to let Pedro into the clubhouse, to which I immediately responded with a resounding YES. I was not about to keep a standing member of the BBWAA out of the clubhouse just because a player didn't want to see him or answer his questions.

As Curt began his postgame Q&A, Pedro did approach the locker, where ten to twelve Arizona media were standing with cameras and recorders to get Schilling's comments. When Curt looked up and saw Pedro, he immediately stopped the interview, as promised. Ever the professional, Pedro turned to me.

"Hey, I'm going to walk away," he said. "It's no big deal. There's no way my presence should prevent everyone else from doing their job and get the Schilling quotes."

THAT'S how a professional works. He didn't want to have his brethren upset with him just because he and Curt Schilling didn't get along. It's been well documented about the article that Pedro wrote regarding Curt the day of Game 7 of the 2001 World Series. A game that Schilling was going to start just hours after the story was written. Again, Pedro was never going to put words in a newspaper or on a website just for the sake of putting words out there. He had sources, several sources who knew the truth and from that information he wrote the piece. As my friend Bill Raftery would say, "he had the onions" to write it and knew it would ruffle some feathers, but he also knew he had a responsibility to the baseball world to write what he knew regardless of how the article would ultimately be perceived. Selfishly, I'm glad that it didn't implode the ballclub before the biggest game most of those guys would ever play in their lives and we all ended up celebrating as world champions.

Despite the fact that Pedro resided in Arizona, as a professional he didn't or couldn't have a horse in that race. He had to do what he was hired to do and for that he should be forever proud. It also showed many other people what Pedro was made of and I have no doubt it was that piece of journalism that eventually afforded him the opportunity to move on to ESPN, where he became a star. He was not just one of the most knowledgeable baseball voices hired by the network, his overall knowledge of sports was utilized to cover all facets and he literally became a household name among all walks of sports.

If I were able to empower people to wish to be cared about as much as Pedro was cared about, I would say just follow his lead. Pedro cared so much about all people. I have no idea how many phone numbers he had stored away in his cell, but suffice it to say no old school Rolodex would have enough room for every piece of paper that needed to be attached to it. Probably the coolest part about Pedro was that he had time for everyone. Even I, in a role as a PR professional who should go out of his way to make time and enhance relationships, do not have the time or patience to be able to converse and share time with that many people for fear of not getting my necessary duties done each day. That was never a problem with Pedro. If you engaged with him, he would engage back and make you feel like you had been part of his life forever.

Do you have any idea how difficult it is to have a great relationship with everybody in Major League Baseball? It's borderline unheard of, because at some point in your career you are going to accidentally step on someone's toes and they will forever remember. Whether you inadvertently said something you didn't like about their organization, or a particular player or staff member that was employed there, it's inevitable in our game. Pedro had a knack of even when he had to be critical of a move or a team, he did it with the security of knowing he turned over every stone to get to the bottom of the story. It may have been hurtful or disarming at the time, but it also made clubs or individuals more introspective because Pedro didn't make it up, someone gave him the information.

Relationships were the key not only to Pedro's success professionally, but also personally. To emulate Pedro Gomez, the first thing you have to do is look in the mirror and see if you are cut out to be loving, caring, funny, honest to a fault and not fearful of stepping on someone's toes if you have all the facts to tell a story. Those are some awfully difficult standards for a mere mortal to aspire to. It's why I will leave this earth some day knowing that there will only ever have been one Pedro Gomez.

Robin and her dad, sportswriter Howard Carr

REMEMBER KGB

BY ROBIN CARR

In the Bay Area sports world, it seems like everyone knows each other. When I was at the San Francisco Giants for a decade starting in 1985, I was close with my PR counterparts at the Oakland A's, San Francisco 49ers, Golden State Warriors and San Jose Sharks. We interacted with each other, compared notes on local sports media and their requests (yes, we did that) and we all became dear friends. As former PR manager for the Giants, I became close with Jay and Doreen Alves, Kathy Jacobson (A's), Kirk Reynolds, Dave Rahn (49ers), Cherie White, Julie Marvel (Warriors) and Ken Arnold (Sharks). This doesn't even include SIDs from Cal, Stanford and San Jose State. We truly are one large Bay Area sports family. This especially carried over to sports reporters, editors and columnists in San Francisco, San Jose, Oakland, Marin, Sacramento. We all knew each other, and may have been competitors, but we were friends and stay in touch to this day.

I thought that the Giants and A's PR folks and media were especially tight. Our teams played each other *all the* time. It seemed like practically every other day (if you include split squads and "B" games) in spring training. We found ourselves at the same watering holes in Scottsdale, Phoenix and Tempe, buying each other drinks and grabbing dinner in some of the finer—and divier—spots in town (admittedly on our expense accounts).

It was at spring training in the early 1990s when I met Pedro Gomez, and I often chatted with him at Candlestick Park during those Bay Bridge Series games between the Giants and the A's. "The Stick" was a cold, dank place, but when Pedro was around, his warmth and happy, friendly aura took the chill away—even at Candlestick. Talk about a guy who became a fast friend. I'm sure that was commonplace for Pedro. My Giants PR boss and mentor, Bob Rose, called Pedro "Dr. Feelgood." He said, "If you saw Pedro, you thought to yourself, 'It's going to be a great day today.'"

Pedro was amazingly accommodating and supportive of PR people, and would assert himself with any Spanish-speaking players, which was so helpful to Bob and me. Even with fellow writers, often competitors—Pedro would serve as the interpreter for many of these players. His personality made everyone comfortable and you could tell that he was just one of those guys who cared so much about people. You could see it in his eyes, his face. It was real. Everyone was always glad to see him.

When Pedro made the transition to network TV, he never forgot where he came from. He always was a part of the scribes. He had a tough job, covering Barry Bonds on a daily basis. Talk about polar opposites!

"I don't trust many of you guys, but I trust Pedro," Bonds once told the media. "He's real."

Pedro had a very good perspective on life and always had a great sense of humor. Even on those rough days covering Bonds, he knew the absurdities that existed and had a healthy attitude, like, "It's OK, it's only sports."

I didn't become really good friends with Pedro until after I had left the Giants in 1994 and took a job managing baseball PR for Nike. I was super fortunate, since I had been at the Giants for ten seasons, to transition to another company and still be able to work in a game that I love. I was also thrilled to still be able to connect with my buddies in the sports media.

One year, I was getting ready to head down to Arizona for a Spring Training Nike event, when I reached out to Pedro to let him know that I would be in town and we should grab dinner. Next thing I know, Steve Kettmann, A's beat writer for the *San Francisco Chronicle*, was calling me at my office at Nike, asking if he could join in on the fun. I had met Steve a few times in the Candlestick press box, when he would occasionally cover the Giants. "Of course," I said, and the three of us had a wonderful, bonding evening. We talked about baseball, our families, our birthdays (we are all Leos!) and cemented our friendships.

That night, I shared stories with Pedro and Steve of growing up with a sportswriter dad. My father, Howard Carr, worked for the *Chronicle* for twenty-five years, and I basically grew up around sports media, hanging out in press rooms and press boxes. In fact, I wouldn't be in public relations if not for my dad.

He was covering the Virginia Slims Tennis Tournament at the Oakland Coliseum Arena in the early 1980s, and my mother and I were watching one of the matches. I was entering my third year of college with no clue what I wanted to do. At twenty years old, I hadn't even declared a major. Between matches, I saw a very fashionable, put-together woman bring some papers to the press table and chat with my dad.

"Who's that?" I asked my mom. "Oh, that's Annalee Thurston, the PR person."

Well, that was it! I decided to major in Public Relations at San Jose State University, with an eye on making it in sports PR. I did a sports internship in the Stanford Athletic Department (my dad's alma mater) and worked alongside tennis coach Dick Gould to manage PR for a scholarship fundraising event with John McEnroe and other tennis alums.

I graduated in December of 1983, but my dad was too ill to attend my graduation ceremony and he died the next month, January 30, 1984. I was twenty-two years old, and basically just getting my act together. And he was gone. I've always felt like he missed everything I did, both personal and professional successes and failures. But when I got the job with the San Francisco Giants in 1985, I got to work with many of my dad's *Chronicle* colleagues: David Bush, Lowell Cohn, Bruce Jenkins and many others. Bruce and I still have long conversations about "Howard," my dad, and how funny and animated he got when talking about Pac-10 football (he lived through some rough Stanford football years).

In chatting with Steve and Pedro that Arizona night, they assured me that my dad indeed "knew" how well I was doing and that he was proud of me. And in a little twist that I love, we realized that Steve and my dad shared a birthday—August 8. My birthday is August 11, and my dad and I celebrated our birthdays together every year. Last year I saw on Facebook some photos of Pedro and his daughter sharing a birthday cake—Pedro, August 20, Sierra, August 22. I thought that was cool. There must be something special about Leo dads and daughters.

Some of my favorite times with Pedro were at Major League Baseball All-Star games. It seemed like Pedro had dozens of friends in every city! And of course, he needed party passes: All-Star gala passes, pregame party tickets, postgame party passes. We were both on the hunt for more passes to accommodate "Pedro's Crew." Boston, Denver, Philadelphia, Seattle—just a few of the locales where we gathered party passes from those curmudgeon sportswriters who absolutely wanted no part of any "gala." Soon, Pedro and I had our own language: "How are you doing on pre?" "I'm good on pre, but need post." "OK, I'm on it."

I read recently where *Chronicle* writer Ron Kroichick called Pedro, "Julie from the Love Boat," due to his social-director personality. Not coincidentally, "Julie" has always been my nickname, so it was not surprising that he and I coordinated what turned out to be one of the most epic nights in New York.

It was one of those times when the moons and the suns and whatever fun planets exist were all aligned: The A's and the Giants were BOTH in New York City for an April weekend in 1997. Pedro and I circled this on the calendar at least a month in advance and led the charge for a night out with Bay Area beat writers, broadcasters and other team personnel and PR folks. With Pedro, Steve, Bob Rose and a cast of dozens, we brought Manhattan to its knees. First, we hit an authentic Russian-themed place on East Fourth Street in Greenwich Village called the KGB. We then went to a Moroccan bar, Fez, where we discovered a basement with live music. That particular night, it was "Bee Gees Night." The unusual twist was that a cast of about a half dozen female singers were featured, all singing the Bee Gees greatest hits in what could have been an off-Broadway production. It was surprisingly fabulous and the rounds of drinks continued throughout the night.

The funfest went on into the wee hours, when we went back to the KGB bar for the mandatory "final final." They started playing classic Russian opera while we polished off our final drinks, and daylight was emerging. I barely made it to a 3 p.m. Broadway matinee of "Once Upon a Mattress" starring Sarah Jessica Parker.

I know that Pedro and Steve tried to live by a code called KGB, for Kettmann, (Ed) Beitiks and Gomez. But from that April evening forward, whenever I ran into Pedro on the road or in the Bay Area, the first words out of his mouth were always, "Hey, RC, remember KGB!" All of us who were there will never forget that night and we will always remember Pedro Gomez.

THE NIGHT WE
TRADED JOSE

BY TONY LA RUSSA

You get a feeling when someone covering your ball club is not really into it. They're doing it because it's a job or because that's what they're supposed to do. From the beginning with Pedro, when he started covering the A's going into the 1992 season, it was the opposite. Pedro loved the game, and he had a personality that matched his talent and his love of the game. He was able to strike a very tricky balance, where he covered the story, whatever the story was, but always with an understanding of the people he was talking to or reporting on. He pushed, that was his job, but he never pushed too far because he wasn't happy with what you were saying. When you give respect the way Pedro did, you get respect back.

From Day One Pedro made a strong impression as a reporter. Even before pitchers and catchers reported in February 1992, he landed a scoop, getting Jose Canseco on the phone to talk about his "allegedly ramming his estranged wife Esther's BMW with his Porsche," as Pedro reported in the *San Jose Mercury News*. Pedro was two years ahead of Jose at Coral Park High in Miami, both of them from Cuban families, so

THE NIGHT WE TRADED JOSE • TONY LA RUSSA

Pedro Gomez (left), Jose Canseco (right), Coral Park High yearbook, 1980

they'd known each other for years at that point.

"It was a very emotional scene and things got out of control," Jose told Pedro. "We got too close and my car bumped hers. It was not intentional. ... It was a humiliating experience, having to put my hands on the car and being searched by an officer. It's the most humiliating experience I've ever gone through."

Pedro reported that Jose had recently bought a 1991 Lamborghini Diablo, a $225,000 car, to go with his $140,000 Ferrari Testarosa—and also that it would be another two weeks before Jose planned to report to spring training. "Six weeks of spring training is too long anyway," Jose told Pedro. "All they can do is spank me. What are they going to do, bench me?"

I thought of that article later that year after we traded Jose on August 31 to Texas for Rubén Sierra and pitchers Bobby Witt and Jeff Russell. Jose was in the on-deck circle and we called him back. I talked to him in the tunnel and gave him the news that he'd been dealt. Jose was very upset. He felt like he had been let down. Pedro had a rapport with Jose. He got the story fresh from Jose in a series of exclusive interviews when he was feeling hurt, and he could have just taken Jose word for word and buried everybody, but Pedro wrote it from a balanced point of view.

Michael Zagaris: "Jose had me shoot pictures of him to put into a booklet we made for Madonna prior to their first get-together."

What he ended up doing was listening to Jose, but then asking the A's, including myself and Sandy, "How did this happen?"

The clips from that week tell the story. This was the first quote Pedro used from Jose in his article he wrote just after the trade: "Tony told me he was going to miss me and then he hugged me."

Pedro summed up Jose's time in Oakland this way: "His moments on the field were many: He was the only player to hit at least forty home runs and steal at least forty bases in one season. He has been on four All-Star teams and was elected to a fifth this season, although he could not play because of an injury. And he has been an American League Most Valuable Player and Rookie of the Year. His moments off the field were many, too, from late-night meetings with Madonna, to speeding tickets, possession of illegal arms to bashing cars with wife Esther. But now he is part of the Texas sports story. The Bash Brothers, Canseco and Mark McGwire, are no more."

Pedro also pointed out: "Canseco's numerous run-ins with the police made him an easy target for skeptical fans and cynical columnists. Toward the end of last season, Canseco stated that unless fans responded favorably toward him he was going to demand a trade."

The day after the trade, Pedro shadowed Jose and was able to report on personal details. "Before the sun even rose on Jose Canseco's Blackhawk home Tuesday, his day had started horrendously," Pedro wrote. "A migraine had grabbed hold of his face in the early morning and refused to let go or let him get a decent night's sleep. And his million-dollar home had been trashed by an egg-throwing vandal. ... The migraine, which attacked at 4 a.m., had left half his face in intolerable pain. 'It was the stress and anxiety,' Esther Canseco said. 'I had to knock him out with codeine.'"

At lunch that day, Jose told Pedro, "I'm not a robot, I have emotions and feelings. ... I'm not happy with the way it was handled, the timing. But I have no bridges to burn. I loved playing in Oakland."

"Throughout lunch, Canseco appeared in a fog," Pedro wrote. "It was as though this was all a joke and that at any minute someone was going to yell, 'Gotcha!'"

Then, three days after the trade, Pedro sat on a plane with Jose and reported that he "pulled no punches in an exclusive interview during his five-hour flight Thursday from the Bay Area to New York, where the right fielder joined the Rangers for the first time."

Pedro asked Jose what he thought of me as his manager in Oakland.

"We had a friendship, but it wasn't what people thought it was," he said. "He's a very smart man and used a lot of psychology to control his players. But he does win with his tactics, and I guess winning is the bottom line."

I respected Pedro for how he handled his reporting that week. The hot story was to get Jose burned by this, talking about a lack of loyalty, but Pedro took on that story and made it more. He basically said: *Hey, this is a guy that got traded. His feelings are hurt, but this is the team that brought him up, gave him a deal to make him the highest-paid player in baseball, and actually warned him, 'Get your shit together.' This is what Jose believes, this is the other side, make up your mind.*

That was Pedro and that was Pedro's whole career. He was special because of the way he could balance the professional and the personal without letting either one dominate at the expense of the other. If he thought that I'd had a bad game managing, and we were close, he would say it. And if he thought that I was being beaten up, his favorite thing on me was, "People keep talking about that you're egotistical." My parents would just be so ashamed if that was true. I was never.

"People just don't know that you always give credit to the players," Pedro would tell me.

He always kidded me by calling me a "push-button manager," and I'd say, "I didn't know you were that smart, because that's exactly what I've been my entire career." You've got a great team, you push the button—pitch, hit—and you sit there. He would ride me about that.

Pedro could understand the personal and professional side of all of this. My father's family is Italian, but my mother was from Spain and I speak Spanish. Pedro and I had that in common. He knew my wife and our daughters. He was very personable and, if I asked my wife and our girls, they would tell you they knew Pedro more than they would know anybody else.

So many of us in the baseball family grieved Pedro because we lost a friend in a really tough business. It's hard to do what he did. It shows how unfair life is. It's a shame. I grieve for our game but I mostly grieve for his wife and family. It's so unfair.

Pedro and Al Kaline in 2013

LET ENTHUSIASM RULE

BY JASON LA CANFORA

I can think of only two people in my entire life who I can pinpoint with certainty the exact day I first encountered them. One is my wife. The other is Pedro Gomez.

It was April 18, 1997. Pedro was on the A's beat for the *Sacramento Bee*, in town with my friend Steve Kettmann, of the *San Francisco Chronicle*, to cover their series with the Tigers. I turned twenty-three that week, somehow lucky enough to find myself as the Red Wings beat writer at *The Detroit Free Press*, already securing my dream job not yet a year out of college, about to cover the second NHL playoff game of my career.

The A's dispatched the Tigers in quick fashion that afternoon in a rare Friday businessman's special to accommodate the big event in town that night: The Wings back in the playoffs, trying yet again to bring a Stanley Cup home to Hockeytown for the first time since 1955. I believe I was able to help Steve and Pedro secure nosebleed seats to the game, at least that's how I recall it, and we chatted above the din of KISS on the PA system during warmups, near the roof of Joe Louis Arena as I leaned out of the makeshift "press box" (it was really just the last row of the place with a long desk added in; they forgot to put a proper one in, which Pedro got a kick out of).

I was already out of my depth, jittery and hoping I'd find the words to do justice to the event I was about to cover. But Pedro put me at ease. He didn't know me, but the way he and Steve treated me, their sincere interest in me, made me feel like maybe I really did belong. It also raised the stakes. They had of course dissected the *Free Press* upon arriving in Detroit, and Steve would tell me, in our first conversation after Pedro passed, how much of a kick they got out of me taking the Wings to task with my off-day story, incurring the wrath of crusty Scotty Bowman in the process. They were genuinely intrigued to see how the kid would cover the rest of the series, and to witness it firsthand.

These dudes were legit. They lived it and breathed it. They had seen quite a bit and done quite a bit. They cared, deeply, and they obsessed over the process of doing what beat writers do. I was raised by ball writers as an intern at *The Baltimore Sun*, and I knew the esteem with which my mentors, Buster Olney and Ken Rosenthal, held Pedro and Steve. They were hardcore newspaper guys. And they would be reading my stuff the next morning with great interest, undoubtedly discussing it over (a late) breakfast at the hotel.

Earlier that day, a short walk away from The Joe, at the corner of Michigan and Trumbull, in a far more spacious but equally dilapidated press box at Tigers Stadium, Pedro had ripped off the following lede after the A's managed a rare victory that day, an easy, 9-5 laugher over a Tigers team that would finish nineteen games out of first place: *The A's didn't necessarily cure their ills Friday afternoon. Instead, they found somebody sicker.*

Yeah, I'd best bring it. I don't remember much about the game I was tasked to cover that night, except that the Wings looked like they might be in deep trouble, having already been shut out in the opener of their series, and through the first two periods of Game 2 as well. History has a way of strangling teams so often on the wrong side of it, and this group had a predilection for choking. However, fourth-line grinder Kris Draper finally scored a shorthanded goal on the net to the left of our perch to end the drought (as Googling the box score confirms), and the Wings won, 2-1, in what ended up being a springboard to them drinking from Lord Stanley's Cup.

What I remember far more vividly than the game is the impact that meeting Pedro for the first time had on me. His joy for life and love of sports and writing and reporting were immediate and overwhelming. You felt it. It meant so much to him; it should mean so much to you, too, if it didn't already. We were getting paid to travel the country—and, at times, the world—to try to tell the best stories about some truly extraordinary people, writing about the sports we have played and loved all of our lives. Who's got it better than us?

I knew innately that I just had made a new friend, someone who would be a willing mentor, who would set an example without even trying. I had found, through Steve, another journalistic soulmate in Pedro. No one had to say it, but when I got off deadline I was going to meet these guys at a dive bar in Greektown and we were going to drink way too many beers and talk enthusiastically about our craft and the writers we loved until they kicked us out. And I would listen much more than I would talk, and class would be in session. I couldn't wait. I figured I could hang, but there was only one way to find out.

Pedro, as always, delivered. There was something so genuine about him. Actually, *everything* was so genuine about him. No bullshit. Never bullshit. Fuck bullshit. He'd leave a little imprint on you. He'd make you better, and make you want to be better. His smile was warm and welcoming. His eyes seemed to light up when you connected about a thought or idea. He lived by a credo the likes of which we all should aspire to. Talk to the guy in the locker room no one was talking to. Treat people with respect. Be accountable. Have fun. Let enthusiasm rule.

If you hung out with him once, you'd want to again, the next night and the next. I left our first bar-closing feeling alive, feeling like this was exactly where I was supposed to be and I was doing exactly what I was supposed to be doing for a living and doing it with the people I was supposed to be with.

But I was also more than a little jealous of the next town and the next beers and the next wave of conversation he and Steve would ride as they tried to suck the marrow out of every shitty game they'd have to cover and find some new or unique angle to take on a Wednesday blowout loss with 10,000 people at the park. I, suddenly, wanted in on that A's beat. After this, who wouldn't?

Of course, none of the losses, nor the mundanity of life on the beat, seemed to slow them down in the least. Somewhere, someone was dying to read about this baseball malady they had just witnessed, and damn right they were going to do it with more zeal and gusto than anyone else. I trudged back to Riverfront Apartments wondering what adventure was next for these two. It might not be as sexy as Game 3 of the Western Conference Quarterfinals in a sold-out arena, but, shit, I wanted to be like them and I wanted to be there.

Most of my experiences with competitors on the beat were acrimonious. I tended to view the other papers in town as the enemy. To see these two veterans bring out the best in one another—actually accentuating their charm as a tandem—despite working for rival newspapers, that to me was kind of astonishing. To see a friendship that rich and real and robust blossom out of that construct, it was almost beyond my comprehension at the time. It opened my eyes. To this day I cannot think of Steve without thinking of Pedro, or think of Pedro without thinking of Steve.

They were so inclusive and welcoming—everyone who wanted in had an invite to this party—and I took note. They took great care to assist young writers. They railed against the Old Boy's Club and wanted to foster a climate that was open to all and broke some of the worst norms of sportswriting. They were staunch advocates for women in this industry and would not tolerate peers or athletes or coaches belittling them. They were always aligned with the little guy. I'd like to think I was already wired the same way on all of the above, but spending time with them further reinforced it: Be an advocate. Anything less made you part of the problem.

They were fairly righteous. And they were goddamn cool at the same time. Not a bad combination.

On the morning of Saturday April 19, 1997, within hours of us calling it a night, I would get a call far earlier than I anticipated, groggy and hung over. It was Pedro. He was excited, more excited than I was. He'd read my game story in the morning paper. He thought I crushed it. I'd captured the moment. He'd captured my imagination. I tear up thinking back about it now.

The last time we talked was shortly after the minor-league baseball season shut down last year. He was one of the first people I thought of; another summer of doing whatever possible to see Rio pitch as much as possible had been robbed by a pandemic, and our federal government's systemic failure to address it. Covid was ravaging Arizona, where Pedro lived, a part of the country he loves so much.

I sent Pedro a text to ask if he could come on my radio show in Baltimore and talk about the impact the loss of MILB was having on players and families, especially those not on Top 10 Prospects lists in *Baseball America*. He got back to me immediately. Couldn't wait to hop on. Of course.

I welled up listening to him gush about traveling to Salem and Wilmington and Frederick and all over the Carolina League and South Atlantic League watching his son from the stands. It was so perfect. He was so happy. He deserved this. My heart swelled for him and his family.

I told Pedro we would absolutely meet up in 2021, whenever the minors came back, whether Rio was in Single A or Double A. My kids and I are minor-league baseball junkies. Whether Rio was assigned to Salem or Portland, my kids and I would make a road trip and we'd watch Rio pitch and cheer him on and drink beers together again.

Unfortunately, that was the last time we would ever talk. That was the end of our journey. Somehow the 2021 baseball season would start without Pedro Gomez there to chronicle it. I am devastated. My kids will never get to meet one of the best people I've ever known. Rio won't get to pitch for his dad again.

But I'll gladly respond to every random email I get from any kid interested in journalism. I'll think of Pedro always and smile. I'll try to match his joy and zeal for what we do. And I'll celebrate the man and journalist he was every chance I get.

Ed Beitiks

TELL THE STORY
WITHOUT PANDERING
TO IT

BY RAY RATTO

The modern American press box is dying, not only as a place to drop your laptop and as a psychic refuge and weirdo job fair. It's the place where sportswriters went to be vetted by the most judgmental bastards there are—the other sportswriters in that press box. And the particularly forbidding press box in Oakland with its Kremlin feel and retrograde lavatories is where a well-encrusted but keenly insightful bag of rumpled laundry named Edvins Beitiks decided that Pedro Gomez could play.

It doesn't seem like much of a discovery in hindsight, we grant you, but Beitiks had an ethereal kind of presence as sportswriters went. He'd been places, and done things, and had things done to him, and thought bigger thoughts than most of the rest of us, which meant he had more pragmatic and yet otherworldly credentials when it came to seeing inside the souls of others. And that's at least moderately less creepy than it sounds.

Anyway, Beitiks was sort of a weird oracle and approval magnet because he'd done the hard things that people inherently respect, even people who work in baseball who view sportswriters as the lowest kind of dilettantes. Beitiks had gone to Vietnam and had been shot through the face as one of several cruelties done to his body during his service, the last of which killed him. Whether he knew he would die at the three-quarter pole of his lifespan or just knew instinctively that time should not be wasted on the soullessly ambitious, the militantly self-absorbed, the aggressively preening or the preternaturally dim, he gravitated toward Gomez and Gomez toward him in their times at the *San Francisco Examiner* and *Sacramento Bee,* respectively. There were people who had stories worth telling, and damned if they wouldn't be the ones to tell them, simply, thoroughly and honestly. And then they would join their colleagues in several acts of beer, because why the hell else would anyone keep these ungodly hours?

The age difference (they died at roughly the same age, twenty years and thirty days apart) was of no consequence. The divide in their cultural backgrounds (no meaningful link has yet been discovered overtly linking Cuba to Latvia) was no divide at all. Beitiks was an immigrant, coming from Germany as an infant with his mother right after World War II. Gomez was the son of immigrants who came to Miami right before his birth and right before the Cuban Missile Crisis. If they found even a tenuous connectivity through that, it was probably in understanding at a cellular level that life is not for the wasteful or incurious.

More likely, it was through their love of baseball, which was expressed through their eagerness to dive into the middle of it rather than the dimensionless monochrome of a favorite team. As part of a larger group of scribes (yes, Gomez liked the old-timey terminology as part of his old-soul-in-new-shoes persona) who understood that baseball was a thing they watched, not a thing they did, let alone a thing they were, they concluded separately but agreed upon jointly that the whole thing was merely a game played by overly pituitaried children, and the real joys came not in the clubhouse but upstairs where the writing and hanging out happened. Their job was to cover it as a thing until it was time to go home to their respective families. They became friends with baseball as the background, not as the cause. But baseball emitted stories worth telling and retelling, and they were just the kids to do that.

Now before you start throwing up into your wastebaskets, this wasn't some decades-ahead-of-its-time bromance of convenience in which they get played in the movie by Paul Rudd with multiple personalities and Steve Buscemi with a helium addiction. They were just like-minded fellows in a larger group of like-minded fellows who took the gig for what it was—a vehicle for storytelling and a happy alternative to forklifting palettes of canned hams on the midnight-to-eight shift at the Burlingame Costco. It not only beat working the desk, it beat damned near everything else. Career-wise, Gomez was going places, while Beitiks had BEEN places, but they enjoyed the four-way stop where their paths had intersected. Gomez had learned what one can learn only by starting one's baseball writing career with a very good and interesting team, the early '90s Athletics, and Beitiks found everything interesting because he had covered everything. Indeed, he didn't become a full-time ball writer until the mid-'90s when the *San Francisco Examiner* gave him the assignment of covering an uninspiring Oakland A's team as part of his weighty resume.

Within two years, Gomez had left the *Sacramento Bee* and been discovered by the *Arizona Republic* as a national baseball writer covering the nascent Arizona Diamondbacks, and Beitiks had become more fully engaged with his fight against the cancer that would eventually consume him, which it did in the early days of 2001.

Now comes the part where they would both break out laughing. Gomez had been hired by ESPN in 2003, which was exactly the weirdest thing Beitiks could have imagined had he lived long enough to see it from this plane of existence. He would have cast no judgment of a friend, but he would have been fascinated to see how a mega-solid journalist navigated the micron-deep/mile-wide world of television. He needn't have worried, of course; Gomez was promptly assigned to the weird world of Barry Bonds, the sort of person and story Beitiks would have wallowed in right up to his eyelids.

That Gomez handled it with the jeweler's eye of a journalist and not a potential chat-show host would have pleased Beitiks. That he handled the required adversarials with Bonds with such immutably professional distance as the story became a daily staple would have had Beitiks laughing with glee. The only affectation Gomez could have brought to it was wearing one of the rumpled hats Beitiks favored, which is not so much a pity as a requirement. They both shared one thing above all others—the skill of telling the story without pandering to it.

It is wrong to conclude that Beitiks taught Gomez to be a genuine reporter. It is wholly correct, conversely, to conclude that they both appreciated the art as they saw it in each other. They both came correct in different eras, but you know what they say about game recognizing game. It's a skill that the old press box environments could provide its most inquisitive and nonjudgmental denizens. Enter freely, enjoy richly, work doggedly, and obey the call of beer—it seems like a perfectly basic set of directives.

If there is a real regret here in the end, it is probably that neither of them could have written the story of Gomez's son Rio's first major-league appearance. Gomez would have written about his son's early mechanical jitters before gaining control of his breaking ball and working six workmanlike innings, and Beitiks would have handled the genetics angle by focusing on Rio's mother, Sandi, and how she surreptitiously but more brilliantly saw and developed the talent that made his father so proud. And then in mutual tribute to the pieces of their lives they shared, unabashed acts of beer while they complained about the lack of pith in Rio's quotes. The way both of them knew how all well-told baseball stories should end.

HE LISTENED

BY RON WASHINGTON

Pedro gave me some of the best advice I've ever gotten in my life from anybody. He called me when I was having problems in Texas. He stayed on the phone with me and talked it all through. Mostly he listened, but he also cared enough to tell it to me straight. This was when I was manager of the Rangers and made a mistake and used cocaine. I did wrong, and I had to deal with the repercussions. I thought we had handled it in house. I went through Major League Baseball and confessed to the organization what I had done. I offered to resign, if that was best for the team. I saw psychiatrists. I went through all of the things that recovery entailed. The Rangers organization supported me and we moved on. Then almost two years later it came out in the press and I had to deal with it all over again, this time in front of the whole world. What Pedro did for me was stay on the phone trying to guide me on how I should handle it. At a time like that, when it feels like the whole world is turning on you, you need to talk to people who care about you, and this is what Pedro expressed to me:

Even though we all have flaws, I care about you, man. I've always cared about you. And if I didn't care about you, I wouldn't be making this phone call. But I'm going to tell you what I think is the right thing: You can't avoid anything, Wash. You've got to face this head on. Sometimes you have to accept the truth, even though it may take you down a little bit for you to get back up. It's not as bad as you think it is. It may hurt, but that's just life. You'll get over it. People are very forgiving. When you run from things, they continue to follow you, but when you take it on and you deal with the repercussions, it makes you stronger and it keeps you happier. At least you have truth on your side. And when that day is over of facing the truth, guess what? It's over.

Those were the thoughts Pedro shared with me during that period of time, when he called me. That's the way I've lived my life. That's my character. But at a time like that it helps when someone cares enough to talk you through it and remind you what you already know. That's who Pedro was. He was showing you the human being first, and then he had to do his job, and that's what I loved about him. I followed his advice, and I was glad I did. It all played out exactly the way he said. Pedro knew what the people in that business expected, and his advice definitely made it easier.

One thing about Pedro as a reporter was he always listened. He allowed you to express yourself. From the first year I knew Pedro, 1996, when he was a *Sacramento Bee* sportswriter and I was on Art Howe's coaching staff in Oakland, we hit it off pretty good. Right from the start he came up to me talking like we were the best buddies in the world. Like he could stand up there and ask me anything and I'd give him the answer. And you know the answer to that is I goddamned did. Pedro wasn't shy and it didn't seem to me like he had an agenda. He was warmly trying to find the answer to what he might ask. I'm a baseball freak, and whenever he had baseball questions, he came to me and we'd take that discussion wherever it went. He used to find me outside on the bench. I had to get out of the clubhouse, and I certainly did. I couldn't make anybody better sitting in that goddamned clubhouse.

Throughout the years, ever since then, Pedro didn't hesitate to call if he had a question about something. He would call just to get my opinion. Like if there was a trade that might happen, he would call to get my take on one player. I've told people to learn from Pedro: *Use your resources.* He was tremendous at using his resources. Not in the sense of *using* your resources. But if you know somebody who knows something, call them. I tell that to kids today: Don't be afraid to ask what you don't know, because then you ask somebody that does know, and guess what? Now you know. You can only really listen to someone if in your mind you're still open, and Pedro had a way of listening closely even when it seemed like he already knew what he thought about something. That's how I try to be when I'm working with a player.

To become a great coach you have to listen. I can't teach you what I know unless I know what you don't know. The only way I can find that out is to allow you to speak. As a teacher, your pupils have to be a part of what you're trying to give to them. You'll never get anywhere if you go in with an attitude of "I know everything" or "You either get it or you don't." It's easy to coach up somebody when you know what you've got to coach them on, but it's tough to coach up somebody when you haven't let them show you who they are. You can't build a strength in somebody if you don't know what their weaknesses are, and the only way you can find out where they're weak is to let them express themselves. When they begin to tell you who they are, what they're about, that gives you an opportunity to see how you should approach them.

It takes patience to be a good listener and that was something Pedro understood. We talked a lot about patience. He would talk to me about his son Rio and trying to teach him patience, trying to keep him in the moment, and when the moment came—that is, the big leagues—you'll still be in the moment. If there's one thing I always expound on with a kid I'm coaching, it's patience: *Don't get ahead of what's in front of you.*

You teach patience by constantly expressing it. You've just got to keep preaching it over and over and over. And all of a sudden patience builds up in people. It really does, especially if you're around them on a daily basis like we are in the game of baseball. You can get a kid to understand what patience is. He may not get it right away. It may take some things to knock him down for him to understand. But when he has that positive reinforcement around him every day, the game begins to show him that it takes patience. Even if you have the ability, you've got to wait for it to happen at the right time.

You think about these young kids today, how they want things to happen right now, and for some of them it does, but for the majority it takes good coaching to make them understand you will get what is due to you in due time as long as you put in the work, be open-minded to learning, and you stay patient. It's like A-B-C-D. You can't jump from B and go to D, because when you get to D, there's going to be something

you're going to have to have in D that you didn't get in C because you jumped C. So what's going to happen? You're going to end up going all the way back. You're not going to go back to C. Your ass will go all the way back to A and you're going to end up starting all over again.

See, I get going, talking about patience, and it makes me think of Pedro all over again. The world is going to miss Pedro. He didn't do anything but pour love into you any time he called you or saw you. My heart just skipped a beat when I heard he had passed away. He will be sorely missed, man, especially by me, but he's in a better place.

Chuck and Alfonso

Pedro and Sandi

OUR COLOMBIA CONNECTION

BY CHUCK CULPEPPER

Of all the marital possibilities on this planet, Pedro Gomez and I both married Colombians, and it never caused him even a hint of awkwardness that my Colombian spouse was, unlike his, male. No, Pedro just embraced our shared enthusiasm for Colombia so unreservedly that, to me, it epitomized his gusto for all the strands of humanity.

Such acceptance might seem commonplace circa 2020, but Pedro's warmth barreled toward me in the early part of the century, back when it always seemed less certain, especially in press boxes and maybe especially in baseball press boxes. I long since had encountered all the mindsets among the sportswriting corps, none of them offensive to me: those who didn't approve but didn't say so; those who didn't mind but didn't ask about anything; those who approved but didn't know what to say; those who approved wholeheartedly and were largely, gloriously female. Still, with Pedro, it ended up as more than that, because of course it did with Pedro.

By some coincidence, he also happened to turn up, in all his vividness, at the very nadir of my time so far in the world. That's when the laws of the United States prevented any of its citizens from seeking a Green Card for any foreign spouse of the same gender, so I'd have to choose between spouse and homeland. Things would have to get wrenching.

Pedro knew about that reality, especially in 2005 when it seared the most, and somehow it was 2005 when we spent the most time together. It was 2005 when he and Sandi took me to dinner in Phoenix and reveled in my connection to Colombia, 2005 when our emotional bond took hold, 2005 when I knew for sure of his unmitigated support, 2005 when he would advise me about certain baseball people during my then-annual Cactus League spring training tour, 2005 which preceded my exile to London, where the United Kingdom accepted our little family of two. It was 2005 when I felt broken and lost in the presence of Pedro and Sandi, and 2005 when they declined to see me as broken and lost.

As of 2005, my worst year, when the stress mounted and the sleep didn't, I knew Pedro as not only a safe human haven for myself, but as someone uncommonly alive and decent, someone who might lend hope just by his essence. When you're in your depths and somebody presents himself or herself as someone who cares, that person takes up a meaningful space in the consciousness, no matter that you might skirt to London and try to handle its soaring stresses and costs and unknowns.

I never had a doubt that Pedro understood all of it, and I never had a doubt he would have done whatever to stem the woe. Maybe even more crucially, I never had a doubt he believed it all would work its way to the best in the end. That essence sat there across the table or right there in the dugout, supportive but also strangely, helplessly hopeful.

Through the ensuing years to London and then agony and then back, he and I mingled now and then but not enough, because it's always not enough. Then, one Halloween night in 2015, after I had worked a splendid Notre Dame-Temple football game in Philadelphia, I drove away to catch him on the radio talking about the ongoing Mets-Royals World Series, which had just finished Game 4 in Queens and would end up the next night at 5. Driving up Broad Street, I listened to him and kept smiling, and it was odd, because shortly thereafter, he texted this: "With Lisa Olson at Foley's in Manhattan. Wish you were here, amigo."

I wrote back: "Want to know a funny truth? Just listened to you on the radio driving back through Philadelphia from the ND-Temple game, and I thought, I'd love to see him again soon. Just an hour ago, this was.

Or two hours if you count the hour we lost."

"Talk about karma," he wrote right back. "Wow! Amazing. Would love to see you again. We will. Our paths will cross. And count my couch in Phoenix as your Arizona home. It's actually going to be a bed so bring Alfonso."

At that point, Alfonso remained in Colombia, awaiting our immigration result in a legal world remade by the Supreme Court, but when I mentioned I would be in Phoenix for the college football title game come January, he wrote, "You have my home. I'm serious."

Two months later, I went for hotel points, one of life's ongoing array of mistakes. But as I finished up with Alabama-Clemson and started on the NFL playoff of Arizona-Green Bay, I ran into Pedro at the Cardinals practice site. His was a presence of unmitigated light, so we hugged and it was beautiful.

Three months later, I turned up as I might at Steve Buckley's house in Boston, and I learned again of their longtime competition about their hair quality, and wrote: "Here in Boston, I have just learned you have the second-best hair in the press boxes of MLB. Don't worry. Silver medals are impressive."

"Oh Chuck, don't let yourself be bamboozled by Buck," Pedro wrote back. "You and I both know Latinos have the best hair. I'm disappointed in you."

"I apologize," I wrote him. "You are right."

There are people we don't see every year because we don't cross paths, or we don't realize the finiteness of life, or we don't cover the same sport as they do. Yet we rely on their light being out there somewhere because of course it's always there.

So that helps explain the wee hours after the blah of a Super Bowl LV in Tampa, with a 31-9 score and limited fans, when I finished the day and the coronavirus stress, and made my way in my triple mask across Tampa Bay and past the prescribed exit and then messily back through the roads of St. Petersburg to Treasure Island and the edge of the Gulf of Mexico. I reached the hotel and the balcony knowing I had two of the greatest fates awaiting: a half-bottle of red, which was enough to help but not too much to hurt, and a sky full of stars, which Jim Murray once extolled when telling of sights he'd like to see after the loss of his eyesight.

With typical unwisdom, I decided to bring my phone outdoors with the bottle and the glass and the stars, and that's what enabled me to learn with shock that hours earlier, the world had gotten less luminous. I would have to cling to having joined the multitudes who had the privilege of knowing Pedro, and carrying along the kind of support he managed to give to everyone, very much including the strays and the outcasts such as myself.

2008, the Grotto: Pedro brought Steve Karsay along to Z's birthday celebration

Tracy on Alpo, a thoroughbred. They both have the same birthday, April 30. In 2021, Tracy turned seventy and Alpo turned twenty-seven.

WITH THE ANGELS

BY TRACY RINGOLSBY

I don't know if there are two people much more different than Pedro Gomez and I were. That is, two people who considered each other good friends. We came from completely different worlds, but, to be honest, I don't know if either one of us ever thought about that.

Our encounters were irregular, infrequent and really tied to being at the ballpark, whether it was spring training, the regular season or the postseason. I had been covering baseball for more than a decade before Pedro came on the baseball beat in 1992, the same year I left my job covering the Rangers for the *Dallas Morning News* to start writing about the Colorado Rockies for the *Rocky Mountain News*.

The thing I remember most about Pedro was he wasn't afraid to ask the hard question. He, however, did it in a special way, one that didn't irritate, but one that would open the door for the athlete, manager or coach to explain a situation that didn't go right.

Pedro always wanted to know what I had been up to and who I had written about lately (other than in a game story), and then to kick around big-picture ideas. In the early years we would chat at length about the importance of respecting the people we covered. Oh, and in recent years, when our times together were primarily limited to spring training ballparks, we would talk (or rather I would listen to Pedro talk) about how proud he was of his son Rio. Pedro was very much a proud papa when Rio was pitching at the University of Arizona, making it to the College World Series in 2016, and then when he was drafted by the Red Sox.

"Who knows what's going to happen," Pedro would say, "but at least he has the opportunity. It's going to be fun to see what it leads to. I think he'll surprise some people."

Knowing Pedro, he's keeping score from above, trying to figure out how to get messages to Rio.

In reading the obituaries and tributes after Pedro's death, I realized how different our lives had been. Let's start with the fact that Wyoming covers 97,809 square miles, 51.5 times bigger than the 1,898 square miles of Miami's Dade County, but Miami's population is five times larger than the entire state of Wyoming.

I'm seventy years old, a fifth-generation native of Laramie County, with family ties to three of the four original families to settle in the county. Let's face it, the big town in Wyoming, Cheyenne, the state capital with a population less than 60,000, is the largest city in the state. But then the state may cover the ninth most land of any state in the United States, but its population, which has bounced around 580,000 in recent years, is the smallest.

My parents and I moved to California in the late '50s for a bit but gladly came back home for my high school years. I broke into the newspaper business on May 1, 1968, the day after I turned seventeen, as the one-man sports staff for the *Wyoming State Tribune*, a six-day-a-week paper. It was with United Press International, after I was transferred to Kansas City in December of 1975, that I first covered baseball. And I still haven't quit covering it, having bounced from Kansas City to Long Beach to Seattle, back to Kansas City, to Dallas and finally to Denver (although I moved home, outside of Cheyenne), which became a running joke between myself and Pedro.

He was a baseball writer from Miami, but he spent much of his life in California and then Arizona and was enthralled with the romance of the Real West. We would often chat about what it would have been like to live in those wild times. Funny thing is as much as Pedro would ask about growing up in "The Wild West," as he would put it, it wasn't until I read his obituary that I ever had insight into the wild world that Pedro grew up in.

Wow. His parents defected from Cuba just weeks before Pedro was born, barely in time to ensure he would be born a United States citizen. They settled in the Miami area, where so many of those who escaped the oppression of Cuba had built their homes. I can only assume hearing the elders discuss the oppression they had faced during their time in Cuba only added to Pedro's upbeat approach to life. It's why he wore that "light up the room" smile and would immediately break into a conversation about what is good in life.

And right now, I can just picture him, up there in heaven, convinced that if they claim to be Angels they must be able to play baseball, and then volunteering to give them advice on ways to refine their skills.

HE MADE THE ROOM BETTER

BY BUD BLACK

I always felt that when I was in his presence, whether in a group setting or one on one, there was a magnetism to Pedro. When I first met him I had already seen his byline and read his stories, so I was like: *Hey, OK, finally in person I get to meet Pedro Gomez!* He was one of the most renowned reporters in our game.

You noticed him right away with that smile and the strong voice, and he always asked good questions. He just had great instincts and understood the setting, so he had a feel for what questions needed to be asked. They were pointed, a lot of times they were tough, but they were the right ones. There was a professionalism to his reporting; he didn't take care of certain managers or certain players.

I liked him. Pedro was a guy I viewed as a friend, even though we didn't socialize. I became aware his son Rio was a pitcher at Arizona and then I followed Rio's career from afar, through video and stats and what I'd hear from Pedro. It was sort of fun following his Arizona years, including that appearance in the College World Series, and then his getting drafted by the Red Sox. By then Pedro was giving me regular updates on what the player development guys were saying. He always kept me involved and I felt what love he had for his son and what excitement for him to be a professional player. It was pretty cool.

We'd exchange friendly texts now and then. He'd be thinking of you and wanted you to know he was, or he'd have something to share. Or you'd run into each other at a baseball game or in an interview situation and he'd follow up later.

I did a Zoom call with reporters in August 2020 during the seven-game losing streak we had that month and Pedro asked: "Buddy, as a player you come from an era when managers would tip over the postgame spread and rant when the club wasn't performing. What's your level of frustration right now?"

Later he followed up with a text: "Thanks, Buddy. I know it's not an easy time. But you answer the bell every day."

I wrote back: "Pedro, thanks. These stretches for players, coaches, managers are rough, as you know. We will come out of this soon. As Winston Churchill said, 'When you go through hell, you just have to keep going.' Good to hear you on the presser. Hoping the lefty is still progressing???"

In a group setting, like in a scrum of reporters, you could feel the respect others in the room had for Pedro, and he treated other reporters with the utmost respect as well. He wasn't bigger than the group, but in some ways it felt that way, just because of his experience and his writing and where he had been. It was always different when Pedro was there. Especially in spring-training scrums or playoff games, I always thought he made the room better.

Pedro was a traditionalist. He believed the purity of the game is what makes it great. I understand the current innovation that's happening in our game to enhance it, but I also think there's another side. This game has been great for a long time because of the way it is played, the measurements of this game, the symmetry. It's in a lot of ways perfect and I think that those of us who see it that way pull hard for it to remain intact. But I'm personally not a dinosaur that has my head in the sand about what can be done to make it better. I'm all about progress and being creative to enhance the game. If we can make the game better, let's talk about it, but not ruin the pure beauty of the game.

Pedro always understood the manager's responsibility for leading this group of players, because he'd been in so many clubhouses, so many manager's offices, and heard so many discussions and talked to so many players. He always saw the managerial position as very important. I think we've started to see again that people in baseball recognize that a good manager is a key part of an organization.

It's like in any walk of life, whether it's a board room, whether it's a baseball field, whether it's an office, any time people are in competition, when it really gets down to crunch time and there are decisions to be made and responsibilities to be given. The manager, the president of an organization, whatever leader it is, they know their people. Whatever the outcome, you're placing your trust in your people, and I think that goes along with baseball. You're in the trenches with people and when it becomes adverse, it gets tough, it gets hot and it's at that peak moment, you have that feeling of who to go to, of who to give that responsibility to, and you feel good about it. We have these decisions to make all the time, each and every night from the time the game starts, and obviously there are decisions that are more magnified based on the game, the inning, regular-season game or playoff game or World Series game.

That's a part of managing and a part of leading that Pedro was always focused on, instinctively knowing your people and knowing what they can do under pressure. Obviously I've never been in a war, but the decisions that generals and admirals have to make, it all comes down to: You know your people. That's what Pedro was all about, always asking questions about people, always seeing things others didn't.

Pedro worked in a period of time when the game was growing and he was part of that growth as the game really took off from the late '80s to where it is now. He was right in the midst of that growth as one of the best. He crossed over because of his background, his heritage, his ethnicity, his language skills. He was able to cover the entire scope of baseball, from the Latin side to just the American side. That made him even more essential as part of this period of growth. I think he'll always be remembered as one of the great baseball writers of all time.

Snafu Lounge, New York: Pedro, ESPN producers Brian Franey and Charlie Moynihan, and Tim

THE WALLS CAME DOWN

BY TIM KURKJIAN

Spring training in Arizona is the best. Perfect weather, great food, salty margaritas, most ballparks within forty-five minutes of each other, downtown Scottsdale on a gorgeous Saturday afternoon. All of which prompted my dear friend Pedro Gomez to smile and greet me with, "Welcome to heaven, Timmy!"

What made spring training in Arizona even better, after a day of baseball in the hot sun, was a night of pickup basketball with our friends with Pedro as one of the ringleaders. I have played basketball in so many different places over the years. In 1989 in Seattle I played with former NBA player Steve Hawes, who is six-nine, and I mean he got *every* rebound. In 1997 in Kansas City, twelve years after Scott Wedman had gone eleven-for-eleven for the Celtics in an NBA Finals game against the Lakers, I wound up in a pickup game with him at an NCAA regional. He had no idea who I was or if I could play, but he whispered to me, "I'm not here to play, I'm just going to shoot. I'm not going to guard anyone or get any rebounds, I'll just be over here on the wing." So we got him the ball, he didn't miss and we won eight games in a row. On Halloween Day

2001 at the Reebok Club in New York, *Sports Illustrated*'s Steve Rushin and I were approached by a couple guys who wanted to play two-on-two. One of them was the worst player ever, the other was Adam Sandler. Since his teammate was terrible, we won every game easily and Adam was pissed, but it was great fun. I called home to tell the kids that we kicked Happy Gilmore's ass.

But there was nothing like spring hoops in Arizona. What an eclectic list of players, led by baseball writers, to name just a few: Pedro, John Shea, Howard Bryant, Steve Kettmann, Mike DiGiovanna. There were executives, including Sandy Alderson, Billy Beane, David Forst, Farhan Zaidi, Jeff Bridich, Thad Levine and A.J. Preller, who was a fucking nightmare to guard, he was so quick, so strong, he could shoot the 3 or get into the lane against anyone. Plus, he would tear your throat out, no matter how small the game. There were managers, including Art Howe and Ken Macha, who brought new meaning to the term "Bull in a china shop." Man, would he lower that front shoulder. There were former players, Steve Kline, Rick Burleson and Lee Smith, who I loved personally but didn't enjoy playing with because he was so good, and so much bigger than everyone else. He refused to take a shot in the lane because it was too easy, he didn't think it was fair. So I would risk my life getting to the rim, pass it to him for a two-footer, and he would pass the ball back out to the 3-point line. "Sorry Timmy," he'd say. "Can't do it." One player, Tony Phillips, showed up and announced, "Don't tell skip I was here!"

"Those games were quintessential Pedro because of the guys that played," said Howard Bryant. "There were writers, executives, managers, coaches and players and ex-players. It was one of the few times that we crossed baseball's professional lines. Depending on the night, I was passing the ball to Lee Smith, or getting yelled at by Tony Phillips. On those nights, the walls came down. It was OK to play with those guys. That's why Pedro was so important to those games. Wherever he went, the walls came down. He made sure of it."

Pedro was one of the great facilitators in life. He always made everyone feel comfortable wherever they were, especially a petrified me when we went to Cuba with ESPN in 2016. Those games in Arizona might have been a conflict of interest. Writers should not be socializing with players and executives when they're covering that team. But Pedro made everyone feel at ease. This wasn't dinner and a movie, this wasn't even beers and nachos, this was a competition, this was a game, this was a 3 from the corner and drive to the hoop. This was, occasionally, a writer beating an ex-player to the bucket, but far more often it was an athlete, or a former athlete, showing writers why they were writers.

"Pedro was a huge part of those games," said John Shea. "I started playing in them when they started in 1988, and I've made sure I have played in at least one game in every year since. We started on an outdoor court at the Giants' minor-league facility. The backboards were made of brick, you had to swish it to make it. And Roger Craig used to play! His wife would come along and watch. And he was old then! And we, the writers, were all in our thirties. Then we moved indoors at the Giants facility, that little blue court made out of rubber. The weightlifters would watch us. Then we moved to the Centre Court Apartments, and I started staying there just so I would have a key to the gym. Howard even thought about buying a place there so we could play. It was built around the Bay Area writers, but the A's were all over that game. Billy Beane, a first round pick, he was supposed to be as good as Strawberry, played. A world-class athlete playing with a bunch of writers. He raised the intensity. He was the best athlete on the court."

Beane has fond recollections of those games as well. "Pedro played basketball very similarly to the way he worked as a journalist covering myself and the A's, he'd push and probe right to the point where you'd get irritated, then he'd just flash that smile and it was impossible to be mad at him," he texted. "I'll always remember our spring basketball games with him and a lot of other now famous sports writers and journalists. Hard to imagine friendly pickup games amongst management and the press could exist today. Of course, Pedro was the ring leader and if you tried to bow out he'd shame you into showing up."

Pedro was a good athlete. He had baseball skills, which is evident from his oldest son, Rio, who pitches in the Red Sox system. The first time I played hoops with Pedro, I told him he looked and played like Kelly Tripucka. Pedro had those big, thick, hairy legs. Big high-top sneakers. And big white teeth, though not as big as Kelly Tripucka's teeth. He had a barrel chest and a thick head of hair. And he liked to pull up and shoot off the break.

"Pedro had a wonderful shot from fifteen feet in," Shea said. "And he had some meat on him, so he could guard someone on the inside, and would go out and guard someone farther out. He always had a great time playing, he just loved being out there with the guys, guys from all over: writers, executives, managers, everyone. He was always smiling. He would make a shot in your face and smile at you. He would block your shot, and would smile. He wasn't trash talking at you, not his style, but who smiles when they hit a shot in your face?"

I always felt that Pedro's hoop game mirrored Pedro the person, and Pedro the writer and reporter: unselfish, decidedly without ego, he did everything with joy, passion and intensity. No story was too big for him, be it Balco or Bonds or Big Papi getting shot in the Dominican. And no shot was too big for him. He wasn't the best shooter on the floor, but he also wasn't afraid to take an open jumper from the elbow with the score tied, 14-14. No story was too small for him because it was never about him, it was always about the team. So many times I saw him voluntarily go into the visitors' clubhouse after a difficult loss, barge ahead with a camera crew on his back, and ask difficult questions. Same with hoops. One night at Centre Court, our team was filled with shooters, with scorers. Pedro recognized that; few read the room, any room, better than Pedro. So he spent the night setting picks, getting every dirty rebound and guarding the best player on the other team. He barely scored that night, but we won every game, and the writers celebrated afterwards with many beers, and relived plays from a meaningless game.

"I don't think I made a shot tonight," he said. "But I enjoyed watching you guys score at will."

It was usually a private game, just our guys, no strangers. One night, the writers, just the writers this time, were playing at Centre Court when a bunch of local guys arrived. They were not happy that these interlopers had invaded their court. And they really weren't happy when we won seven straight games, they would lose and have to sit and watch. In the final game, it got testy, one of the locals wanted to fight. So Pedro the peacemaker took over.

"Fellas," he said. "We're old baseball writers. We're just getting some exercise. Calm down."

He loved being with his writer friends. He loved telling stories, many of which he repeated, but no one cared because they were great and they were funny. His favorite story about hoops in Arizona was the famous night that DiGi messed with the wrong Marine.

"Oh, myyyyy," Pedro told me many, many times. "Greatest moment in basketball history."

"I started playing my first year on the beat in '95, I didn't know a lot of guys, but I knew Pedro, and he introduced me to a lot of people because he knew everyone: that was Pedro," said DiGiovanna, who like Pedro was born in August 1962. "And I want you to know that this story has appeared in three books, only this time, I'm a going to tell it correctly. When the A's guys showed up, the games were ultra-competitive. I was thirty-two. We were playing four-on-four full court. Sandy Alderson was guarding me. He was guarding me hard on every possession. So the ball went out of bounds at midcourt, Pedro retrieved the ball. Play had stopped, but Sandy's back was to the play, so he didn't know the ball had gone out of bounds. So he was still guarding me. Hard. So, famously, I said, 'At ease, soldier.'"

Steve Kettmann was in that game, and remembers Pedro flashing him a wide-eyed "Holy Shit!" look as they ran down the court just afterward, and saying, "Did you hear that?" and telling him what DiGi said to Alderson.

"Well, from that minute on, Sandy guarded me even harder, like it was the NCAA Final Four or the NBA Finals," DiGi continued. "Damn, he was crushing me. This poor sap—me—didn't know what had hit him. He blocked me out so hard. After the game, I told Pedro what I said, and his eyes just lit up. He said, 'Are you kidding me? He's a decorated Marine!' I had totally insulted him. I had no idea he was a Marine. I knew he worked for the A's but I wasn't even sure if he was Sandy Alderson."

John Shea played in that game.

"Sandy wasn't just an ex-Marine, he posed for the poster that recruited guys to come to the Corps," Shea said. "After DiGi famously said, 'At ease, soldier,' the next time down the court, Sandy hip-checked him into that brick wall at the end line. DiGi didn't even know who Sandy was at the time. We went for beers after the game. That's when we told DiGi who that was that knocked him into the wall. He said, '*That* was Sandy Alderson!?'"

Twenty-seven years later, DiGi disputes small details of that story, but is required to tell it.

"Well, we made amends, Sandy and I," DiGi said. "We laugh about it now. I will never live that down. And I never should live that down. Pedro, Steve and I would always laugh about that. They still bring up that night. Pedro always laughed. Pedro always had a great laugh."

Pedro helped build the bridge back between Sandy and DiGi. Pedro built bridges, he knocked down walls, he built them back up and he always did it with a smile, especially in those hoop games in Arizona, surrounded by his favorite people, those who loved the game.

"We're playing tonight!" he would tell me on a spring training field. "Don't miss it. It'll be great!"

And then he set an imaginary pick for me, lifting his elbows, smiled that Pedro smile, laughed that Pedro laugh, and walked away.

Jack and Pamela

Pedro and Sandi

THE MUSIC NEVER STOPPED

BY JACK CURRY

The texts would ping on my iPhone at the most random of times. It could be 8 a.m., it could be 8 p.m., or there could be a flood of texts at 1 a.m. And they weren't boring texts. They were effervescent texts, I-must-respond-now texts. They were Pedro Gomez texts and they were almost always about our shared passion for music.

I met Pedro almost thirty years ago because we were both baseball writers who covered American League teams. When Pedro covered the Oakland A's and I covered the New York Yankees, we had conversations about baseball, but I don't recall them because I had those types of talks every day. What I do remember was how deeply Pedro and I bonded over our passion for new wave and alternative music from the 1980s.

Since Pedro was born in Miami in 1962 and I was born in New Jersey two years later, we discovered that we were buying the same albums, cassettes and CDs while we were in high school and college. Sure, we could have discussed Rickey Henderson and Mark McGwire or, later in our friendship, dissected Derek Jeter and Mariano Rivera. And we did. But we really wanted to talk about the Clash and the Cure.

The baseball press box can be a lonely and demanding place. It's just you and your laptop and the challenge of finishing your story and doing a better job than all of the competitors working beside you. And once you've finished one story, you must start working on your next assignment. The deadlines and the pressures are endless.

To help conquer that stress, I've always turned to music as a soothing influence. If I heard a song over the public address system, I would guess the artist and the title or I would sing backup vocals. That singing development would always be horrendous on everyone's ears. If I liked a player's walk-up music, I would comment on it. If I disliked it, I would suggest a replacement song. Or I would force my colleagues to listen to some of my music or even persuade them to attend concerts of bands they barely knew.

Live music enthralls me. I know it enthralled Pedro, too, which is why I so cherished his texts. Pedro, the great, kind and unforgettable Pedro, helped me vicariously attend many concerts with him. Only Pedro. Only Pedro would be so generous and so observant to grasp how meaningful it would be to me to receive a fifteen-second video from a concert. Yes, I wanted that clip of the B-52s or the English Beat or the Cure or OMD. Those were my bands! Correction: Those were OUR bands. And Pedro made sure our bond, a bond that started in a baseball press box, remained strong through venues both of us visited, stretching from California to New York, from Arizona to New Jersey and from Ireland to St. Kitts.

Flash back to July of 2015 and Pedro texted, "I'm going to the English Beat tonight. Should be great."

"I love them," I responded. "They are nonstop fun in their shows. I'm jealous. Enjoy!"

A couple hours later, Pedro sent me a video of the English Beat doing "Twist and Crawl," and it seemed like everyone in the audience was twisting and crawling. If you attend an English Beat show, it's virtually impossible to stand still. They are a ska band who deftly mix reggae, soul and punk rock and even the most stoic person would be challenged to remain in place.

But guess who wasn't moving? Pedro! What the heck? I deduced that Pedro wasn't moving because he was holding his phone steady so that he could send me a smooth video. Pedro was about fifty feet away from Dave Wakeling, the lead singer, and the videos (of course, he sent more than one) were perfect.

"That's how close we were," Pedro texted. "Great show."

After Pedro gave me that musical gift, the only return gift I could muster was to tell him I once shared beers with Wakeling after an English Beat show in Hoboken, N.J. And, yes, Wakeling was as cool a guy off-stage as he was on stage. Pedro, the '80s music savant, loved that tidbit.

Sometimes, Pedro opted for short, descriptive texts, especially when my fellow music man behaved like an on-site correspondent.

"Hollywood Bowl. Right now."

That was Pedro's video text to me in May of 2016 to announce that he was at a Cure show. The sights and the sounds were unmistakable as Robert Smith, the lead singer with the unruly black hair and the unmistakable voice, stood on stage with blue lights flashing around him and sang "Just Like Heaven." Just like Pedro, I felt like I had been transported to the 1980s to see the British post-punk icons.

Pedro was about a hundred feet away from the stage, a prime position to eyeball one of his favorite bands. At the end of the song, I heard another fan screaming, "Woooooo hoooooo" way too long. You know the type. He's the kind of raucous fan you'd like to muzzle so you can listen to the music. But knowing the genteel Pedro, he probably befriended the guy and took a selfie with him.

As always, I thanked Pedro and told him I hadn't seen the Cure since 1995 or 1996, but I've always loved the band. That's when Pedro became a Cure maniac, for both of us.

"They are playing EVERYTHING," he texted. "I mean, EVERYTHING. Smith is way into it. Google this tour. He's been playing thirty-five-song sets with five encores. Amazing. And this is how close me and my wife are. Splurged. It's well worth it."

Pedro's enthusiasm was infectious so I behaved like a Cure maniac, too.

"Looks like they are in New York in June," I wrote. "I'm going to try and check them out. Thanks! Get your '80s on."

Pedro responded: "Ha, ha! Exactly. He is playing all the great stuff. The Cuban 80's alternate fan highly recommends."

That text made me laugh. So Pedro. So sweet. And I appreciated that

The Clash at the Warfield, 1980

Pedro had sent me a snippet of "Just Like Heaven" because that high-energy song is on many of my running playlists.

Along with a video of the Cure's "A Forest," Pedro texted, "Still going strong. It's 10:09 here. They started at 8:07." Do you notice how precise Pedro was with the details? Obviously, the reporter in him was reporting on this show. Yes, that's exactly what he was doing. He was giving me play-by-play.

"10:44," was the next text with a clip of "Let's Go to Bed."

"10:47," came next with a clip of "Close to Me?"

"10:51," followed that with a clip of "Why Can't I Be You?"

It was almost 2 a.m. in New Jersey and I was riveted by a concert unfolding 2,800 miles away because Pedro brought me there with him. Even if I wanted to go to bed, as the Cure had just sang, I couldn't. I needed Pedro's updates. I needed to know what the Cure played for an encore.

About ten hours later, Pedro texted me the encore information.

"They finished with 'Boys Don't Cry,'" he wrote. "Really sorry for the flood of texts last night. I hope you were O.K. with them. If not, a sincere apology."

I responded quickly and emphatically.

"O.K. with them? You made my night. Seriously I love them."

"You and I always shared our love for the same style of music," Pedro texted back. "But I was hoping your wife wasn't saying, 'Who the hell keeps texting you at this hour?'"

"She was asleep," I told Pedro. "It was just me, you and Robert Smith."

Then I told Pedro I planned to buy tickets from StubHub to see the Cure at Madison Square Garden. As much as I adored the Cure, I wasn't even thinking about going until Pedro's passionate texts.

"I also had to buy from a secondary broker and it was costly," he said. "But it was incredibly worth it. The way I see it, and I think you are similar in this respect, I'm not a frivolous person. My money goes to my family (wife and kids). So every once in a while, it's OK to splurge on something I really want. Plus, my wife is a huge Cure fan."

Along with the text, Pedro sent me a picture of him and Sandi smiling at the Hollywood Bowl during the concert. Sandi's cheek is pressed against Pedro's cheek and their powerful love for each other shouts from the image. The picture resonated with me then. It resonates with me so much more now.

"The happy couple," I wrote. "Great pic. You guys look like you're in your 30s."

Pedro texted back, "Maybe mentally. Ha ha."

Five months later, Pedro was covering a San Francisco Giants game and he texted me about an innocuous pitching change. Well, again, with us, it wasn't about the baseball as much as it was about the music

"Derek Law has to be one of your favorites," he wrote. "His walk-in song is 'I Fought The Law.' The Clash version, the only version that matters."

Anyone who has spent

Z and Joe Strummer of the Clash

five minutes ruminating about music with me knows the Clash, the punk truth tellers, are my all-time favorite band. The savvy Pedro played off the Clash being described as, "The only band that matters," in his text. But there was a humorous wrinkle regarding me and Law's walk-up music. Mark Gonzales, another baseball reporter, had already tweeted the same sentiment about how I probably loved the song because of the Clash. So I playfully told Pedro, "Gonzo beat you to it."

A day later, Pedro, perhaps deciding that he needed to redeem himself, sent me a clip of the Sex Pistols' "Anarchy in the UK" and asked, "Is Gonzo sending you this?"

Of course not, I told Pedro, because Pedro was the only person who would do that. On that same night, I went to see Squeeze and the English Beat. I did my best Pedro impersonation and sent him a video clip of Squeeze's "Pulling Mussels From A Shell." Well, no, if it had been my *best* Pedro impersonation, I would have sent him five or six songs.

Soon after the 2017 baseball season ended, I received another one of those enthusiastic texts from Pedro.

"Jackie. My wife and I are heading to Ireland at the end of the month and I bought tickets to see Peter Hook in Dublin. He apparently does a thirty-two-song set jam with sixteen Joy Division songs and sixteen New Order songs. Here's a taste."

Naturally, he included a concert clip of Hook, the talented bass player who was also the cofounder of Joy Division and New Order. I've always been entranced by New Order, a British band that helped inject electronic and dance music into the rock world and made some spellbinding music.

"That sounds fantastic," I responded. "Hope you have a great time. I'm in St Kitts and I'm going to see a local Reggae band. Peter Hook vs the local Reggae band? You win."

"St. Kitts sounds pretty good," Pedro said.

And, on the first day of December, my concert play-by-play man was back.

"Dublin. Right now," he wrote and included a video of "Bizarre Love Triangle." It seemed as if Pedro was about thirty feet from the stage as Hook and his band followed that by roaring into "Temptation," a song that includes the wonderful, mysterious and apt lyrics, "Oh, you've got green eyes. Oh, you've got blue eyes. Oh, you've got grey eyes. And I've never seen anyone quite like you before. No, I've never met anyone quite like you before."

I thanked Pedro profusely for escorting me to Dublin with him and Sandi and he responded immediately, the excitement bursting through with every text.

"He played 150 minutes with a 7-8 minute intermission. Amazing show. If you get a chance to see Peter Hook And The Light, I highly suggest it. Because he's not making new music, it's hit after hit and he truly enjoys it."

I thanked him over and over, thanked him for sharing the experience with me. Again, as I pondered our friendship, I asked myself, "Who is that thoughtful to do this?" Pedro loved live music, loved the experience. Just like me. But, in the middle of that experience, he wanted to selflessly share it with me. It was a beautiful gift that he gave me and a beautiful gift that he has left me. Sometimes, it leaves me speechless.

Most sports fans were focused on football as the New England Patriots played the Jacksonville Jaguars in the AFC Championship on January 21, 2018. But I'm a baseball guy so I shared a cool Cure video with Pedro during the game. Several fans had used videos from their iPhones to stitch together an entire Cure concert.

"Wow," Pedro wrote back. "I'll check it out after this game. Thanks for passing it along."

"I was going to wait until after the game," I told him, "but Robert Smith's team won out over Robert Kraft's team. Lol."

Ever the Cure fanatic, Pedro agreed: "Robert Smith always wins that battle."

Regardless of whether it had been one week or six months since I'd heard from Pedro, his texts were always as warm and welcoming as if we'd seen each other a few hours earlier. During a steamy day in August, my mind mired in the baseball world, Pedro texted me the following: "Berlin, OMD and the B-52's tonight." I liked all three bands, but I told Pedro I had only seen the B-52s in concert. So you know what happened next.

First, Pedro sent me a Berlin video of the song "Metro" with Terri Nunn, the lead singer, parading around the stage. Then he sent me OMD playing "If You Leave," a song that dominated my mix tape collection back in the '80s. Finally, he sent me "Rock Lobster" by the B-52s and, this time, the camera was moving so that meant Pedro was moving, too.

I loved it, just like I loved every text I received from him.

I woke up feeling gloomy on October 18, 2019. Terribly and devastatingly depressed and sad. It was the twenty-fifth anniversary of the day my mother passed away. I think about my mother, who was my hero, every hour of every day. But the magnitude of twenty-five years walloped me that day. I realized it had been 9,125 days since I had heard her voice or hugged her. I rarely do this, but, needing some sort of outlet, I posted about it on social media. Guess who sent me a sweet and timely text? Saint Pedro.

"Jack. Never met your Mom, but my favorite story has to be when Steinbrenner called for you at your house and she scolded him for calling during the dinner hour. It still brings a smile to my face. Hope all is well, amigo."

And, with that recollection, Pedro brought a smile to my face. And he was right about the details of that memorable story. In my early days of covering the Yankees for *The New York Times*, I couldn't get George Steinbrenner, the principal owner, to return my calls. I left messages for him for six straight months. Nothing. I can still recite that 813 number in my head because I had nightmares, wondering if he would ever call me. A Yankee writer who didn't have access to Steinbrenner was a hamstrung writer.

Finally, a Yankee official told me George had researched me and liked what he had heard and was going to call me soon. And, one day, the phone rang and a voice said, "This is George." I had recently graduated from college and wasn't yet married so I was still living at home with my parents in a four-room apartment in Jersey City. It was 1992 so we had one phone with one extension. Obviously, there were no cell phones.

I was nervous and elated to hear from George. The first thing he said was, "I've asked around about you and I've heard you're fair. That's why I called you back. But I don't want you to ever lie to me. If you lie to me, I'll never call you back. But if you tell me the truth, I will return your calls and answer your questions."

I thanked George for returning my call, told him I would always be honest and then I started to ask him questions. And George, very quickly, transformed into vintage George with some intriguing comments about his players, his executives and even the Mets.

The more George spoke, the more I realized I had a tremendous scoop. Finally, George had called me back! My mind was spinning. George was comfortable talking about a variety of topics and our conversation pushed beyond thirty minutes. Then, suddenly, there was a crackle in the phone line and a female voice was heard saying, "Doesn't anyone know there's a dinner hour around here?" And then the voice and the crackle disappeared.

"What was that?" George shouted. "Who was that? And what did she say?"

Remember, at the outset of the call, George stressed that I needed to always be truthful with him. So, as worried as I was to admit what happened, I said, "Uh, George. That was my Mom. She wanted to remind me that dinner was ready."

I waited for George to verbally explode, tell me that my mother shouldn't have interrupted our call and say that he'd never call me again. Instead, George reacted in a much different way.

"She's right, she's right," George bellowed. "Dinner time with the family is very important. You should be with them. You shouldn't be talking to me. We'll talk again."

And then George hung up the phone. So that's how my mother silenced George and ended my first interview with the man I'd been pursuing for six months. And that's the story that Pedro loved. It meant so much to me that he mentioned it on that dreary anniversary.

Two months later, Pedro did a huge favor for me during baseball's winter meetings in San Diego. Scott Boras, the agent, decided to stage a press conference in front of a massive Christmas tree near the hotel lobby. Reporters swarmed toward him. I was about fifteen feet away from Boras, but it might as well have been 1,500 feet because I couldn't snake my arm around the bodies to get my YES Network microphone close enough to Boras. But Pedro, without saying a word, reached back to take my mic and held the YES mic and his ESPN mic close to Boras so that we would both secure the interview. That's a friend.

On Feb. 21, 2020, which would have been my mother's eighty-first birthday, I heard from Pedro again. He didn't know it was my Mom's birthday, but, based on his text from a few months earlier, it was symbolic when he reported in from another show.

"Seeing the Motels," he wrote. "Certainly not an '80s A-lister, but not the bottom by any means." And, of course, he sent me a video of

Debbie Harry in the Hall of Flowers in Golden Gate Park, 1977

"Suddenly Last Summer," which is their most popular song.

"Classic '80s tune," I texted.

Pedro: "Indeed. By the way, Martha Davis, the Motels singer, is sixty-nine."

Me: "That saddens me."

Pedro: "Because it means we are getting older."

Seeing that "getting older" text now gives me chills. And so does this one, which Pedro sent a few months later.

Pedro: "Our feeling old reminder of the day. Debbie Harry is seventy-five today."

Me: "And I can still see her on the 'Parallel Lines' album cover. Feels like it was yesterday."

Flipping through the channels on Father's Day, I was grateful to see a feature Pedro did for ESPN about him and Rio, his son who is a minor-league pitcher in the Boston Red Sox organization. I quickly texted Pedro and told him it was a great piece.

Pedro: "Thank you, Jack. I truly appreciate the note."

During a painful and depressing 2020 in which tens of thousands of families experienced heartbreaking losses from the coronavirus outbreak, a truncated baseball season was played. Both Pedro and I covered the stories of this surreal season. A day before the postseason began, I found out that I had tested positive for Covid-19 so I was unable to cover the Yankees' games. Pedro didn't hear about my diagnosis until after I had recovered.

"Holy shit, Jack," he wrote. "I had zero idea. So glad you're doing better."

Me: "Thanks a lot, Pedro. Scary to hear I tested positive. But I am happy to be feeling somewhat normal again."

Unfortunately, that was the last time we texted. After Pedro's passing, I spoke with some of his friends about what made him so special. And, as I thought about how influential Pedro was for so many of us, it was alarmingly obvious that Pedro thrived on being a giver. If he saw a way to help you or connect with you, Pedro seized upon it.

In our friendship, Pedro was the ultimate giver because he uncovered a way for me to enjoy these shows with him. Every time I see or hear one of OUR favorite bands, I'll think about him. I already have. The day after Pedro left us, I clicked shuffle on my trusty iPod and went for a run. One of the first songs that filled my ears was the Cure's "Just Like Heaven." Thank you, Pedro. Thanks for everything, amigo.

Pedro with Z and his son Ari

DEFINITELY A
STONES GUY

BY MICHAEL ZAGARIS

Pedro was one of those people, as soon as I met him, I just knew he was simpatico. It was like: *I've known this guy all my life.* I met him in the '90s when he was covering the A's as a beat writer and I was team photographer. Pedro was just a hip cat. Baseball was one touchstone, but only one of many.

We talked a lot about the Rolling Stones, not just the music, but the Stones as lifestyle, the Stones as attitude. They were always rebels and that was Pedro, he was a rebel in his life and in his persona. Based on the family members I met when I was with him in Miami, they were all pretty conservative, and he was 180 degrees from that in just about every way. And yet, he was a likable rebel. If you were on the road, after a game, you wanted to roll with him, not even knowing where you might go to eat or where you might go after that. It was cool and easy. He was the guy you always wanted to hang with. Even if you were going to go to war, it would be more fun with Pedro. If you were under attack, it would be a lot cooler with Pedro. Even if you were getting shot at, you could look at each other and go, "What the fuck," and have a laugh. And the Stones were that. He

"The Golden Greek"

loved to hear the stories about the 1972 tour and what it was like to be around the band, because he recognized a part of himself in the Stones. That was one of the unspoken bonds Pedro and I had.

A lot of people only half-listen when you tell them a story, but not Pedro. He never did anything halfway, least of all listen. When he saw pictures of me playing football for Enterprise High School in Redding (class of '63), where I signed my yearbook picture "The Golden Greek," he laughed and then wanted to hear all about me as an athlete. He'd heard about me meeting Pierre Salinger in California, and through him landing a job working in Washington as a legislative assistant to Senator Bobby Kennedy from 1965 to 1967, and Pedro wanted to know what that was like. I was just an errand boy, a glorified page, I told him, and that made him *more* curious, not less. Sometimes I'd run things over to the Floor. I was given a pile of newspapers to read every morning, twenty-four big-city papers, and I'd have to go through every paper to see if there was anything on Bobby or the Kennedy family. I wasn't actually a speechwriter for RFK, that part has been greatly exaggerated, but I did do research for the speechwriters, Adam Walinsky and Jeff Greenfield. I'd go over to the Library of Congress to gather information to back up their arguments in speeches they were working on.

When I've told other people I was in Los Angeles at the Ambassador Hotel near Bobby the night of the California primary in 1968, they're eyes go wide, but they rarely ask many questions. Pedro always wanted to hear more. I told him how I started to walk into the kitchen area, following the crowd, and I heard sounds like someone had fired off a string of firecrackers. The photographer Bill Eppridge, who had been covering the Senator for both *Time* and *Life*, ran past me, knocking me into the door jam, yelling "9 millimeter!" My first thought was he was talking about a fisheye lens. A gun was the last thing on my mind. As I continued walking, I almost slipped on what I thought was cooking oil, but it was blood.

That night was it for me and politics. JFK was dead, Malcolm X was dead, Martin Luther King Jr. was dead, and now Bobby was dead. I flamed out at Santa Clara Law School, filling several blue books with a screed on the depraved state of the country for one exam, and then started hanging around the San Francisco music scene as much as I could. I'd go to the Fillmore with my tape recorder, a couple joints in my pocket and my camera, and I could usually bullshit my way backstage. I was working on a music book focusing on these English guys who, using our blues roots, changed our culture while changing theirs. I never really considered myself a professional photographer until Eric Clapton looked over my work one time at the Sausalito Inn in 1971. I showed up unannounced and asked if he'd like to read over an interview I'd done with him for the book. He was more interested in the pictures I'd brought with me.

"Mind if I look?" he asked politely. "Fucking hell, these are fucking great. Can we use these? Albums, song books. The writing is all right, but you should be doing this for a gig."

A month later, I told Peter Frampton what Clapton had said. He agreed.

"You've got to come to London," he said. "You can stay with us."

I took him up on his offer. Mary Lovett, Peter's first wife, would take me around to antique markets and night spots all over London. I soaked up the music and the vibe and after a couple months, I went back to San Francisco focused on being a great rock-and-roll photographer.

I'd caught the Stones on their U.S. tour in '69 and thought they were at their zenith, and then came "Exile on Main Street" and the '72 tour and with the next album it seemed they were even better. I decided I had to

Z won't say where he picked up that hat, somewhere on Haight Street
most likely, but the bomber jacket he's wearing was worn by his father,
Nick Zagaris, a waist gunner and bombardier on more than twenty Flying
Fortress (B-17) bombing runs over Hitler's Germany during World War II

DEFINITELY A STONES GUY • MICHAEL ZAGARIS

cover that tour—be *on* that tour. I was just starting out as a photographer, but thought I was hot shit, as you can only think when you're young and starting out and really don't know. I was always looking at fashion magazines for photo ideas and had a copy of English *Vogue*. I saw that Leo Lerman was the photo editor, which gave me the idea to call Jo Bergman, an assistant to Mick and the band, and pretend to be Lerman. It took me about a week to get a hold of her, through two or three different people. I finally got her on the line, and I *became* Leo Lerman, right down to the plummy British accent.

"Right. Hello, Jo. Leo Lerman here, *Vogue* magazine in London," I started off. "So listen, we'd love to do a story on the lads on this tour. We've got this great new photographer, Michael Zagaris. We're assigning him. It's going to mainly be photo driven, but we'll have some text."

"Listen, Leo," Jo said. "Thank you. We already have a photographer. It's Ethan Russell. And anything that you need for the story, we'd be glad to make available to you, but we're not adding anybody at this time."

"Right. Sorry, love," I told her. "We can't really take handouts, now can we? Maybe next tour we can work something out, but thanks for your time."

"Wait a minute, wait a minute," she said. "What's this guy's name again?"

"It's Michael Zagaris. And again, he's a younger guy but he's a great photographer."

"Well, if he can make his way up to Vancouver, we'll put him on the plane," she said. "He can shoot the show up there and the gigs in San Francisco and Los Angeles, but that's the best we can do."

Pedro loved that story because it's just what he would have done if given a chance. Can you imagine trying that now? Keith was pretty spaced out on that tour and yet they were playing fucking great, they were channeling this incredible, incredible music. On some of the nights it transcended any of the music of that time. This was not long after 1968, the nadir of the political global revolution, and three years removed from Altamont, where the Hell's Angels stabbed and beat someone to death in front of their stage. Things were much darker now. And *this* was the Stones' music in 1972.

To anybody that was really into the Stones the way I was, and the way I think Pedro was, it was much more than music. It was about a feeling.

Eric Clapton

We both recognized parts of ourselves in them. You were almost out of body when you were at those shows. I look back now, and I realize they're just people and like us, they were caught up in it, too. None of us realized it at the time. Mick was always a great showman, very theatrical, but he was *more* than that. *They* were more than that. They were what they played. What you saw on stage, that's who they fucking were. *That* was the Stones. And when I was around them, I felt like I was *in* the band. And that was *me*. It was *more* than music or attitude. It was about something that I think we all wanted to project, and Pedro fucking loved that stuff.

I remember telling Pedro one story about an off day when I was in Keith's room with Danny Seymour, who was doing sound for Robert Frank's documentary on the Stones. Freddie Sessler, who Keith described as almost a father to him, was there. When you're sitting around high, the conversation goes all over the place, but it was mainly about women and good times. At one point Mick came in for a few minutes and made some remark about, "Women, sometimes it's tough to be with them."

I laughed.

"Oh yeah, women," I said. "Like *you* have a real problem? You can have any woman you want."

He stopped and looked at me, like: *Who the fuck are you? You think it's like that?*

"Well," he said to me, "how'd *you* like to be with someone and you're in the middle of balling them, and they're looking at you like, 'Is this *it*? Is this all it is?' Because man, that's fucking *pressure*."

Pedro and I laughed over that story so many times. He loved it because he loved the Stones and loved seeing people for how they really are, not how they're built up to be.

I'll never forget the look on Pedro's face when he saw what I'd given him for his fiftieth birthday: it was a shot I'd taken at the Cow Palace in 1975. The Stones performed on a custom-built star-shaped stage, and there was a giant snake Mick would ride. Keith hadn't slept for three days.

"Hey, this is a little birthday present," I told Pedro, wanting to downplay it, but Pedro's eyes went wide.

"Z," he said, "this is going straight onto my wall at home."

Pedro was always himself. He was *real*. He never needed to be anyone else. That's something you're born with. You can't learn it from somebody. And I think that's one of the reasons we connected. It's a quality that people like Bobby Kennedy and Mick Jagger had, where

500 people could be in a ballroom talking and when that person walks in, even if they're behind you, you *feel* their presence. Pedro had that certain something. It's just who he was and he was always both curious and engaging. And he had the kind of a personality where even if you didn't agree with him, you respected him and you listened. Pedro was such a unique individual, his death hit me so hard, at first I refused to believe it. He's not going to be in my life anymore? That's wrong. There are very few people whose death hits so many so hard. There are billions of people in the world and there aren't many like that.

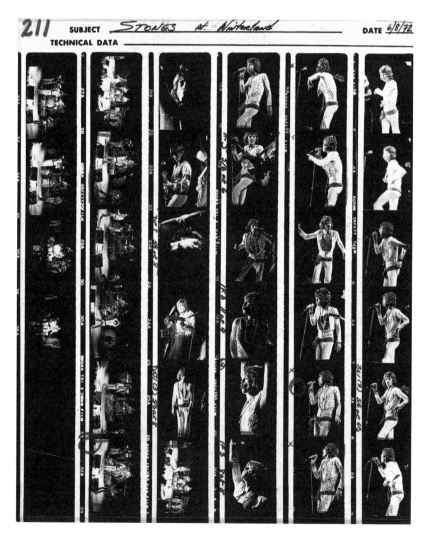

DEFINITELY A STONES GUY · MICHAEL ZAGARIS

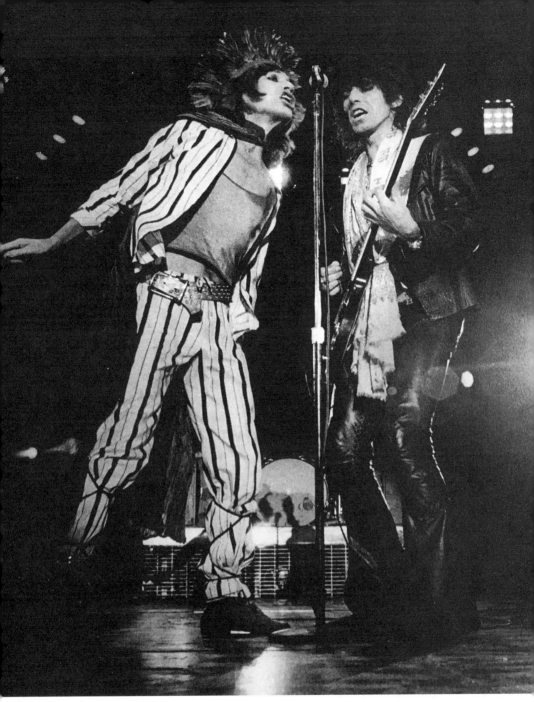

The Stones shot Pedro hung on his wall at home

Pedro and Rio with Micah Kinsler and Ken Griffey Jr. at
the Fiesta Bowl, 2014

Paul with his sons Patrick, Billy and Charlie

SHOW ME WHO YOUR FRIENDS ARE

BY PAUL BEGALA

Aside from my family and my faith, my two great passions in life are politics and sports—especially baseball. They are alike in many ways: binary events with one winner and one loser. The contest is carried out in public, and the whole world judges who is more talented; everyone knows who the winner is. They tote up the score, and one side is exultant, the other crestfallen. Afterwards, analysts pick over the entrails of statistics, seeking insight from the obscure.

Character, they say, is revealed in adversity. I think that's true. But character is also revealed in victory. A great public victory can breed arrogance; a humiliating defeat can be bracing. Baseball and politics are also team sports; no one wins alone. That's why so many politicians talk about "we" rather than "I." Barack Obama became the president with the slogan "Yes, We Can," not "Yes I Can."

Pedro Gomez knew baseball. But what he really knew was people. That means he knew politics. He was a kindred spirit: witty and kind and generous with his insights. We hit it off immediately. And, as the father of four sons who were all jocks, when the boys learned that I actually knew the legendary Pedro Gomez, well, for a brief shining moment, their Dad was cool.

For several years Pedro and I kept up an email relationship that I treasure. I would quiz him about baseball: Can the Nationals bullpen ever stabilize? Is Houston's young talent for real?

He would indulge my questions, and provide me with insights that made me look smarter than I am when I'd go to games. But what he really wanted to talk about was politics. He was an astute observer. He was also a darn good political strategist. A week after Donald Trump was inaugurated, he emailed me with this suggestion:

> During the campaign he loved to hang his cute nicknames on his opponents; "Little Marco," "Lyin' Ted," etc. Someone needs to start calling him "President One Term" and just continue to do so. It will drive him crazy.

Pedro was prescient, of course. He was convinced from the start that Trump would be a one-term wonder. Just five months into Trump's first year, Pedro saw the writing on the wall more clearly than most political pros:

> This has the same feel as when a coach/manager is going to get fired. There's just too much momentum to stop it and go backward. Feels like, even though it's not going to happen in days, weeks or even months, it just feels like there's too much momentum moving toward the same result that usually happens with a coach/manager who everyone knows is going down.

And that wasn't the only time. Here's what he wrote on August 17, 2017—sent to me while I was on the air at CNN:

> Watching now. I know there's a ton of talk about how he [Trump] is keeping his base happy and that's how he got elected. Didn't he also get elected because all Republicans voted for him? I think he's fracturing the R party and that halfway intelligent R's would never vote for him again and that would be enough for him to lose. Think about intelligent R's in Michigan, Ohio, Pa, Wisconsin who swayed the election by less than 100,000 votes. He's losing those. I

think I will actually vote for Flake here in AZ because of how he's standing up for himself.

Spot on. Trump did in fact fracture the party, driving principled Republicans like Senator Jeff Flake of Arizona to retire. And, sure enough, Trump's divisive brand of politics caused him to lose Michigan, Ohio, and Pennsylvania, as well as Arizona.

Here's another example of Pedro being able to see around corners, written to me in June 2020 when leftist protestors were marching in the streets of our major cities, protesting the death of George Floyd:

He said, "There will be retribution" when asked about protesters. Oh, how profound those words one day may wind up being toward him.

Oh, how right you were, Pedro.

Pedro had an abiding love for America, and a visceral hatred for bullies. He was at the pinnacle of his profession—a position of real power. And yet he always identified with the underdog.

Little in life is worse than a fake tough guy. This guy is at the top of the list of fake tough guys. He's the punk standing behind the biggest guys and saying things he'd never say if he was alone.

Frequently he would reason by analogy, arguing that our political divide could be analogized to the most bitter sports rivalries:

It's now Ohio State/Michigan or Yankees/Red Sox. It's, "We're right and you're wrong" for all the wrong reasons. Everyone is on separate teams now. We are, as a society, forgetting that the only uniform that matters is red, blue AND white!

Pedro followed world affairs as well. Here's an email he sent me from overseas, just an email to a friend, but written with such style and wisdom—and humor:

My wife, Sandi, and I just finished twelve days in Ireland and Northern Ireland. Truly a wonderful and magical place. I was glad to get the reminder of what Clinton did to finally bring peace to Belfast. They are still so appreciative of what he and George Mitchell did to stabilize Northern Ireland. We did a Black Cab tour where we visit the highly segregated areas on Falls Street. Amazing to see the wall separating Catholics and Protestants still in place. Our Irish driver was a wealth of information and a sage philosopher. A few of his more memorable lines:

"After what Clinton did for us, we Irish don't care one bit what Clinton did with Monica Lewinsky. He's the single-biggest reason we no longer have daily violence and deaths on our streets. Having boots-on-the-ground in Senator George Mitchell was the difference-maker."

"What Trump doesn't realize is that if America sneezes, the rest of the world catches a cold. He doesn't understand the importance America plays and how they impact everything throughout the world."

"Anybody who thinks walls help should come to Belfast and see how they do anything but. Trump should come see this wall for himself and how it never worked."

As an aside, we heard so much Christmas music while here that I had a lightning bolt hit me with an idea for a joke for Bill Maher or Jimmy Kimmel that I just know they'd love and use. They could start talking about Trump and his supremacist quotes and anecdotes and then something along these lines:

"It's Christmas and it brings about memories of such fantastic holiday hits such as 'Have Yourself a Merry Little Christmas,' 'Jingle Bells' and 'Silent Night.' It got me to thinking about Trump's all-time favorite Christmas song for obvious reasons: 'I'm Dreaming of a White Christmas.'

Sandi broke out laughing. Hope you liked it, as well. Hope all is well, amigo.

His Cuban heritage, and his family's flight to freedom, informed Pedro's political philosophy, causing him to send me one heartfelt email about Trump's immigration policy that was especially personal:

Geezus, if this was the case in the 1960s, there isn't a single Cuban family that would have been allowed in, and look at what we have done as a community. And it's never ever the first family that winds up doing the most, it's the children....Almost every one of the children of Cuban refugees, those that are my age range, are major contributors. Our parents came just wanting the chance and fighting every day. None came in able to speak a word of English. 45 does not get it at all.

Pedro would usually sign his emails by referring to me as his amigo. In one email, he told me:

"My Cuban grandmother always told me this saying: 'Show me who your friends are, and I'll show you who you are.'"

I hope she was right, because I am honored to say Pedro Gomez was my friend, and I am a better person for having known him. Thanks, amigo.

'GOTTA LOVE THE SHOOTERS'

BY BRAD MANGIN

When writers cover a baseball game, they are nestled upstairs in air-conditioned press boxes with padded seats, clean bathrooms and free hot dogs. Must be nice. Photographers are down on the field where we are exposed to unpredictable weather, batted balls and drunken fans. The divide is real between the scribes and the shooters, but Pedro was one of the few who crashed through that barrier and always treated photographers at the ballpark with the utmost respect. He realized some of the best characters on the field just happened to have a camera in their hands and if you came up with a shot that wowed him, no one raved with more conviction and enthusiasm. Pedro loved photographers, and we loved him back.

I first encountered Pedro in the early 1990s when he started covering the Oakland A's for the *San Jose Mercury News*. The way everyone gravitated toward him, I could tell he was one of the cool kids, with his distinctly warm personality and infectious smile. Watching him on the field and in the dugout before games, the way he related to people, no matter how big of a star they were—or weren't—was amazing to this shy photographer. He was so comfortable in his element and never afraid to

ask a question or give manager Tony La Russa a hard time.

"To-neeee!"

Around this time, I had become the official Christmas card photographer for the Bud Geracie family. Bud is an old baseball scribe who has spent much of his career as *Mercury News* sports editor. For several years, I drove out to Bud's house and photographed his young son, Nick, in front of the Christmas tree while Bud paced and smoked cigarettes. In December 1995, Bud drafted me for another job: shooting a family photo of his good friend Pedro Gomez, his wife, Sandi, and their first child, Rio, who was just fourteen months old. We met in a park close to Monte Vista High School in Danville, where they lived, and got some nice family pictures. It was special to shoot their first Christmas card as a family, and from then on, like so many others, I considered Pedro a close friend.

Once Pedro moved to the *Arizona Republic* and then ESPN, I didn't see him as often at the ballpark, but it always was a special occasion when I did. It meant I was at a big game. An All-Star Game. A World Series game. Then came the Barry Bonds watch, and Pedro was a main

February 2006: Barry dresses up as Paula Abdul for "Giants Idol"

man on the beat. That was one of the great things about it. Pedro was back in town, and I got to see him all the time. I covered the Bonds home run chase in 2006 and 2007 extensively for *Sports Illustrated*. Pedro was extremely busy but never too busy to say hello or roll his eyes when I saw him on the field during batting practice.

In spring training, Pedro was a fixture at many of our Scottsdale gatherings, especially when we were honoring the birthday of legendary Oakland A's team photographer Michael Zagaris at the Italian Grotto in Old Town, which sadly is gone forever. In 2008, Pedro showed up

Brad and Garry at the Grotto

loud and proud, wearing a Cuban baseball jersey from the 2006 World Baseball Classic. Outfitted in bright white with red and blue trim, Pedro was hard to miss telling stories with a glass of red wine in his hand. The stories got louder and louder as the night progressed, especially when Grotto owner Garry Horowitz instigated his usual brand of trouble.

We all knew about Pedro's Cuban heritage and his proud family history, but only one photographer accompanied Pedro to his homeland in March 1999 when he made his first trip to Cuba. That was Dave Cruz of the *Arizona Republic*. Pedro was employed at the newspaper at the time, and this was an amazing opportunity to travel as a journalist to cover a baseball game between the Baltimore Orioles and the Cuban National Team.

"Pedro's first mission was to find the home where his father grew up in Cuba," Cruz said. "Pedro did not know what to expect when and if he could find the house. We found the house and found old family friends that remembered his father. They invited us inside and offered us something to drink. We both said, 'Yes, please.' Two boys ran out of the backdoor of the house. One went climbing a lemon tree to make some fresh lemonade while the other went to a neighbor's house to borrow some sugar. We had no idea that the family had offered us something that they did not have for themselves. We were so grateful to the family for taking in two strangers that just walked up to their home."

At a local night club, with just one light bulb and some candles, Pedro and Dave ordered rum and Coke. "A few minutes later, we were both served our own bottle of rum, two bottles of Coke and a tray of broken ice," Dave remembers. "We looked at each other and started laughing, 'Now, that's a drink!' We enjoyed the rest of the evening with our new friends, sharing baseball stories and eating and drinking. There was a man in his 70s having the time of his life. He was dancing the night away with all the pretty women in the club."

The bill for the eight people at Pedro's table added up to $12 U.S. at a time when Cubans were making the equivalent of $10 a month, working sixty to eighty hours per week.

"Without hesitation, Pedro pulled out his wallet, placed a twenty-dollar bill on the tray and told the server, 'Please keep the change,'" Dave remembers. "You should have heard the gasp from everyone at the table. 'What do you mean keep the change? Do you know how hard we have to work to make eight U.S. dollars?' Pedro right away opened his wallet and offered more money. They all refused to take it. That evening was the only time in my life I felt we were the richest men in the world. It was like Bill Gates giving out $10,000 and not blinking an eye. I'll never forget that moment with Pedro."

In 2012, I fell in love with my iPhone 4s. The first day of spring training in Scottsdale, I began shooting pictures and turning them into Instagram posts. By the time the Giants won the World Series in Detroit, I had a set of pictures that would become a book, entitled *Instant Baseball: The Baseball Instagrams of Brad Mangin*. The first person I turned to for a foreword? Pedro. It was such a thrill having Pedro involved with this project. He was so supportive of the book and everything I was doing. After he saw an early copy of the book in March 2013, he texted me, "Man, I'm not sure you're even going to take my calls in the near future. I *USED* to know Brad Mangin."

Right around this time, I got a call late at night from Pedro. It was loud on the other end, and I could barely hear him. All I could make out was Pedro

Pedro's favorite picture of Art Howe

'GOTTA LOVE THE SHOOTERS' • BRAD MANGIN

screaming: "Brad!" He was in New York at Elaine's, an epic establishment. It was 1 a.m. in New York, and he was hanging out with my old boss and friend, the legendary photographer Neil Leifer. Knowing Pedro, in the time it took him to order another round, he'd have talked to Neil about his iconic shot of Ali looming over Sonny Liston in 1965, about selling pictures to *Sports Illustrated* as a sixteen-year-old kid, and about photographing Ronald Reagan, Fidel Castro and Charles Manson. When Pedro discovered Neil knew me, he figured they had to call me. Of course, they did. "Brad! I'm with Neil Leifer!" Pedro kept screaming. It was hysterical. Knowing Pedro and Neil were thinking of me at Elaine's meant everything to me.

Working on this book as picture editor, reading how important Pedro was to so many people in baseball, it seems like no one man could have made so strong an impression on so many different people. Then you start talking to photographers and you're blown away all over again.

"He was a genuine soul who I treasured," said my great friend Elsa Garrison, who has covered big-time sports all over the world for Getty Images for more than twenty years. "I knew it was an important game when I saw him on the warning track during batting practice. Always happy. I could be having the worst day, and his infectious laughter would brighten my day. I never saw him sad or upset. He never had a bad day. I was insanely jealous of it. He was a gem."

Scott Clarke is one of my oldest and best friends in the business. He has been a senior event photographer for ESPN for more than thirty years and worked with Pedro countless times. "Sometimes in life," Scott said, "you are lucky to cross paths with people that are so kind, so generous, so happy to just be alive and doing what they are born to do. I was lucky to have crossed paths with Pedro Gomez, a baseball poet, the kindest man you could hope to know. He had a thousand best friends. When it was just the two of you, you were one of those thousand. The world was a better place with him in it, far better. This hurts, and it hurts more because I was lucky enough to know him."

In the summer of 2019, I was assigned to photograph the All-Star Game in Cleveland for *Sports Illustrated*. After my run of seventeen straight World Series ended in 2016, I had not covered a big event until this one. When I showed up early at Progressive Field on Monday afternoon before the team workouts and Home Run Derby, I felt like the oldest person in the house. I went into the photo workroom and didn't

Darren and Dusty

know anyone. I was thinking the game had passed me by. I felt all alone with no one to talk to. Until I found Pedro.

In the service corridor near the clubhouses was a tiny closet where ESPN had set up a makeshift studio to tape player interviews. This was Pedro's home for the next two days, and it became a safe place for me to visit. I can't tell you how comforting it was to see an old friend while I was practically having an anxiety attack.

The highlight of our talks in Cleveland, as they had been over the years, was of Pedro's son Rio and his pitching exploits. Funny how things come full circle. The fourteen-month-old I photographed in 1995 was now a minor-league pitcher in the Boston Red Sox system and having a terrific season throwing strikes, missing bats and getting outs. Pedro was losing his mind with excitement.

Since the 2020 baseball season was a Covid nightmare, and I didn't shoot the World Series, I never saw Pedro after Cleveland. His loss is crushing to so many people for so many reasons. He has an amazing family that he never stopped talking about. And then there were his thousand best friends. How Pedro was able to keep track of everyone without a scorecard, I will never know. We lost one of the all-time greats. Pedro could do it all, even hang with the photographers. "Gotta love the shooters," Pedro once texted me. And the shooters loved *you,* Pedro.

THOSE YEARLY
GLIMPSES OF THE
GOMEZ FAMILY

BY JEREMY SCHAAP

ESPN is a big company, with thousands of employees. Most of us work regularly at our headquarters in Connecticut—but we have colleagues who live all over the country, all over the world, working in sales, in marketing, in production, as journalists and commentators. At an event like the Super Bowl or the World Cup, we might all come together, scores or hundreds of us, but otherwise you might cross paths only occasionally, rarely, with fellow employees outside your immediate group who don't work in Bristol.

If you're a host or a reporter, you will speak frequently, for broadcast, with colleagues who are in other locations, in studio, out in the field, via satellite, Skype, Zoom—but you might never spend time with them off the air. It is a strange dynamic—and yet we are all accustomed to it, those of us who do it for a living and anyone who watches TV.

It's hard to put a finger on it, but when you have that kind of relationship with a colleague—a relationship that consists mostly of your interactions on TV—you develop a sense of each other. Something is heightened, maybe even distorted, in those moments, when you are both working, cognizant not only of what you are saying but how you are saying it, and how you appear saying it, but you come to have an appreciation of each other's strengths, weaknesses, self-confidence, knowledge, wisdom, etcetera. Sometimes the chemistry is good, sometimes not so good—often for no discernible reason.

Pedro Gomez and I never hung out. I'm not sure we ever shared a meal, or a drink, not one-on-one anyway. I started at ESPN in 1993, and by the time Pedro was hired in April 2003, I was no longer covering very many baseball games, as I once had, which would have presented opportunities for us to work closely together. We probably spent more time talking to each other on live TV, via satellite, than in person. Yet Pedro is someone I felt I knew.

When I heard the awful news that Pedro had died, the first thing I thought about were the Christmas cards. They arrived unfailingly every year. The Gomez family Christmas cards. I came to expect them, and to look forward to them. They stood out, because they were from a colleague with whom I hadn't spent much time. But more than that, they stood out, too, because they so strikingly conveyed what I perceived as real love and affection. All of it came bursting forth with such authenticity—no forced smiles, none of the winking "Here we go again" attitude we sometimes see in this ritual. Pedro so clearly relishing the moment, being photographed with his wife and kids, in his glory. And each year, when the card arrived in December, I would think, *this is great, and meaningful. Pedro is sharing his love of family, and showing us what family means to him.*

I suspect Pedro's family must send out hundreds of cards—if the Schaaps were on the list. But somehow that simple gesture always struck me as significant. It suggests a desire to create and maintain a connection beyond the professional. It emphasizes the personal—and above all else it spoke to Pedro's pride in his family.

Look, I know it's easy to attach too much meaning to a holiday card. Of course. For most people, it's just something that's done every year, the list of intended recipients rarely fluctuating, it's merely a courtesy, a nice one, but not much more than that. But I choose, especially now, to think that with Pedro it went beyond that. Maybe that's irrational, but I don't think so. Sometimes the smallest gestures are significant, and not small, at all.

To me, it's all of a piece with what I knew about Pedro, as a man, as a father, as a colleague, as a journalist. You could feel, without even trying, what made Pedro tick. The compassion. The generosity of spirit. The principles. Pedro wasn't all about Pedro. That came through in his work, which was imbued with such a humane touch.

That was true whether he was chasing history with Barry Bonds—a tough assignment that he negotiated so well—or on a baseball trip to Cuba, his ancestral home. Pedro's uncommon touch shined especially for me on one story in particular, the story he reported for ESPN's newsmagazine show E60 on the life and death of the Miami Marlins' pitcher José Fernández.

Fernández and two other men died in a boat crash in 2016 in Miami. Fernández was driving the boat—and at the time he had cocaine in his system. Pedro delivered a story that encompassed the full scope of the tragedy, speaking with Jose's survivors, and not shying away from the reality of what happened and why. It was fair and compassionate and true. To achieve that, it takes skill—but it also takes heart. Pedro had plenty of both.

By the time Pedro had died, on Super Bowl Sunday, we had cleared out our 2020 Christmas cards. They'd been taken down from the wall they'd been taped to and discarded. Now, of course, I wish we had held on to the card from the Gomezes. As much as I've tried, I still haven't quite fully articulated why that card always seemed so special, and NOT simply de rigueur. I don't think I am attaching these feelings to that piece of cardboard only now, in the aftermath of losing Pedro. No, searching my feelings, that really is how I always felt about those cards, and about Pedro, and I know I am not unique, that there must be so many who feel the same way, who were touched by Pedro, and all the things that made him the man he was.

At some level, I think we both expected that at some point we would spend some time together, maybe just sharing a beer, or a meal, some night after a game, or on one of those off days during a series. That would have been fun. After talking baseball, and shop, I would have wanted to know how he did it, how he managed to spread so much love, and to make so many friends.

After he died, I said on the air that I had never heard anyone say a bad word about Pedro. That can't be said—not with total honesty—about too many people in this business, which is so competitive. But in Pedro's case, it is completely true. Pedro was beloved—and respected—by all who knew him. Which is almost as rare as an unassisted triple play.

I hope we still receive those Christmas cards. It won't be the same, of course, but I suspect Pedro would want everyone to be able to open those envelopes and see his family, and to be reminded of all that he has left behind.

Rio Gomez

THE BIG QUESTION

BY JEFF PASSAN

Every day, around the same time, concentric semicircles would start forming in the San Francisco Giants' dugout. I found myself on the outside by design, content not to jostle with the troglodytes inside who wielded their television cameras like unregistered weapons. I stood in back with my friend Dave, and I would bite my tongue to stifle the laughter as the person everyone was there to see started to speak.

It's almost impossible to convey the size of Bruce Bochy's head without actually basking in its glory. Bochy was in his first year as manager of the Giants, and though he would later go on to win three World Series and secure himself an eventual spot in the Hall of Fame, at that point in his career he was the guy whose neck was straining from under the weight of his melon. And between the cartoonish size of it, and his voice, which sounded like it had been bathed in molasses, all rich and slow like, I'm sorry, but I couldn't help myself. It didn't matter what Bochy was talking about—his starting pitcher that day, the game the night before or, typically, Barry Bonds, who was the real reason I was there. I would laugh, because in 2007, I was a twenty-six-year-old who missed his pregnant wife and just wanted a little levity.

I should've swallowed the excuses and shoved my way to the front and asked questions, though the important ones always managed to escape the lips of the same person, who made sure he was inside that first ring. I knew Pedro Gomez a little and respected him a lot. Even though he'd sold out and gone to TV, to ESPN, to this maddening assignment that necessitated him following Bonds around the country for years, he was a newspaperman at heart, a grinder, someone who knows a deadline doesn't begin and end when a camera light turns on and off.

His job wasn't a job as much as it was an identity, "ESPN" forever an appendage on his name, like Jr. or Esq.: "Pedro Gomez, ESPN." That's how I saw him, and that's how the world saw him, and little did I understand at the time just how familiar that would become to me, how bits and pieces of Pedro's life always would pop up in mine, how at the time I took for granted what his job really was, which was not to chronicle the same-shit-every-day ruminations of a soon-to-be home run king but to get back home and hug his wife and kids.

◆ ◆ ◆

This thing we do, me and Pedro and everyone else gifted the opportunity to clack away at a keyboard and empty a thousand words at a time: It's the best. I never wanted anything else. Just me, a story and an empty screen to fill. It is challenging and fulfilling and maddening and edifying. It has taken me to places I'd never have been, tested me in ways I'd never have imagined possible, broken me, beaten me, lifted me, sustained me. It's so deeply ingrained in me that I spent ninety-six words here anthropomorphizing a job.

And that's how it has to be, right? Right? I tell myself that, because it's what I see in everyone who's great. I see them there, in the front of the semicircle, not just present but a presence. I see an assignment that lasts years, and you do it, because it's the job. I see afternoons at the playground spent on the phone, texting, missing a smile, or maybe not there at all. I see late nights. I see dark nights. I see cognitive dissonance. I see years melting away and boys growing and neon lights that flicker with a question: Is it really the best?

I never answer.

I saw what it did to Pedro, how it salted that resplendent dark mane, and if that was the worst of its damage, it's clear he won. He figured out how to be a father, a husband, enough for both. How to play catch. How to tell a bedtime story. How to dance. How to laugh. How to be there. How to balance.

I want to believe I can have everything, a consideration that exists somewhere between optimism and hubris, though I lean toward the former. Because I saw it. Pedro had it all.

◆ ◆ ◆

Every night I'm on the road, my older son calls me before he goes to bed. His voice is in that awkward stage, between a boy's and a man's, cracking involuntarily and much to my amusement. I ask about his day. He mumbles that it was fine. I tell him about mine. He humors me and listens. I ask about his brother—whether he's doing those push-ups and sit-ups we've been working on. He gives me status updates. I tell him I love him. He says he loves me, too.

The conversations don't last long. They don't need to. There will come the days when we can talk for hours on end, when that time manifests itself, when our divergent paths merge, our problems are the same, our experiences match. When I go to him for advice because he has seen things I never did and father-son relationships need not be one-directional. When he understands why Pedro dying hit me so hard.

That confused him. I didn't talk about Pedro much. He didn't realize why I revered Pedro. Every now and then I mentioned him. There was that one time I sent Pedro video of my son pitching, and he wrote back with a detailed breakdown of everything he saw, including comments from Rio, and that earned me a few dad points. A real baseball player, looking at him and treating him like a peer.

My son is at that age where he's starting to understand the gradients of friendship—that not everyone can be a best friend and those who do exist on the periphery, flit in and out of life, can be loved just the same. That there are people you may see once a year for a meal or a drink, just a few hours, and you tell stories and laugh and reminisce and hope the night creates a new memory or two so the next time you see one another, 300-odd days later, it's not just the same stale tales. Though even if it is, they never do seem to get old.

Someday he'll know someone like Pedro, who isn't your age but feels like a brother, who is a phase ahead in life but cares enough to always ask how the present one is treating you, whose little kindnesses added up to feel like something big. I kept hearing that from friends the night he died. He was just ... such a good guy. He was just ... so cool.

That latter one feels out of reach. But being a good guy? Listening?

Helping? Caring? Pedro modeled it for Rio, and I'm trying to model it for my son, who's thirteen, the same age Rio was when I first got to know Pedro.

Turns out my boy is a pitcher, too. It's funny to see—him growing, getting stronger, throwing a ball harder than I ever have. I remember the first time Pedro talked to me about Rio. "He's got a chance," Pedro said, and all those years spent around scouts had given him a sense of just how good he was. I'm not sure how good my son's going to be, but I wish I had Pedro to ask.

Instead, I've got another person I can. I got a text from Rio in March asking whether Minor League Baseball was going to delay its season. I made a couple calls, gave him the answer he was seeking and said I'd be in touch. I'm going to be, too, and not just rooting for him as he makes his way to the major leagues.

The big question isn't going away. It's omnipresent, lingering, challenging, vital. And one day, when I'm feeling it, really feeling it, that's when I'll call Rio and ask him to tell a story about his dad. And just like I did from the back of the pack all those days in San Francisco, I'll laugh.

Phil Garner

DON'T BE AFRAID TO GO OUT ON A LIMB

BY BOB MELVIN

I've been trying to put into words what it was that set Pedro apart. He wasn't the only baseball reporter you ever talked to who was so genuine and real, he made you feel like every conversation with him was special. He wasn't the only one to give you his full attention, totally engaged in what you were talking about, no matter who might walk by at a given moment. He wasn't the only one with deep knowledge of the game and decades of experience on the beat to give his insights authority and color. What Pedro did was put all that together with a sense that he cared deeply about you as a person. He cared and he wanted to understand what you went through. He was always stretching to have a little more empathy and a little more perspective on the unique pressures of the job.

I remember Pedro's reaction when I told him a story about a conversation I had years ago with Phil Garner about managing. This was in 1999, which turned out to be the last of his eight-year run as manager in Milwaukee, and I was his bench coach.

"You're never going to feel like your players or coaches or anybody takes a loss as hard as you do," Gar told me. "It's just impossible for them to realize until they actually manage."

No truer words were spoken, but at the time I couldn't see that.

"Gar, I die for you every game," I told him. "I die for us."

"I know that," he said. "In that respect you do, but you'll see."

I didn't know then that one day I would be a big-league manager, but for some reason Gar did. What's that Gordon Gekko line from *Wall Street*? "Old Russian proverb—'a fisherman always sees another fisherman from afar.'" Gar saw that I had the qualities for the job, which as he put it were: "good evaluation skills and relating well to players."

Fast forward four years, I get the job managing in Seattle, and we open the season in Oakland and drop two straight to the A's. Boy those words from Gar just rang so true in my ears! I'm sitting there in my room—I couldn't have told you what was on the TV—just playing back the game in my head, over and over. What could I have done differently? Should I have started this guy running on that 3-2 count? Phil Garner had it right.

When I told Pedro that story, his eyes just kind of bugged out of his head, he was so engaged, really trying to grasp it. I think that conversation captured something important about Pedro. You could tell just by the way he was listening to me that he wanted to understood as well as he possibly could.

Pedro just loved baseball. He saw it from a fan's perspective and saw it from the perspective of someone in the game and understood the nuances. He certainly wrote it that way, which was so much more personal and personable than just writing down the facts and then critiquing things. There was a special way he intimated the game that I think connected him to fans and whoever read or watched his stuff.

You knew Pedro was genuine because he would follow along with you, no matter what the subject. If you wanted to talk restaurants, great places to go for local color, he could take that subject and run with it—for hours, if there was time. He loved talking about his family, but he was just as focused if you talked to him about yours.

I remember talking to him about my daughter Alexi when she was diagnosed with Type 1 diabetes in 2003 when she was fourteen. He brought it up and we talked about how cool it was that she could raise awareness, for example as the honoree at the Juvenile Diabetes

Research Foundation gala in Phoenix in January 2009. He told me he thought she could be a big hit in the Type 1 community. He turned out to be right about that, by the way. I'm so proud of her, she's also an actor and writer and her voice appears in two of the *Star Wars* movies. When people reach out about your family, certainly your daughter, and you can tell how genuine the interest is, that just makes you a little bit closer.

Pedro was never afraid to go out on a limb. To me, I'm happy to be part of this book to make the point that we need to remember Pedro's example, which I'd sum up as: Don't be afraid to show some emotion and certainly don't be afraid to be yourself. It's important that you really have a passion for what you're doing. Pedro always looked like what he was doing was his favorite thing in the world to do. And it certainly was. So don't be afraid to show some passion and some compassion for people. Pedro was very compassionate, you could feel that as well. It's tough to emulate what he did or really even explain it, but it hits you in the heart.

Be yourself. Remember who you are. That should be easy, but often it's anything but. You lose sight of what matters most. You're always trying to keep your job and you're worried about what somebody thinks. I understand that, and there are times in this job when I've fallen into that. But you're never going to be your best unless you're authentic. Pedro was definitely authentic, which is why I think so many baseball people have reacted to his death the way we have. You felt about Pedro the way you did some of the great players in the game we've lost. It's a difficult task for a writer to get that kind of emotion and response from guys in the game, even though he didn't play, but they had the same kind of feeling for him as if he actually did. He was one of us.

Scott, Pedro and Greg Papa

Scott and Bob Melvin

WHAT IT WAS REALLY LIKE ON THE ROAD

BY SCOTT OSTLER

Let me tell you about the night Pedro Gomez and his crew scared the shit out of me. It was the 1992 ALCS, A's versus Blue Jays, so the A's beat writers and Bay Area columnists all jetted to Toronto. I had been at the *Chronicle* for about a year, up from Los Angeles, but this was my first road hang with the Bay Area gang.

It's one thing to know other writers from home games, but it's on the road where you really get to know people. I still felt kind of like the new guy in school, a bit of the outsider. First night in Toronto, everyone's at the same hotel, most of the crew winds up in the bar. I guess the library was closed. A few drinks in, I hear someone say quietly, "Let's go upstairs and do it." "Oh, you brought the stuff?" "We got it. It's on."

They beckon me to come along. I'm thinking: *OK, someone's got weed. Possession of weed is probably a major felony in Toronto, but why be a wuss?*

We go to one guy's room. There are about ten of us, including Pedro, Ray Ratto, Bruce Jenkins, Bud Geracie. Big crowd, little room. Air of tension, or was that just me?

"Get the stuff out, man, let's go," someone says.

One of the fellows goes to the closet, gets out a gym bag, and begins unloading the goods. He tosses each of us a golf-ball-sized ball of aluminum foil. My thought: *Black-tar heroin. What the hell else could it be? Free-base product of some kind, perhaps?*

I knew these guys liked to have fun, share a laugh or two, drink a beer, but holy shit. The fellas back in L.A. enjoyed their weed, and maybe some blow, but I guess I'm in the big leagues now. Well hell, nothing to do but see what goes down, and make a plan to sneak out the door, if necessary.

Not necessary. I have been invited to a game these guy play on the road. It's a weird offshoot version of H-O-R-S-E. The tinfoil ball is your basketball. When it's your turn, you place a hotel-room trash can anywhere in the room, and you declare your shot.

Bank shot off the window and couch cushion. You get to try it first, then everyone else gets their turn, amidst nonstop hooting and hollering and fake-announcer commentating. I mean nonstop.

Ratto: Here's Bud Geracie, who is a freelance urinal-cake tester in his spare time and an avid competitor in the Soap Box Derby.

Just howlingly funny stuff. Incredibly stupid and crude. Without doubt the least-mature activity in which I have taken part as an adult, and that's saying a lot. It was also a window to the Bay Area writers' collective soul.

They had a brotherhood going on, you better not take yourself or life too seriously. And in their spare time, they did some quality writing.

Pedro? He wasn't the leader that night, that would be Ratto, but everyone contributed, and I remember Pedro just having a better time than anyone else, laughing 'til he cried. Pedro, I would learn, wasn't the loudest of the crew, but he was not quiet. He always had something to contribute, fun or serious, and he always had the best laugh, just a hearty, head-back roar. When it came to hairline, laugh and smile, Pedro jumped the freakin' line. Cheater.

The press box was a more fun place back then, before everyone was nonstop consumed with tweeting and beating killer online deadlines. There was a ton of conversation and commentary and camaraderie, a lot of sarcasm and fun and laughing. Of all the crews I ran into back then, the Bay Area guys had the most fun. And Pedro was so super-sharp, so funny and on it, but never trying to dominate, kind of like a good point guard, getting everyone involved. He left the Bay not long after that, so I didn't get to know him as well as I would have liked to, but when I read all the stories about the acts of simple kindness that were his MO, I was not surprised.

When I would run into him through the years, he always greeted me like an old pal, and it felt genuine. He wanted to hear about how you were doing. Good listener, yes.

Also: One thing I appreciated about Pedro was his name. I know his folks were from Cuba, but to me Pedro Gomez was the most Mexican name I could imagine. I grew up in SoCal and I love the Latino culture. My high school girlfriend was pure Mexican. I have felt sad for Mexican Americans I know who try to pass as Spanish, as if that was an upgrade. Pedro Gomez? That was like: Wear your heritage proudly, hombre.

I remember Pedro telling me when he and his wife were pregnant that they were going to name their son Rio. I thought, Damn, this kid's going to be a rock star. Sure enough.

I ran into Pedro frequently when he was on the Barry Bonds home-run-record beat for ESPN. That was the strangest assignment any sports journalist ever got. It was like being a star reporter who also gets to clean the press box toilets. We're a bitchy and whiny lot, we sporting scribes, but that wasn't Pedro's style. He treated that Bonds beat like it was a cool gig. I'm not sure if many of us would have survived a week shadowing Captain Cantankerous, but Pedro pulled it off beautifully, and professionally, to the surprise of zerobody.

With his intelligence, sense of humor, and awareness of humanity, Pedro brought journalistic integrity and dignity to what easily could have been a clown show. Surely he taught Barry a thing or two about being a human being.

Reflecting back, I can see how Pedro was such an integral part of that Bay Area sportswriting scene (and it wasn't just guys—Joan Ryan, Ann Killion, Gwen Knapp). Such distinctive voices and personalities. Welcoming, but you had to bring something to the party, and Pedro brought the laughs, the personality, the smile, and so much more. I just wish he would have tipped me off about the goddamned tinfoil balls.

The King flanked by David Cone and Reggie Jackson (yes, that's Gay Talese in the background)

THE GOMEZ GLIDE

BY GEORGE A. KING III

Nobody hits with the infield in their entire life. Not Barry Bonds, Pete Rose, Mike Trout or Derek Jeter. From the outside looking in that quartet seemingly did, but that is what the public saw, not how it is inside the velvet rope. They made a very difficult game to play appear alarmingly easy.

Ditto Tom Brady, Joe Namath and Paul Hornung. Who wouldn't want their lives? Michael Jordan, Magic Johnson, Kareem Abdul-Jabbar or Muhammad Ali? Think it was difficult being Walt Frazier in New York City when he was driving the Knicks train to two NBA titles and answering to Clyde? Mickey Mantle and Joe DiMaggio had Manhattan in their palms.

Nor was the world that easy for Pedro Gomez, sportswriter turned ESPN television personality. However, Gomez didn't so much walk through the globe covering events as he glided, which made it appear the infielders were playing on the grass. Armed with an infectious smile highlighted by piano-white teeth that played off dark eyebrows he said weren't painted and bouncing off a full head of gray moss, Gomez made athletes, executives and anybody else he came in contact with instantly comfortable.

You watched Gomez work a clubhouse and it was impossible to see even a sliver of discontent in his world. Of course, there had to be, but Gomez enjoyed everything about his job. I never asked him what he didn't like about a gig that at times was seemingly designed to eat the young and middle-aged and send dinosaurs running for Social Security, Happy Hours that start at 3 p.m. and early-bird dining with the blue-hair set. Outside of taking him away from his family, I would have been shocked if Gomez whined about the red-eye flights, cancelled flights, delayed flights, bad games that took four hours to finish, rain delays and boorish behavior by players.

Many knew Gomez longer and better than I and they spoke glowingly of him in the aftermath of his sudden death in his Arizona kitchen at age fifty-eight. A lot of the compliments centered on Gomez's love for his family. Love that the family returned hours after it lost its leader. "Pedro was far more than a media personality. He was a dad, a loving husband, loyal friend, coach and mentor. He was our everything and his kids' biggest believer," the family statement read.

I didn't know Gomez's wife, Sandi, daughter, Sierra, or sons Rio and Dante, but in the profession that isn't unusual. What I know of Gomez's family is that Rio is a left-handed pitcher in the Red Sox minor-league system. Of course Gomez was a proud father, because what dad wouldn't have been? And from those closer to Gomez than me he was just as proud of Dante, Sierra and Sandi.

On February 26, 2018 I texted Gomez and asked him if he was coming to Florida for spring training, and he said yes. "Not to work but for this." The words were typed under a picture of a Red Sox jersey hanging in a locker. The crisp red shirt had GOMEZ above 74 in white letters and numbers.

How many times have you heard a parent complain that their son or daughter wasn't getting a fair shake by a coach or manager? Or how good their offspring is? Gomez was sure proud of his son, but those words were ones I never heard. Instead, he talked about Rio's development, which took a step up on June 5, 2019. In a text string about how each of us were doing, Gomez wrote, "Good here. The kid got promoted to High A recently."

It read as if you were getting change from the convenience store clerk for a newspaper and a bottle of water. Having made his living covering baseball for thirty-five years, Gomez knew the road was going to be a long one for Rio, who was selected in the thirty-sixth round of the 2017 draft out of the University of Arizona. In 2012 MLB shortened its draft from fifty rounds to forty. The dreams of most late draft picks end on the backroads of minor-league baseball.

Like all minor-leaguers in 2020, Rio didn't pitch an inning, due to Covid-19. He is twenty-six and a reliever who held Single-A left-handed hitters to a .203 batting average and .653 OPS in 2019. So, the longshot is still in the fight, which means wherever Gomez is he is smiling.

Gomez was well known due to the ESPN gig but nothing was too trite for him. In the middle of October, 2018, a text surfaced on the phone screen. "Interested in a possible note? Not a high note by any means. Just a little filler if you ever need. Look who is still playing in the Mexican League at forty-five." It was none other than Ruben Rivera, once the Yankees' top prospect in the mid-'90s who hadn't played in the big leagues since 2003 with the Giants and never came close to reaching what turned out to be unrealistic expectations.

Gomez's popularity with players, coaches and managers is legendary. However, when the hammer was required, he had no problem swinging it. In January when Curt Schilling asked the Hall of Fame to remove his name from next year's ballot, and reached into a tired bag of gripes about sportswriters, I texted Gomez to remind him of his column in the *Arizona Republic* the morning of Game 7 of the 2001 World Series. Gomez that day called Schilling "something of a con man who was bent on polishing his image through whatever means possible." Twenty years later his description of Schilling stands true.

Gomez left a big hole in the business. In the hours after his death, he was celebrated for a life well lived, for his professionalism and for being someone who could be trusted. We all lose friends, because that is the cycle of life. In the business it is a little different because your neighbor, brother, mother, father, sister or most folks who die aren't remembered on ESPN, the back page of the *New York Post*, the *Dallas Morning News,* the *Boston Globe* or the *Delaware County Times* outside of Philadelphia. Gomez, *New York Post* photographer Anthony Causi, Dallas baseball writer Gerry Fraley, Boston baseball columnist Nick Cafardo and Phillies beat writer Bill Brown were and it was different. Dying has a rhythm and it doesn't usually include seeing a friend in a big spotlight.

From that spotlight it was hard to understand that Gomez wasn't going to glide into a clubhouse wearing a smile, a jacket and a tie when the temperature in Texas was in triple digits. Others have written about Gomez for this project and their interactions with him. Ours was a friendship that rose out of the weird but amazingly rewarding business of writing about baseball.

When 2-1 games didn't last three hours and forty minutes, I offered out-of-town writers a ride from Yankee Stadium to their Manhattan hotels. Most of the rides consisted of small talk and what song was on WFUV, Fordham University's radio station, but Gomez was looking forward to the next game, the pitching matchup, what was wrong with so-and-so.

The same would be in play when we ran into each other in road cities. A beer at The Lodge in Chicago was something I had aged out of years ago when Gomez suggested a visit to Division and Rush. It led to one of those wonderful saloon nights that ended far too early in a town that stays up very late.

Yankees third base coach Phil Nevin appreciated Gomez interacting with his son, who was in the Rockies' minor-league system before being dealt to the Orioles. "He would go over to Tyler and just talk," Nevin recalled. "He liked talking to the young prospects just about the game or life. It was kind of cool."

Assigned to cover the Tampa Rays against the Cuban National Team in Cuba in 2016, Gomez spread the ashes of his father and brother in his dad's native land. Most of Gomez's reports for ESPN were done long after the stadiums had emptied either late at night or early the next morning and delivered with the same smile and a mountain of enthusiasm. Talking that day about releasing his father's and brother's ashes Gomez's voice cracked several times. It was the only time I didn't see Gomez smile.

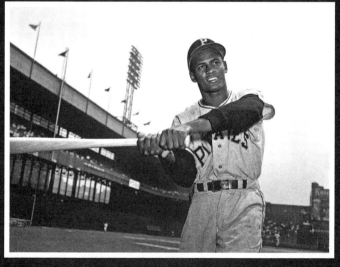

Young Roberto Clemente at the Polo Grounds

HIS EYES LIT UP

BY TERRY FRANCONA

I grew up just north of Pittsburgh in the borough of New Brighton, Pennsylvania, so Roberto Clemente was one of my favorite players. People talk about baseball lifers, well how is this for a distinction? I've been paid by baseball since I was a newborn baby. My dad had a hot streak playing in the big leagues the year I was born, 1959. He hit in nine straight games and was leading both leagues with a .407 average. Frank Lane, the Indians general manager at the time, was so excited when my dad hit a pinch-hit three-run homer to beat the Yankees in the tenth inning on May 1, nine days after I was born, he sent my mother a $250 check made out to me. Lane told the Associated Press at the time that he knew it was against the rules to pay a player a bonus, but "I can give a player's kid presents if I want to." Said my dad at the time: "If I can keep this up, my baby's gonna be rich."

I was thirteen when all Pirates fans were shocked by the death of Roberto Clemente in a plane crash on New Year's Eve 1972. He'd been on his way to deliver supplies to Nicaragua after it was hit by an earthquake. Less than three months later, in a special vote, Clemente was elected to the Hall of Fame, not only the first Puerto Rican but the first Latin American player enshrined in Cooperstown. I tell people all the time that watching Clemente run out a triple, just chewing up ground with

HIS EYES LIT UP • TERRY FRANCONA

that unique gait of his, was like watching art. Or watching him go into the right field corner, pivot, and make a throw to third base.

Pedro loved Clemente. In fact, his son remembers that Pedro's Clemente Pirates jersey was the only team-issued gear he ever saw him wear. Pedro loved how Clemente played with so much pride and intensity. He talked about him playing with "fury," that was the word Pedro used for the way Clemente attacked the game. I'd call it "pants on fire," but I think we're on the same page.

"My family comes from Cuba, but Robert Clemente was a god to our people," Pedro told Bob Ley on "Outside the Lines" in 2016. "If you're Latin American, he was *the* Babe Ruth, *the* trailblazer. Even though he wasn't the first Latin, he was the first Latin superstar in major-league baseball, and that separated him from everybody. I just remember my grandfather crying over a baseball player dying. That's how much Robert Clemente meant."

Pedro, seeing a picture of a young Clemente staring down a photographer, once commented: "Wow, even his eyes shot lasers!" It pained Pedro to think about what Clemente went through as a Latin player in the 1960s and early '70s. I'm sure Pedro wished he had been around at the time, to interview Clemente live on national TV, offering real-time translation of his eloquent Spanish so the American people could get to know the man.

The world has changed, thankfully, but I remember sportswriters calling Clemente "Bob" and accusing him of being injury prone and unwilling to play hurt. I remember them making fun of him for the way he talked. When you think back on it now, how unfair was that? This was a guy, born and raised in Puerto Rico, speaking to reporters in his second language. If anything, there should be a respect for that. My goodness, man, we all dabble in Spanish, but I can't do an interview. Instead of laughing at somebody, now I think we realize: *Hey, man, this is hard!* I went to winter ball a total of six times, counting managing. I got firsthand knowledge of what it felt like when somebody would say something to me and I would just nod because I didn't want them to think I was dumb or didn't understand. You think about Clemente and the other trailblazers and how things were pitted against them. I can't imagine how some of these guys even survived, let alone thrived, and if they dared to speak back, they were castigated. They were talked about,

HIS EYES LIT UP • TERRY FRANCONA

which is embarrassing to think about now.

Pedro helped push that earlier era farther into the past. When he would interview Latin stars, like at the Home Run Derby, and go back and forth seamlessly from language to language, it just humanized everybody. And it was really cool. He took flak for that work. In 2013 he live-translated Yoenis Céspedes after he won the Home Run Derby and for most of us it was amazing—but a few vocal critics complained. Articles were written about the "ugly" reaction from some, and Pedro had a good comeback to people outraged by hearing Spanish: "I'd like to know if any of these people moved to Germany, in two years would they have German mastered? And I believe that the answer would be no."

One thing Pedro loved talking about with me was the University of Arizona, where I went to school. I was at U of A when we won the 1980 College World Series. So when Pedro's son Rio went to U of A the Wildcats became our favorite topic of conversation, even before they made it back to the College World Series in 2016. Regardless of what was going on with baseball, as soon as I asked Pedro, "Hey, how's Rio doing?" he went from professional to dad in about a half a second and I would get the biggest kick out of that. The first time I asked him about Rio at U of A it was like he almost pulled a hamstring. I was just doing it to be polite, because of the U of A connection, and he stopped in his tracks and the rest of the conversation was about Rio's breaking ball. I just thought that was great.

What I'll remember most about Pedro was the way his eyes lit up when he talked about Rio playing baseball. He was so positive, it reminded me of what my dad was like with me. As I told a reporter once years ago when I was still in college, "The only time I can remember him yelling at me was a time when he saw me hang my head after I'd struck out. He taught me to think positively. His advice was always constructive, never negative."

As good a writer as Pedro was, as good a reporter, it will always stick with me how he would transition so fast it would make your head spin when I asked him about his son. He knew Rio didn't throw 98, and might never pitch in the big leagues, but it really didn't matter. You could just see the excitement in his voice and then his eyes, just sensing the pride that Rio was still on his journey.

Pedro snapped this shot of Derrick at the Floridita in Havana

Pedro interviews Tony Castro, Fidel's son, in Matanzas, Cuba

A UNIFYING FORCE

BY DERRICK GOOLD

Eager to share a story, Pedro Gomez reached for his phone, swiped until he found what he was looking for, and turned the screen so I could see. On it was a video he had sent to me twice before and I had watched even more than that. He beamed—he so often beamed—as he played his report for ESPN about the lost minor-league season, his son's minor-league season. Highlights of Rio Gomez pitching in college and pitching in the minors scrolled by with photos of a proud father at the ballpark and his narration, an ode to the minors.

He had seen so much history, so many amazing moments on baseball fields around the world as a celebrated reporter, but it was clear none could match one moment of watching his son pitch. The cancellation of the 2020 minor-league season was more than news to report, it was personal. It embraced the game, his son, and, as he said in the report, the loss of opportunity. Baseball, family, and opportunity were the connective tissue at the heart of stories he told.

In the press box at Petco Park, huddled over his phone watching his video, was one of the last times I saw Pedro in person before his sudden death left baseball less. I have been looking through the few photos we've exchanged trying to find the right words. There's one of him in Matanzas, Cuba, interviewing Tony Castro, Fidel's son, live on ESPN from a ballpark named after the Bay of Pigs. Not pictured is the sheer, undeterred hustle it took Pedro to get the interview. That's off camera, but with Pedro it's assumed. There's a screenshot of a Zoom meeting address he slipped me because he knew I had tried unsuccessfully to be included. There's the photo he snapped of me beside a full-sized statue of Hemingway at the Floridita in Havana. He found it and another one from a World Series while looking through his phone—almost five years later. And there is a photo of his son Rio signing his first professional contract with the Boston Red Sox. The accompanying text reads: "I cried so much when I saw this picture."

At an airport while we waited on a delayed flight, Pedro told me once that "baseball is a universal language." Through his work, I saw it as more than that. Baseball was a unifying force. So was Pedro, a longtime newspaperman who became a trailblazing reporter on ESPN.

One of the reasons Pedro means so much to other baseball writers is because all of us can point to a peer he mentored, a story he alone was brave enough to tell, or a moment we shared with him that made us better. A great fireside storyteller and fervent reporter as well as benevolent mentor, Pedro is the best of us. In a business consumed by what a reporter can get—get the story, get the scoop, get to this place, get the interview, get ahead—Pedro gave as much as he got.

When I first met Pedro I was a young reporter aiming to be a baseball writer. There were plenty of people telling me how I couldn't be one, wouldn't last as one, didn't belong as one. And then there were journalists like Pedro. He told me why I could be a baseball writer, why it was worth chasing and trying, and then showed me how. Assigned the important and unforgiving beat of Barry Bonds' historic home run chase, Pedro overcame the obstacles of covering the same, disagreeable person daily with will, creativity and zero compromise. Any of us who spent a day or a season on that same story saw the hard, determined work Pedro put in before several times a day telling a fresh story with grace and ease.

Pedro's smile arrived before he did, and it was the outward symbol of how inclusive he was—for other reporters and players. There are examples galore of interviews going sideways because of a language barrier that Pedro, for the benefit of the player and reporters, deescalated. Many times, while interviewing a player alongside Pedro, I benefited from the warmth of his reputation. Within baseball circles, he radiated credibility, with enough to share. He could pull off the feat of serving as both reporter and interpreter for a Latin player on live television with a mix of empathy and accessibility. He gave voice to players and their stories so they could be heard, in any language. His own voice was buoyant with enthusiasm—either ready to launch into a story, conspire to get one, or excited to hear one.

Throughout the shortened 2020 season, I drove from city to city, Cardinals series to series, to avoid airplanes and crowds when I could during the pandemic. Pedro was one of my friends who called during a long drive, for company. I was somewhere in Arkansas, returning from the World Series, when we swapped stories about covering Tony La Russa as a beat writer and listed all the flamboyant players La Russa managed and didn't care about their style or bat flips as long as they won.

On another drive in another country, Pedro held court in the back of a bus on its way from Havana to Matanzas. He was one of thirteen of us covering Major League Baseball's "goodwill" tour to Cuba—the first step, officials hoped, toward stronger relations and a safer route for Cuban players to professional baseball. With Pedro at the lead of our caper, we scouted out the best, most consistent spot for Wi-Fi in a hotel and set up a bureau for the writers to work—it just happened not to be at the hotel where the reporters were staying. We would tell that story later about how we contrived a way to send our stories back. Or the one about going to Havana's La Esquina Caliente—the Hot Corner, a hub of baseball debate—where the locals swirled around Pedro as if he was a ballplayer because here was a chance to "not just talk baseball but talk baseball with Pedro," ESPN's Marly Rivera recalled.

Back on the bus ride, Pedro educated some of us on the legend and importance of Orestes Kindelan, El Tambor Mayor and the home run king of Cuba. Again, baseball segued to personal. He told us about his parents, the map his father drew him to visit their Cuban home, and how they fled from Cuba to Miami three weeks before he was born ("I always say I was made in Cuba," he joked). They left to give him a world of opportunities but made sure he remained proud of his Cuban roots. They nourished and were nourished by a bond to baseball, the sport and profession that would bring Pedro back to Cuba.

Family. Baseball. Opportunity.

These same adhesives holding together his best stories—on TV, in print, or in person— explain why they will stick with us. My first trip to Cuba was Pedro's fourth, and at the Havana airport, as we waited for our return flight, we recorded a podcast about the experience. He helped me understand what we had just witnessed with Cuban players like Jose Abreu returning and Tony Castro hosting, and how this act of baseball diplomacy could be the abutment for a bridge between the countries. I asked him how he, the son of two Cubans who left the island, felt about interviewing the son of Fidel Castro. He explained it was part of getting a story he wanted to tell.

"You have to be a professional," he told me. "First and foremost, we're journalists. We're here to document and describe what we see."

What prompted him to reach for his phone years later in the Petco Park press box was our ongoing conversation about the stories that would evaporate as the minor leagues contracted, as access shriveled for reporters. We expressed how some of the best stories would not be told, that some of the game's personalities and players and voices would go unseen, unheard or unwritten. And we worried an invaluable thread of the game we cherished could come undone. Pedro captured that concern in his video about the missing minor-league season. Without the opportunity to tell those stories, baseball would lose what can make it feel like family.

Those are the words I was searching for, the ones echoing in the video Pedro shared or the conversations we did. We should do what he did—seek out those stories, protect those stories, and most of all take this opportunity to tell his story and all stories as he did, as he lived, fearlessly and generously.

Alex and her dad, author Wayne Coffey

Vuc

MAKING TIME FOR
EMPATHY

BY ALEX COFFEY

It was telling that on one of the biggest days in the sporting calendar, Super Bowl Sunday, and on the heels of one of the greatest quarterback matchups in recent history, Tom Brady versus Patrick Mahomes, Pedro Gomez's warmth could not be eclipsed. News of his passing spread as the clock was winding down, and red and white confetti began to fill the Tampa air. For many, even weeks after his death, the news had yet to feel real, to feel final, to touch the ground. Pedro's warmth is a big reason why.

Sportswriting can provide a fraternity that lasts a lifetime, and it can just as easily lend itself to jealousy, resentment and a stiff hierarchy that doesn't always welcome newcomers. Of course, it's easy to succumb to these emotions, especially in a sport like baseball, that consumes 162 days of your life a year (or more). But the beauty of Pedro Gomez was in his uncanny ability to cut through all that nonsense, to see the humanity in any situation. To see the humans involved, and recognize that they were just that—humans—and should be treated as so.

This should not be a novel concept, but in journalism, far too often it is forgotten, kicked to the wayside. We focus on what's in front of us, whether

Steve Vucinich

MAKING TIME FOR EMPATHY • ALEX COFFEY

it is being "first," or getting a scoop, or seeking proper accreditation. Far too often, it feels like there is not enough time to consider human impact, to think things through with genuine empathy. But Pedro Gomez always made time for empathy, and for that, he was different.

I only met Gomez once, and it was brief—in the A's clubhouse during spring training of 2020. His warmth shined through, even if only for a few minutes. I was young, new to this. I still am. But even when I had covered the A's for a grand total of three months, Pedro made me feel like I mattered.

It was telling that on the evening we learned of Gomez's passing, tributes began to ride in, tributes from all sorts of people. Few of them were short. Many of them were long.

"What a special, special, man he was," said longtime A's equipment manager Steve Vucinich, who has been with the organization for fifty-three years. "From San Jose to Miami to Sacramento to Arizona, I always cherished spending a few minutes with Pedro when I could. When he moved onto ESPN, the first time I saw him I kidded him about his hat collection, as we do with players that play with many teams. He laughed. Since he passed, I've heard from writers that he would casually mention visiting with me in my office. He always made it a point to stop by, sit in my Comiskey Park Stadium Seat, and talk about the game, ESPN, our families and life. He would say, 'You never know who you're going to run into in Vuc's office. It was always special!' He was friendly to all who came across him. Club personnel, security guards, ushers, clubbies, all would call him a friend. I wish we would have been photographed together somewhere. I would display that picture proudly and call it 'just two special friends.'"

We heard from athletes, managers, club officials, writers, TV personalities—folks who had overlapped with Pedro over the course of his thirty-seven-year-long career—but we also heard from people who only overlapped with him once. This is where it gets *really* telling.

Take, for example, Alexis, a Cubs fan who met Gomez in 2017. They sat next to each other at a pub after Game 3 of the NLCS. The Cubs were on the verge of elimination, and Pedro asked Alexis if she thought they'd pull it off. She said she didn't, and he was impressed with her reasoning as to why. "You know your stuff!" he exclaimed, and dug into his backpack, pulling out a cork.

Pedro with Cubs fan Alexis Bernardireis after
Game 3 of the 2017 NLDS

"This is for you," he told her. It was a Champagne cork from the Cubs' celebration after winning the NLDS against the Nationals a week earlier.

"He said that one of the perks of his job was meeting different baseball fans and since he would be going to the winning team's city next, he always made sure to pick up some locker room corks to make some of those fans smile," she wrote on Twitter. "And smile I did."

Alexis still has the cork, and now, a memory of a man who touched more lives than we'll ever know. It is overwhelming to think that the Pedro Gomez that we loved, as a colleague, as part of the fraternity, touched so many lives outside of it. He transcended sports media, and this was just one interaction. Just think, over thirty-seven years—including twenty-five World Series—how many more there must have been. How many more corks must have been delivered to a passionate fan. *This* is how someone eclipses the biggest day on the sporting calendar, a day that features Mahomes and Brady at the highest of stakes. *This* is Pedro Gomez: father, husband, fan, friend, and first, above all, human.

Alexis Bernardireis: "And yes I still have it!"

Will Ferrell at short for the A's in a spring-training game

LET ME TELL YOU 'BOUT SOME FRIENDS I KNOW

BY SEAN McADAM

Steve Kettmann was doling out assignments, like some substitute teacher in middle school attempting to herd a classroom full of restless students into some form of order.

"I'm going to have Jack Curry do something with music," he said, running though his checklist. "Bob Ley is going to write about his interviewing style, Kurkjian will talk about playing basketball with Pedro...."

The names kept coming and the topics kept flowing. I listened with interest, nodding in agreement at the choices paired with their prospective writers. Yup, I thought a few times, that makes total sense.

In the back of my mind, however, I kept waiting for the big reveal. What would my assignment be? What topic could link me with my friend, Pedro Gomez, who had tragically passed only days earlier? Like every other contributor for this book, I had spent time reminiscing, taking a mental inventory of past phone conversations, shared meals and random text messages. What would Kettmann pick for *me*? My mind raced: What single topic connected me inextricably with Pedro? What was the shared DNA of our friendship?

It's the kind of question you don't ask until circumstances dictate a sort of inventory. Who cares what it is that connects you to someone special? Friendships, especially ones that last decades, just *are*.They don't always hold up to closer inspection. I had no idea where this was going.

"I'm sure you know where this is going," said Kettmann.

"Umm, not really," I said with more than a hint of embarrassment and plenty of trepidation.

"*ANIMAL HOUSE!*" Kettmann finally blurted out.

Of course. *Animal House.* For the uninitiated—or for millennials blissfully ignorant of any pop culture touchstones that dared exist before their birth—*Animal House* was a 1978 comedy about the exploits of a particularly raucous fraternity, set in the days of the Cold War. It was sophomoric, proudly politically incorrect, irreverent and defiantly crude. In other words, it's like countless other comedies, including the entire Will Farrell oeuvre. Except *Animal House* is actually funny. Hysterically, unapologetically, relentlessly funny. And did I mention groundbreaking?

Without *Animal House*, there's no *American Pie, Old School, The Hangover* or countless other "gross-out" comedies. Talk about a legacy. But this much remains unassailable: *Animal House* was, and is, funny. And eminently quotable.

Long before "You're my boy, Blue!" became a staple of marauding twentysomethings enjoying a night out came: "Fat, drunk and stupid is no way to go through life, son." And "See if you can guess what I am now...A zit....get it?"

A confession: I don't remember when or where I first met Pedro, though it's a safe bet that it was either at Fenway Park or Fill-in-current-corporate-title-sponsor Coliseum in Oakland in the early '90s, when he was covering the A's and I was covering the Red Sox.

Second confession: I don't remember what it was that made us bond over *Animal House*. And that's entirely appropriate, I guess. This isn't *Casablanca* or *Citizen Kane* or *The Seventh Seal*, revealing new intricate layers with each rewatching. *Animal House* is just *there,* always ripe for another viewing, a dependable comedic pick-me-up. I'm sure its emergence as our mutual touchstone began organically enough. One of us probably cited a line from the film in the other's presence, eliciting a chuckle or an appreciative nod, and off we went.

If you're looking for some sort of cinematic serendipity, the movie was set in 1962, the year Pedro was born. For now, I'll take some small comfort in that bit of harmonic convergence. It was released in between my freshman and sophomore years in college, the perfect sweet spot with which to appreciate its examination of college life—even one made to look like college sixteen years earlier. Pedro, some three years my junior, would have been in high school when it first played in theaters. I wonder if it scared or thrilled him with its glimpses of the college experience that awaited.

The texts would come out of the blue, sometimes unprompted, sometimes in response to the events of the day. They could come in the late innings of some game in the swelter of August, designed to break the boredom of a season's dog days. Or they could emerge from the chill of December, spurred by yet another viewing on TBS, where *Animal House* seems to play with the regularity and predictability of a metronome. (Naturally, we strongly decried these airings on TBS—or any others edited for regular cable audiences. Those were bastardized versions of AH, with all the glorious profanity edited out. And where was the fun in that? It's like watching a PG version of some Richard Pryor standup bit).

As a rule, we tended to avoid the most obvious lines of dialogue. So we would seldom resort to "Was it over when the Germans bombed Pearl Harbor?" or any mention of "double-secret probation." These were examples of low-hanging fruit, best left to newbies just discovering the movie for the first time. In musical terms, we went for the deep cuts, the offhand remark that might not be endlessly quoted, but nonetheless revealed a deeper, human truth—and, snobs that we were, would identify us as true connoisseurs.

Stuff like: "The time has come for someone to put their foot down. And that foot is me."

Or Tim Matheson's desperate plea to Peter Riegert, "Tell those assholes to shut up," resulting in Riegert restating the request, loudly, word-for-word in the middle of the famous disciplinary hearing scene.

It was code. I could be walking through the bowels of Yankee

Stadium or entering the media dining room of Dodger Stadium, and a recognizable voice would shout a completely out-of-context quote from a forty-year-old movie, and suddenly I knew my day or night was about to get exponentially better.

I've devoted an inordinate amount of time in recent weeks to attempting to discern what it was that made *Animal House* so endlessly appealing to Pedro. He had other favorite movies and would quote from them liberally. He loved *The Godfather,* I suspect because Francis Ford Coppola's epic take on immigration to America, and, crucially, assimilating in America was an experience to which he and his family could surely relate. And he was partial to a line or two from *Scarface,* which might have been because it told the tale of a Cuban coming to Miami, but more likely, because it was so ridiculously over-the-top and full of comedic fodder. He was not above reaching for an easy laugh. But what drew him to *Animal House*? Or, more to the point, what drew *us* to *Animal House* and somehow came to cement our friendship?

After some reflection, I decided I was being too literal. Pedro hadn't found any hidden message or Grand Theme in a 1970s examination of early 1960s collegiate mores. He just took immense joy in the broad comedy, the sight gag or the devastating comeback.

Seen through a more modern lens, *Animal House* could rightly be categorized as homophobic or misogynistic—even if its time travel back to 1962 allowed for a certain amount of revisionist laughs. But what Pedro derived from it was not sociological; instead, he wanted some laughs—for himself, and anyone else who shared his view that life was to be enjoyed. He didn't revel in the subtlety or the clever quip. Pedro wanted the bend-at-the-knee, so funny you feel faint, big laugh. Because why settle for less?

I should stress: *Animal House* was not the only topic Pedro and I discussed. Particularly over the past two years, we shared more personal and family triumphs. I was forever updating him with tales of my infant grandson, Lucas. He, naturally, was immensely proud of all three of his children, but talk often centered on Rio, a pitching prospect in the Boston Red Sox minor leagues. As a reporter/columnist covering the Red Sox, I would share what I heard from those in the organization.

In March of 2020, just before the pandemic struck, I was in Lakeland, covering a Grapefruit League contest between the Red Sox and Detroit Tigers. Rio had been added to the "travel list" of players who were chosen to take the trip. (Teams often choose young players from the lowest levels of the minor leagues to take the longest bus rides, not wanting to require a more established player to take a five-hour round trip for the sole purpose of tossing an inning of relief or taking a late-game at-bat or two).

Pedro texted me excitedly that morning to alert me to the fact that Rio would be with the team, though he realized it was highly unlikely his son would see his first Grapefruit League action. I told him I would keep him updated nonetheless. Everything played out as expected, with Rio stationed in the visitor's bullpen, barely moving. Then, after the Red Sox had raced out to an early lead, the Tigers began inching closer and closer and the Red Sox kept trying to repel them with a succession of pitching changes.

By the ninth inning, the Sox were down to two remaining pitchers— the guy on the mound, and, still in the bullpen, Rio. I narrated every development on the field, including, to my chagrin, a premature call of a pitching change that turned out to be just a mound visit. Along the way, Pedro was a mess. I envisioned him pacing madly in some other ballpark, wanting desperately to be in Lakeland. Instead, he was like the expectant father in some 1960s waiting room: equal parts excited beyond words, desperate for news, beaming with pride and scared half to death. Rio didn't get into that particular game, though he did appear in others later that spring. Pedro would go to great lengths to find a video feed on the occasions when he couldn't be there in person.

Our last communication came via text, about two weeks before he suddenly passed. And yes, it was about You-Know-What. In a series of rapid-fire exchanges, we set about to cast *Animal House—The Sequel,* with inspiration drawn exclusively from members of the Trump Administration.

He had the trigger happy Douglas Neidermeyer played by Michael Flynn and tragic kiln-explosion victim Fawn Liebowitz in charge of funding for the arts. I, on the other hand, imagined an impeachment speech being delivered on the floor of the Senate, detailing behavior "so profound and disgusting that decorum prohibits me from listing them here"—just as Neidermeyer had done in attempting to get Delta House thrown off campus.

And that was the last time we communicated. Since Pedro's passing, I'm told by some of his friends that, beyond the broad comedy and the endlessly quotable lines, Pedro actually identified with some of the misfit pledges in the film—the outsiders, the ones who had to fight for acceptance.

And given his own origin story, that makes some sense. Surely, as the son of immigrants, he sometimes felt marginalized and perhaps even unwelcome. I suspect, like many of us, Pedro found himself on an endless quest for acceptance. When he switched from newspapers to television, he worried how he might be viewed in a new field of work. Would he always be seen as "the former writer" by those in the TV industry? Would he have to work twice as hard to earn their respect?

That self-doubt seems silly to the rest of us who saw Pedro display an unmistakable ease before the camera, adapting to his medium with a natural comfort. He smiled effortlessly and had the ability to put both interview subjects and viewers at ease. That happened with TV viewers and in real life.

About a dozen years ago, while in Southern California covering a playoff series between the Angels and Red Sox, I organized a group dinner at my favorite Mexican restaurant in Newport Beach and asked Pedro to join us. From the moment he walked in, Pedro commanded the place like, well, a movie star. Every Spanish-speaking waiter, busboy and bartender wanted to meet him.

After a while, everyone else at the table ceased trying to get the waitstaff's attention for drink orders or refills of our water glasses, and had Pedro act as our point person. A simple raised hand or quick bit of eye contact with one waiter would bring a handful of workers to our table, each more eager than the next to attend to his every need. Pedro put people at ease. He was everything you would want in a TV personality—accessible, approachable and relatable. Even if Pedro didn't recognize that quality in himself, others did. Once, he was in Washington DC, getting out of a cab in front of a hotel, and spied singer/actor Tony Orlando. Orlando, in turn, recognized Pedro.

"You're the guy on ESPN, right?"

Orlando went on to say that he was a big fan of Pedro's work, remarking on his on-air persona. He recalled some "touch-and-go" moments between Pedro and Barry Bonds and how well Pedro had handled himself in what were clearly uncomfortable situations.

"You should give movies a try," advised Orlando. "You should go read for a role. Just walk in and read. You have a presence on-camera.... You could give George Clooney a run for his money."

No doubt he could have.

At the end of *Animal House*, there's a postscript in which we find out what happened to the various characters later in life. One turns out to be a tour guide at a theme park, and so on. I've thought about that coda and the closing credits a lot since Pedro passed, and wonder what might have been ahead for him. His favorite of those final scenes was the shot of Senator Blutarsky, the great John Belushi, grinning at the wheel of a massive convertible, in pirate costume. If I squint a little, and blink a couple times, instead of Mandy Pepperidge squeezed up next to Bluto, I see two Senators sharing the front seat of the convertible, both flashing grins to light up a stadium, driving off into the distance, having a great time and ready to raise a ruckus.

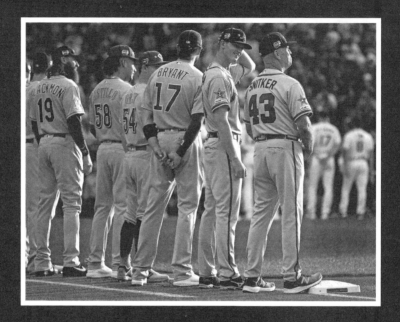

Walt Weiss in his days as A's shortstop

LIKE A GOOD BENCH COACH

BY BRIAN SNITKER

I can't tell you how many baseball people I've talked to who all said they had been in touch with Pedro the week before he died—and I was one of them. The first Wednesday of February, I went into my office at Truist Park in Atlanta, packing my bag for spring training, and my phone rang. When I saw it was Pedro, I picked up—and we had a long talk. He'd texted me to ask if we could talk for a book on managers he was working on with Steve Kettmann. So when he called, I put him on speaker phone, sat down at my desk and kicked my feet up. God, we must have talked for an hour. It was like that with Pedro. The time just raced by because he was such a good guy, and you enjoyed talking to him so much. Pedro was always exuberant about talking about baseball. He was as honest and genuine a lover of the game as you'll find. You could tell.

Four days later, when I heard the news, it just blew me away. My God, I hated that. Pedro was such a wonderful person and it was such a rough year overall in the industry. I turned to my wife and said, "Is this ever going to end here?" Baseball had just lost Hank Aaron, Tommy Lasorda and Don Sutton in January, after losing Phil Niekro, Al Kaline,

Bob Gibson, Joe Morgan, Lou Brock, Whitey Ford and Tom Seaver in 2020—ten Hall of Famers in ten months. Then on Super Bowl Sunday we lost Pedro.

Shoot, I liked him. He wasn't looking for anything from you. We were talking baseball and experiences and it was never anything other than real—and I really appreciated that. I'd seen Pedro on ESPN for years before I ever met him. The first time Pedro and I talked was after I got this job as manager of the Braves in 2016. All I ever heard about him was: "Yeah, this guy's a pro." Nobody ever had anything bad to say about him. Everything was always so professional and real and honest. And I just really liked the person, quite honestly.

Pedro had an honest interest in what you had to say, and what you were doing about your team, and he always let you know he understood this was a tough job. That's what I try to do as a manager. This is a hard game to play. This is a hard game to coach. This is a hard game to manage. It may look easy to the fans, but it's hard. I saw that any time I got thrown out of a game during my fifteen years managing in the Braves' minor-league system. I'd go sit in the stands and watch the game and from there it looked totally different. I kept thinking: *God, everything slows down.* The game is so slow from afar, but so fast when you're in the dugout or on the field. This is a tough game to navigate. I think Pedro got all that. Especially with managers, he always had a very deep understanding of how challenging a job this is and all that you have to do.

Pedro listened the way a good bench coach listens, and he paid attention to the game the way a good bench coach does. One of the first things he noticed about what we were doing in Atlanta was the coaching staff I'd put together. He told me that when he was trying to get a handle on a new manager in the big leagues, he always took a close look at who he was able to bring together on his staff. His first season on the baseball beat was in 1992, covering a Hall of Fame manager in Tony La Russa, and Pedro respected Tony for surrounding himself with strong personalities who were good baseball men, like his pitching coach, Dave Duncan, and Rene Lachemann, Tommie Reynolds and the Cave Man, Art Kusnyer.

He loved that for my bench coach, I'd hired Walt Weiss, Tony's shortstop on that '92 A's team. I have a rock star coaching staff. It might be the only one of its kind in major-league baseball right now. In spring training two years ago, I had an umpire tell me: "Snit, you've got three coaches out there, they're probably guys that eat donuts and all that in the morning." You know what I mean? Instead of bird feed. And the beauty of it is, they all love the work and really love the teaching, which you're not seeing in the game any more. Our guys have managed, coached and played in the big leagues. They've been through the wars. They all bring instant credibility for who they are in the game.

Ron Washington, one of two former big-league managers on my staff, has a reputation as one of the best teachers in the game—Eric Chavez gave him one of his Gold Glove awards—and he really enjoys that work. No. 1, the man doesn't realize how old he is. He has the energy of a thirty-year-old. But more than that he has instilled a work ethic in all our players, which comes down to consistency, consistency, consistency. You can set your watch on the way Wash does things. He does the same thing every day, every day, every day, every day. There's no change. That's the way to get the focus you need to be a successful big-leaguer, a flat-lined, boring pro. You do the same thing every day and stay consistent, because if you ride the crest in this thing, if you ride the ups and downs, you'll drive yourself crazy.

I got hives a couple of years ago when Walt Weiss' name was mentioned as a possibility as my bench coach. You're talking about a perfect complement for me. Unbelievable. This guy is off the charts, and he's managed. He learned from one of the best in Tony La Russa, a Hall of Famer, and he and Tony remain good friends.

Walt's a classic bench coach in that he's like an extension of my own brain. He'll think two innings ahead during a game and bring me ideas. Like: *What do you think about doing this?* And that's huge, because there are so many things going on in your mind when a game starts, my God dude. Walt and I go over every game, prior to it. We don't script it, but run scenarios and get ideas. We'll talk about pinch-hitters and pitching moves and when we might double switch, looking ahead. He has my back every day.

Walt's the guy that can bring me bad news. He'll come in to my office and pull me aside and as soon as I hear him saying, "Hey Snit," I know from his tone that something's up, like, "Oh gosh, here we go." A bench coach like that is somebody we all need, whatever our job. If we're making big decisions, we all need a bench coach. I'm not stupid enough to think I can do this by myself. My ego won't allow me to believe that it's me. It's a combination of players and coaches and others around the team. If we're doing good, it ain't about me. If we're going bad, I'll take the fall. I've got big shoulders, I can handle that. But I will never, ever in my life, as I do this job, think that the success is me. It ain't.

I think in life too we all need a good bench coach, someone who helps you think ahead, and think through challenges. My wife is that for me because she's truthful as hell. She'll let me know. And then I'm sure there's a friend that we all have that we lean on. We all have to have somebody that we can talk to or we'll go nuts. The more I heard about Pedro, after his death, the more I learned about all the lives he touched, all the people he reached out to at a given time, the way he did the last week of his life, and how often he was really there for people when times were tough—including Ron Washington and AJ Hinch.

2012, Phoenix Muni: Pedro with Yoenis Céspedes and Ariel Prieto

A NATURAL TEACHER

BY BRETT KURLAND

The last time I saw Pedro Gomez in person was in a baseball clubhouse, smiling that megawatt Pedro Gomez smile, going out of his way to help our students. That was Pedro. I am the director of sports programs and a professor of practice at the Walter Cronkite School of Journalism and Mass Communication at Arizona State University, and that day left an indelible mark on me, an exemplar of everything Pedro did for our students, our school, and for me.

It was early in spring training, in the Colorado Rockies clubhouse at Salt River Fields at Talking Stick in Scottsdale, Arizona. Our program partners with media outlets from around the country to augment their coverage of spring training, with students reporting on teams across the Cactus League. I walked into the Rockies clubhouse with two students, helping to acclimate them to spring training.

A baseball clubhouse can be an intimidating place. I often tell students "clubhouse" is the perfect word to describe this place—during the 162-game season, and six weeks of spring training before that, it is the players' home away from home. They live there, laugh there, play there, find respite there. And the media on the baseball beat is an extension of that—the day-to-day drumbeat of baseball fosters a close-knit community. Walking in as an outsider to that environment can be challenging. But to Pedro Gomez, there were no outsiders. Pedro made sure everybody felt like a friend, felt like part of the club.

On that day in the Rockies' clubhouse in late February 2020, I said hi to Pedro and immediately: "Are these your students?"

"Hi, I'm Pedro Gomez. What are you working on?"

He turned to introduce the students to the media relations staff. He made suggestions for whom they should talk to for their stories. He gave them tips for how to navigate baseball coverage. As players held court, Pedro made sure they knew about the Cronkite students there reporting for the *Denver Post*.

Pedro welcomed the students into the baseball journalism community, signaling through his words and his actions that they belonged there.

◆ ◆ ◆

Always a big fan of Pedro's work, I was thrilled when my friends Jim and Dustin Farrell introduced me to him in 2013. Through their Arizona-based company Crew West, they worked closely with Pedro, shooting just about every story Pedro did in Arizona. When I first started teaching a spring training class at the Cronkite School that year, I asked them about Pedro, if they thought this journalist I admired from afar would ever be willing to visit my class. Their response— "Absolutely." They could not stop telling me what a wonderful person Pedro was. They passed on his contact information, I reached out to Pedro and he immediately got back to me: "Where and when?"

My students were transfixed as he told the class how to cover baseball, how to find a good story, and, most important, how to ask good questions. Pedro and I shared a passion for interviewing—to me, it's the most important tool in a journalist's toolbox. And a tool that Pedro wielded like the master craftsman he was.

Early in my time at Cronkite, I received an invitation to attend ESPN's interview workshop in Bristol, Connecticut. Three eight-hour days in a conference room, led by ESPN's terrific interview coach John Sawatsky, every editorial employee at ESPN went through some version of this workshop multiple times over the years. It was fantastic, and among the many lessons drawn from those three days are three simple tenets of good questions—they should be open-ended (no yes/no questions!), lean (short and to the point) and neutral (avoid bias). Ask good questions, you have a pretty good shot of getting good answers. Ask bad questions, and, well, you're on your own.

A few weeks after I returned, I ran into Pedro in a stairwell at Cronkite. He had just finished yet another class visit. (Pedro was everybody's friend. He was a frequent guest speaker across our sports journalism classes, always a highlight for our students.) I told him about my trip. Without missing a beat, he immediately looked at me and said, with a huge smile, "Open, lean and neutral!"

For Pedro, it was just that simple. Go back and watch any interview Pedro did. The deep, insightful answers he elicited didn't come by accident. His interviews were a master class in how to be a journalist.

Pedro loved the craft of journalism, and even more, I think, he loved sharing the craft with others, leaving every journalist he came into contact with a little bit smarter (and a bit happier—Pedro lit up every clubhouse, press box and classroom he entered). Spreading the gospel of good journalism brought Pedro such great joy.

Back in the winter of 2014, Pedro made one of his visits to my reporting class, imparting that wisdom of asking good questions, and answering every question students asked. But his dedication to teaching those students never ended when the class session ended. He would often follow with an email or a text, like this one he sent to me a few days after that class, following Super Bowl XLVIII, in which Peyton Manning's Denver Broncos fell to the Seattle Seahawks. Pedro saw a journalist ask a bad question of Manning following the game, and Pedro's first instinct was to share that with my students:

"... (Manning's) reaction was all over SportsCenter and is a clear example of how NOT to ask a question. The reporter put the subject in an antagonistic mood and, while it led to an interesting sound bite, it shows how you're not eliciting a true response to the game that just ended. All the question did was elicit anger toward the question, not an answer to what happened in the game. I thought of your students when I saw that question and answer. Hope you're well and I had a great time last week."

The assortment of emails and texts only begin to tell the story of his commitment to our students that he carried well beyond a one-hour Q&A in a classroom, beginning with the moment class drew to a close. His class visits would linger well after the end of the session, as students would line up to talk to him. He wouldn't leave until every single student had the opportunity to ask whatever they wanted to ask, to connect with this role model for all of them.

After his passing, a student named Marco Peralta shared a story with me of a conversation he had with Pedro at the end of one of those frequent class visits. Marco asked Pedro if he would be willing to share his email address for career advice. Not only did Pedro immediately say "Of course," but he turned to the class full of students and, almost apologetically because he hadn't said it earlier, yelled out "All of you can email me!"

Pedro wanted to teach as many students as he could, build a connection, share whatever lessons he could share. He encouraged students to reach out, becoming a mentor to many, including the student in the anecdote above—reviewing their work, giving them career guidance, encouragement, passing down whatever he could.

When he passed away on Super Bowl Sunday, my Twitter feed flooded with an outpouring of reflection from so many current and former students.

Marco Peralta shared some of what Pedro had passed on: *"Use your gift of being bilingual." That's advice that the late #PedroGomez gave me one day. I heard that advice before but when it came from him, it meant so much to me. Now that he's gone, it means the world to me! RIP @ pedrogomezESPN! I hope to make you proud someday.*

Pedro was a regular guest in the sports reporting class of Katherine Fitzgerald, an *Arizona Republic* sportswriter: *Pedro was someone who I looked up immensely to growing up. When I got to know him in AZ, I was taken aback by his kindness. He spoke to my class each year because he cared so immensely about the next generation. We were all better for him, & for his caring spirit. I'm heartbroken.*

Chris Cadeau, a recent Cronkite graduate now working at Fox Sports Arizona, built an instant connection with Pedro just after one class visit: *"Stand on my shoulders kid. That's how I got to where I am, and that's how we're going to get you to where you're going." This is what Pedro said to me when we first met. Forever grateful for his text convos, mentorship and love over the last few years. I'm crushed.*

We all stand on Pedro's shoulders, on the tremendous legacy he left behind—to work hard, to pursue a good story, to ask good questions, to help others, to enjoy what you do. And always, always to smile.

Seeing what a natural teacher Pedro was, and how much he loved teaching, I asked Pedro to teach a sports reporting class at Cronkite, knowing we were just scratching the surface with his class visits and mentoring and speaking appearances and impromptu meetings in a clubhouse (although that was still so much!). He told me he would love to do it, if his schedule ever opened up. (Pedro was one of the most prolific reporters at ESPN. I'm still amazed at how much time he found for our students.) I told him to let me know when he was ready and we would find him a spot.

Sadly, Pedro is gone far too soon, before his schedule slowed down enough to allow him the time to be a professor, to lead his own classroom, to pass on even more to future generations of journalists—how to ask good questions, how to be a good reporter, how to treat other people.

But that legacy lives on, through the Pedro Gomez Foundation Fund at Cronkite, impacting those sports journalism students Pedro always went out of his way to help. But it's not just the funding. Our sports journalism faculty is dedicated to sharing his lessons, carrying his wisdom forward long after he is gone.

Alden and Pedro with Alanna Rizzo and Amaury Pi-Gonzalez

HE CARVED A PATH
FOR ME

BY ALDEN GONZALEZ

I can't stop watching Pedro Gomez talk about Cuba. It seems the only way I have been able to process his shocking death has been to continually pull up the clip of that March 2016 standup hit that has populated the Internet in recent weeks, where Pedro—remarkably vulnerable yet resilient—breaks down while explaining his connection to an island he really only knows in spirit.

"A big part of me," he said, "is Cuban."

I feel this in a way that is still difficult to describe. I'm the son of Cuban immigrants—as proud of my family's heritage as I am spiteful of the communist regime that suffocated them—and I'm navigating a career in journalism largely because Pedro carved a path that I otherwise couldn't have imagined. The only way Pedro's parents could board a flight out of Cuba in the early 1960s was for his mom to lie about being eight months pregnant. The only way my parents could get on a boat out of Cuba in the early 1980s was for my father to lie about having an engineering degree.

Pedro talked about having a brother who was "one of the most

Cuban people I'd ever come across," which reminded me of my own brother. Pedro's father used to tell him he wouldn't return to Cuba so long as the Castro regime was in power, which made me think about the conversations I had with my dad as I prepared to travel to Cuba as part of Major League Baseball's goodwill tour in December of 2015. As my trip was winding down, I met up with a cousin who still lives on the island, drove to my parents' old neighborhood in Havana and brought back pictures that made my father weep—three months before Pedro famously spread the ashes of his father and brother along an ocean shore nearby.

I honestly haven't felt much resistance in my attempt to climb the ladder of an industry with scant Hispanic representation. And that's because Pedro thawed some of that along his path, traversing the United States—through Miami, San Diego, San Jose, Sacramento and Arizona—at a time when this country was even less accepting of minorities with strong voices. I remember how awed I was watching Pedro conduct an interview while translating for Yoenis Céspedes on live television after he won the 2013 Home Run Derby, how connected I felt hearing someone speak with that distinctive Cuban flair that routinely filled my childhood home. And it wasn't until after Pedro's death that I learned how much vitriol that triggered.

I was offered an internship with MLB.com by a man named Bill Hill, the deputy managing editor at the *Arizona Republic* while Pedro worked there from 1997 to 2003. As I approached my mid-20s, Bill told me I could be "the next Pedro Gomez"—a thought that seems every bit as unfathomable now as it did then. He told me about how Pedro came up as a beat writer and how he found his voice as a columnist before becoming that recognizable face chronicling Barry Bonds. Bill told me the foundation of this business is the desire to report, the willingness to ask questions and the ability to foster meaningful relationships, and he told me Pedro did that better than anybody.

I first met Pedro in 2011, on a southbound 4 train out of Yankee Stadium in the Bronx. By then I had heard so much about him, I made it a point to introduce myself. He was so warm, so engaging. We bonded over Westchester, the Miami neighborhood where he grew up and where I was born, and he made it a point to remind me of that every time we ran into each other in the years that followed. Nobody worked a clubhouse better than Pedro. Nobody was better at striking the balance between competitiveness and empathy than Pedro. Nobody, anywhere, was better about making you feel important.

The significance of what he did for people with my background didn't really strike me until the night of February 7, moments after I blew out the candles for my thirty-fifth birthday, when I got a call from a colleague informing me that Pedro was suddenly, tragically, gone. I broke down in front of my two-year-old daughter that night. The next morning I received a call from Bill. He told me Pedro had been scheduled to speak at his journalism class two days later and asked if I could take his place. It was my first step in what might be a lifelong attempt to honor his legacy.

Sarina on the set of SportsCenter:AM

HE WAS MY IDOL

BY SARINA MORALES

I was a teenager playing baseball in the Bronx when I first saw Pedro Gomez. He was covering baseball on ESPN. He stood out to me. It was the first time I had seen a Latino reporter covering baseball on national television.

Baseball is everything to us Latinos growing up in the Bronx. It was the thing I cried over and got excited about. I wrote speeches for school on the Yankees winning the 1996 World Series. I wrote my college essay on being the only female in my baseball league. I played baseball for ten years, until I was seventeen.

It's why I ultimately applied to go to school at Syracuse. I thought I could be a Latino voice for those baseball players who played the game just like me. If a reporter like Pedro Gomez could make it, maybe I could too? The Newhouse program bragged about having the best reporters coming out of their school. However, once I got in, I struggled with my identity and felt like I wasn't good enough.

That's why Pedro Gomez was so influential. He was a familiar face on a TV screen that had mostly white men. And yet his on-camera presence made everyone, Latino or other, make you feel like you were his friend. His amigo.

He was my idol. I religiously watched him cover baseball. And

HE WAS MY IDOL • SARINA MORALES

by the time I made it through my junior year at Syracuse University, I was set to figure out how to be the next Pedro. I helped start the first National Association of Hispanic Journalists school chapter at Syracuse and ultimately became the president of the organization my senior year.

It was the summer heading into my senior year that I met Pedro for the first time. Syracuse sent a handful of NAHJ Board Members to the national convention. Pedro was standing by the ESPN booth. I recognized him immediately and mustered up the courage to walk up to him. Looking back, I probably could have thought through my "elevator pitch" a bit better, but I think I spilled my life story to him instead. And he listened. I remember I told him I wanted to be a baseball reporter for ESPN and that I played the game for ten years and that I went to Syracuse. He made me feel like I was the first person to ever tell him I wanted to be a reporter for ESPN. I remember we ended up talking a handful of times that weekend and he was kind enough to connect me with ESPN producers, fellow baseball writers and other media folks.

That was just the beginning. Pedro opened the door for me and he didn't have to. And thinking back to that first weekend I met him, everyone gravitated to Pedro. And yet, he still made me feel special and included me in conversations about baseball and news despite my youth

Sarina, Pedro and Sinhué Mendoza

and being a female. I was never included in these conversations before.

Before that weekend ended, I asked Pedro if he would come up and speak to students at Syracuse University one day. It was a big deal to bring up professional speakers. I wasn't sure he would have the time or ability or interest to come, but he kept his word. I remember picking him up from the airport in my old Saturn. I was slightly embarrassed because my car was old and here I was, picking up *"The* Pedro Gomez."

That day was one of my highlights at Syracuse. I ended up conducting the interview with Pedro. He packed an auditorium with students eager to hear his baseball stories and his journey into journalism. Afterwards, he took the time to shake hands and speak to students after the event. The next morning, I had planned to take him back to the airport, but he ordered himself a cab, and flew home without any complaints or bother.

That was just the beginning of my relationship with Pedro. I texted him here and there over my journey to becoming a sports reporter. I got even more excited when I saw him cover the World Series. I will never forget him telling me, "When ESPN wants you, they will call you." He also told me to keep working, keep my head down.

Then ESPN called. Well, it was an email. But I got called up to the big leagues and who was the first person to reach out? Pedro Gomez. Who was the first person to text me when I anchored SportsCenter? Pedro Gomez. Who texted me when I went to the Super Bowl with the Rams in 2018? Pedro Gomez.

I've heard that you never want to meet your childhood heroes because they will disappoint you. Pedro Gomez did anything but disappoint. His actions taught me what was important: kindness, listening, generosity with time and work ethic.

He has set the bar so high for me and my fellow Latino reporters, the next group of us has to take note. He made his work his life, and now we need to make sure we represent him as he has left a huge void in the sports world. He has been very important to me. I hope to never disappoint him.

Miguel Tejada's first major-league hit, Dodger Stadium, 1997

A BEACON

BY MARCOS BRETÓN

To me, he was Pedrito. It's what I called him for the twenty-five years of our friendship and it's how I will remember him for the rest of my life. When one calls a grown man named Pedro by the name of Pedrito, it is meant in affection—cariño, as it is said in Spanish.I shared a great deal of cariño with Pedro Gomez.

He was my Cuban brother and I was his Mexican brother. Our fathers taught us to love our ancestral homelands and we clung to them and built a loving friendship on that bond. Many people, myself included, loved Pedro Gomez the man. But I also loved and respected who he was as a professional.

Pedro Gomez was a towering figure in the community of media professionals who descended from Latin America. I would argue, he was a historical figure. Pedro achieved national recognition for his coverage of baseball—he was a made man for years at ESPN, no less—and he accomplished that without denying who he was, where he came from, who his people were.

Pedro Gomez radiated his love for his Cuban ancestry while maintaining a dignified and proud persona in countless national broadcasts for nearly the last twenty years of his life. Pedro never allowed himself to be a caricature in all those years. He was buoyant and

full of life on the air, but never a fool lampooning an accent or lowering himself in any way.

Neither the game of baseball, nor the United States, ever emasculated Pedro Gomez or marginalized him. He was strong enough to show us his tears of joy while standing on Cuban soil and reporting for ESPN what it was like for him to return to the county his ancestors fled. Listen, I cried with Pedro as I watched that report because I understood what he was feeling. But beyond the emotion, the power of that moment was in the pride demonstrated by the American son of a father who loved a country at odds with American foreign policy and American financial interests.

This is where our immigrant stories from Latin America differ from those of our Irish and Italian American friends. Our ancestral homelands have all been menaced by the American superpower. The relationships between the nation we now call home and the nations where our people come from are fraught and fractured by the massive footprint of American-style colonialism.

So when Pedro Gomez cried tears of pride for his Cuban ancestry, and poured the ashes of his father and brother into the Cuban surf as the ESPN cameras rolled, I shook my head in disbelief. Our dear friend was telling us all to be proud of who we were. He was showing us how to remain true to our blood, to our relatives, our experiences, our complex narratives. He was urging us to remember who we are.

In the game of baseball, we extol the leader who leads by example. That's who Pedro Gomez was to us, to me. He was our friend, of course. Over twenty-five years, I had some fun times with Pedro Gomez after work hours, though not nearly enough of them. I was so much taller than this guy, so much bigger in stature, and yet that Cuban drank me under the table in such a comical way that we laughed about it for years. But on the job? He was a role model to me and many, many others.

He showed us that we could be successful and kind. We could assimilate into America while being who we were without reservation or shame. Pedro knew very well that this was not true for past generations of baseball players from Latin America. The American pastime was hard on post-World War 2 pioneering big-leaguers from Cuba, Venezuela, the Dominican Republic, Puerto Rico, Mexico and Central America.

Every one of those nations and territories have suffered at the hands of the United States in the last century and beyond. And when the

players from those nations arrived in postwar America, they didn't fit America's rigid racial order of Black or white. This was true even for the Black players from Latin America. Their accents and foreign passports placed them in another, forsaken category of discrimination.

The late, great Minnie Miñoso, a Cuban like Pedro's parents, was also Black and also faced Jim Crow-style segregation and violence on baseball fields dotted with racists in opposing uniforms. This happened to Miñoso in the 1950s while he was trying to learn English and American customs.

By the time my path crossed with Pedro's on the baseball beat in the 1990s, the players from Latin America were starting to make big money. But it was still rare for a baseball writer to be fluent in Spanish. There was still little understanding about life in the countries and territories feeding generational talents to Major League Baseball. Players from Latin America were still in their own corners in MLB clubhouses, their language barriers keeping them at arm's length from full acceptance in the United States.

That's why Pedro's ascension from Oakland A's beat writer for the *Sacramento Bee* to national baseball writer for the *Arizona Republic* to an outstanding baseball correspondent for ESPN made him the perfect man to chronicle the explosion of big-league talent from Latin America. Pedro covered every aspect of the game and, outstanding reporter that he was, he had sources across the game. His ease with players from Latin America was essential to telling their stories. Why was that important? Because that didn't used to happen in the old days.

I wrote a book about the legacy of Latin American players in the big leagues called *Away Games*, and when I was doing my research I found out why so many of the great old Latin American players didn't get their due in the U.S. Their language barriers relegated them to supporting roles or comic relief in the grand narrative of the game. Mike Cuellar, the left-handed ace with the Baltimore Orioles in the 1960s and 70s, was another Cuban whose great talents were never accompanied by breakthrough acceptance because the coverage about him and who he was as a man was slim to none. When I began interviewing Miñoso and other great Latin American players of the 1950s, and talked to them in Spanish, I found an enormous chasm between the hilarious and lyrical way they spoke Spanish compared to the remedial way they were quoted in English.

The late, great Roberto Clemente, as venerated as he is today, was an outspoken critic of how he and other players from Latin America were lampooned or damned with faint praise in the media. It pained Pedro to think of Clemente being called "Bob," and he winced when he talked about it. To him, the image of Clemente playing with what Pedro called "fury," digging the ball out of the right-field corner and wheeling around to unleash a rocket throw to third base, was as close to baseball perfection as it got. There was no figure in baseball history Pedro held in as high a regard as both a ball player and a man as Clemente, and he knew how thoroughly the sportswriters of his day had swung and missed on reporting the truth of the man.

Pedro gave the Latin players we covered the platform to speak and be understood as the consequential men they were. Pedro did this without being a shill or cheerleader. My boy Pedrito was an old school print scribe to his bones, which meant you didn't write PR. You covered the game and followed the truth as you saw it and shared that truth with readers and viewers.

The reality was, by the late 1990s, baseball was energized by players from Latin America. So Pedro simply reported that phenomenon with clear understanding. His readers and viewers were the beneficiaries, as was a game where it is no longer unusual to see media people covering baseball who speak Spanish.

Even before he joined ESPN, Pedro's reputation among Latin American players was lofty. My book placed Miguel Tejada, a Dominican who went on to become the 2002 American League Most Valuable Player, at the center of the narrative. And when I was writing it, I took Miguel to dinner in Phoenix during spring training. Pedro joined us and Miguel was star-struck when my Cuban brother sat down at our table. I witnessed similar moments in big-league clubhouses as Pedro's reputation grew when he joined ESPN in the early 2000s.

My boy always kept one foot in two worlds and he moved gracefully through both. He could communicate beautifully in English and Spanish. He was American and he was Cuban. He shared each side of himself freely and joyfully. He became a big success while remaining uniquely himself. It sounds so simple, but it's really not.

Pedro's life was a blessing to all of us who knew him, but to those of us who shared a profession and an ancestral language with him, his life was a beacon. Each one of us shares a personal story with him that involves something in Spanish that linked us until he left us. For Pedrito and me, it was the Spanish word for moon: *Luna*.

On my birthday in 1997, Pedrito, his wife Sandi and their son Rio, who was just a preschooler at the time, drove up ninety minutes from the East Bay to the northern part of Sacramento where I lived. It was a long round trip and I was flattered he made the gesture. Later, when I had my own children, I realized how hard it could be to schlep a long way, at night, to a party with your child when you were probably exhausted by said child.

Yet there they were and Rio, like his dad, had a magnetic sense of charm and he sidled up to the girlfriend of a buddy of mine. My friend's girlfriend, Laura, looked a little like Uma Thurman. Rio took her hand and tugged her toward my back door, pointed up at the night sky and said, *"Luna."*

He wanted to take her outside to show her the moon and he did. The adults left behind in the room stood there, jaws agape, and marveled at the moxie of a tiny boy with the presence of mind to ask an attractive young lady for a glance at the moonlight. For more than twenty years, Pedro would work the *"Luna"* story into our conversations. When Rio made his debut in professional baseball, Pedro called from the ballpark and just before we hung up, he said *"Luna!"*

I think of Pedro every time I look at the *luna* now. I hope one day I'll get to see Rio pitch in the big leagues, under a big bright moon like we saw that night on my birthday years ago.

It's just a daydream for now and in it, after Rio records the last out of a win for his team, I'll look up at the moon and see his father's smile.

John with his wife Melanie, daughter Natalie and
son Jack (that's George in front)

Pedro with an Al Kaline baseball card a fan sent him

VOICE TO THE
VOICELESS

BY JOHN D'ANNA

The voice on the other end of the telephone line was excited, overwhelmed, emotional. It belonged to a man who was making a pilgrimage of sorts to the homeland his parents had fled nearly forty years earlier, never to return. It was the voice of a sportswriter, and he was calling me from Cuba to dictate a column for the next day's newspaper. The voice belonged to Pedro Gomez, and I was his editor.

It was spring 1999, and Pedro was the national baseball reporter and columnist for *The Arizona Republic*. He was covering the first ever game between a Major League Baseball team and the Cuban National Team. It was a momentous and unprecedented diplomatic milestone, a thaw in one of the last vestiges of the Cold War. It was a political story as well as a baseball story, and Pedro was crafting the proverbial first rough draft of history around it because, well, that's what journalists do.

We were an odd pair. Pedro was a sports guy, one of the best in the business, and I was on the news side. I'd never worked in sports, but our bosses put us together because we shared a passion for making journalism richer, deeper and more meaningful. It was the start of an amazing professional relationship, but more importantly, it was the start of a friendship that lasted nearly twenty-five years and only ended with Pedro's death, which I am still trying to comprehend.

As I write it's already been weeks since that horrible Super Bowl Sunday when I heard the news, and I still cannot wrap my mind around a world without Pedro Gomez doing the kind of journalism that matters, especially in a time and place where journalism itself seems not to matter at all for some. From the beginning of our journalistic careers we are taught to be objective (whatever that means), to be dispassionate observers, or "disinterested observers" in Walter Lippmann's influential phrase, to be flies on the wall. We're taught to never become part of the story.

Pedro and I shared those values, even though we took our journalism training at different ends of the country, he in Miami and me in Tucson. But there is also a higher journalistic calling that we both shared, and that is speaking truth to power and giving voice to the voiceless. Sometimes, that requires us to set aside some of those aforementioned journalistic conventions, summon our courage, and allow our humanity to shine through. It is something that many journalists can't, won't or simply don't do.

But Pedro did, and he did it often. And when he did, it not only brought him closer to the people he covered, but to the people who read his stories or watched him on television. In 2013, long after he'd left the *Republic* for ESPN, I watched Pedro on TV as he interviewed an Oakland A's outfielder named Yoenis Céspedes, who had just won the All-Star Game's Home Run Derby.

Céspedes was a Cuban refugee and spoke very little English. He had come to this country with nothing by escaping Cuba via a harrowing speedboat ride over dangerous seas.

In the league just a couple of years, Céspedes was not an All-Star, and in fact was the first person to win the Home Run Derby without being selected to play in the game. It would have been easy for an interviewer to toss questions at him in English and let him fumble his way through a few *muy biens* and *muy felizes*. But that's not what happened.

What did happen was not just extraordinary, it was vintage Pedro Gomez. Pedro seamlessly translated his questions to Céspedes into Spanish and then translated the answers into English for the audience.

Yoenis Céspedes

Without Pedro's conviction that everyone's voice deserves to be heard, that young man would not have been able to share his unbridled joy with the world. It's not easy to explain just how difficult it is to interview someone and serve as their translator at the same time. To do it in a live standup, in prime time, in front of a national audience takes not just a special kind of skill, not just a special kind of fearlessness, but a special kind of commitment to giving a voice to the voiceless. To doing journalism that matters.

That kind of humanity wasn't just the hallmark of a great journalist, which Pedro was, but it was the hallmark of an amazing friend who always gave more than he got. Whenever Pedro talked with you, it didn't matter if he'd just gotten off the phone with a billionaire team owner or a millionaire player because you were the most important person in the world to him at that moment. Or at least he made you feel that way. And

341

your family was his family.

When my wife was teaching at an elementary school in a low income, heavily Latino area of suburban Phoenix, she was struggling to find ways to get her fourth graders, many of whom were immigrants or children of immigrants, to believe they could someday go to college. I asked Pedro if he might be able to speak to her class. It was, in hindsight, a stupid question. Pedro showed up with a bag of ESPN tchotchkes and a story to tell.

I'm not exaggerating when I say it was a life-changing moment for those kids. Standing in front of them was someone who looked like their fathers or uncles or big brothers. Someone who, like them, grew up speaking Spanish as their mother tongue. Someone whose parents came to America for a better life for their children, as their own parents had.

That someone like him could be on television and make a nice living interviewing the baseball players they all knew and idolized didn't just captivate thirty bright-eyed kids for a day. It planted the seed that their education mattered, that it was possible for them to someday not only have their own voices heard, but to have them heard on national television. It was vintage Pedro, and while there wasn't a broadcast segment to air or an article in the paper, it was storytelling at its finest. It was journalism that mattered. Pedro never cared about the size of the audience that received his journalism. Whether it was a national TV audience in prime time, a classroom of thirty kids or a single teenager contemplating his future, what mattered was that success was something to be shared.

A few years after Pedro spoke to my wife's class, our son Jack was accepted to the University of Southern California and was toying with the idea of going into sports management. I suggested he talk with Pedro, because he knew all the big-time sports agents and team owners. It was a busy time for Pedro. Baseball season was in full-swing, and he was traveling a lot. When I asked him if he could take a few minutes to talk with Jack on the phone, Pedro suggested we go to lunch in a few days. I was hesitant to ask him to take away valuable time from his family, but he insisted.

At lunch, he carefully listened to Jack's hopes and dreams, and made him feel like he was the most important person in the world at that moment. And then Pedro threw Jack—and me—a curve and said that he should consider not majoring in sports management at all. Instead, he should look at majoring in economics.

That was what many of the best minds in sports, like then-Dodgers GM Farhan Zaidi and Rays president Matt Silverman, had majored in, he said, and if in the end Jack decided he didn't want to spend his life dealing with athletes or schlepping his way through minor-league town after minor-league town while climbing the ladder to the bigs, he'd have a versatile degree that could take him in a lot of different directions. Econ wasn't anywhere near Jack's radar, but he took his advice. Whenever Pedro would come to Los Angeles to cover a story, he'd call or text Jack to check in on him and take him to lunch.

In the end, Jack changed his mind about sports, but not about economics. Today I am writing this from Washington DC while helping Jack move as he embarks on a new career in the defense industry, confident that the voice he brings to the table will be heard. I wish I could tell Pedro that he was part of Jack's success, but I'm sure he'd just tell me it was no big deal and to just pay it forward. And I can hear him saying to me in that voice, that same voice I heard on the line that day in 1999.

Over the course of his week in Cuba, Pedro did the dispassionate observer thing, documenting the balls and strikes, both literal and political, as Cuban President Fidel Castro, flanked by Baltimore Orioles owner Peter Angelos and Major League Baseball Commissioner Bud Selig, looked down from his box at Estadio Latinoamericano, the second largest baseball stadium in the world. But over the course of that week he also documented the misery Castro had inflicted upon his own people and how four decades of the U.S. embargo against Cuba had only compounded their suffering. It was a suffering Pedro knew well before he even went to Cuba.

His parents had fled the island in 1962, just weeks before he was born. They literally left everything behind, their home with every stick of furniture, every family heirloom, every piece of jewelry and even every photograph, to give him a better chance at life in the United States. Pedro could not ignore their sacrifice any more than he could ignore what he saw and heard in Cuba.

"You have no idea of how lucky you are," a twenty-seven-year-old man named Armando Ochoa told him. "I would give anything to change spots with you. Anything. This system does not work."

Those words, Pedro wrote, reinforced what he was already feeling, making the contrast between the pre-Castro Cuba his parents knew and Cuba of today even more stark.

"Standing on the main artery of 23rd Street at night and closing my eyes, I am placed back in a time when roulette wheels spun and salsa dancers took center stage every night of the week until dawn...But then the stench of pollution in the air fills my lungs and settles in my eyes, and I am reminded of the afflictions strangling Cuba. The current decay is unmistakable and indelible."

Pedro was speaking truth to power, and not just to Castro. In a subsequent column, his Open Letter to President Bill Clinton, he called for the end of the four-decade U.S. trade embargo, which had done just as much to strangle Cuba's economy and impoverish its people. Pedro's people. It was not a popular opinion. Just a few years before he wrote those words, a Gallup poll found that 87 percent of the Cuban-American exiles living in Miami/Dade County, also Pedro's people, favored maintaining the embargo.

But having a popular opinion was not what mattered to Pedro Gomez. What mattered was that historians would someday read his first rough draft of history and know he told the truth. And what mattered was that he gave voice to the voiceless, like Armando Ochoa. Because, well, that's what journalists do.

Pedro with Mark Fainaru-Wada, Steve Fainaru and Bud Geracie

Carlos Carrasco

CUBANIDAD

BY STEVE FAINARU

Cubans, they're different than you and me. They fear nothing and have opinions about everything. They imagine things we can't see, and with their audacity and stubbornness they can make the most fantastical stories real. To say Cubans have balls has nothing to do with gender, because the women are the same as the men. When Orlando "El Duque" Hernandez escaped Cuba on Christmas Day 1997, he and his compatriots had to wade through the water to reach their vessel, a broken-down fishing boat anchored off Caibarién.

"This boat is a piece of shit," one of the men said, and for a moment everyone hesitated.

"We've made our decision," El Duque's girlfriend and future wife, Noris Bosch, shot back. She was a lithe modern dancer and the water was nearly up to her neck. "Better to drown than turn back now."

There's a line in Pedro's extraordinary Open Letter to Bill Clinton after he saw Cuba for the first time: "After gazing into the eyes of the Cuban people, I have discovered that I see so much of myself." It's surely one of the truest sentences he ever wrote. Pedro grew up in the States but was conceived in Havana and the spirit of the place radiated off of him, much like El Duque or any number of people I met on the island. Pedro was so humble, so optimistic and self-evidently decent, I think people sometimes missed his fearlessness, the remarkable things he did. On ESPN, he routinely performed the high-wire act of conducting live interviews in Spanish and translating them flawlessly—in real time on national TV.

Pedro's *Cubanidad*—his essential Cubanness—wasn't something I really thought about until suddenly he was gone and I was flooded with thoughts and memories, like everyone else who loved him. When we met in the early '90s. I was in my last years covering the Red Sox and he'd just started covering the A's. An old girlfriend recently sent me a picture from back then—Pedro, Bud Geracie, my brother and me at Bruce Jenkins' wedding. I stared at it and thought about what happened next—all the things none of us could see coming. Pedro, as many people noted, made the seamless transition from beat writer to columnist to TV, but to me it was much more. In thirty-five years, I have worked with only two other reporters as naturally gifted as Pedro—sports journalist Jackie MacMullan and Anthony Shadid, who won two Pulitzer Prizes reporting from Iraq before he died in Syria in 2012. As with Jackie and Anthony, in Pedro there was an alchemy of charisma, curiosity, hard work and, especially, passion; you looked at him and thought: *I wish I could do that, but I can't.*

We worked together on a Covid story last spring and it was classic Pedro, which is to say full of laughs and insight. Among Pedro's many gifts was his ability to elevate people's moods just walking into the room— even a virtual one. On our first Zoom call, everyone was waiting around in awkward silence when Pedro noticed one of his favorite producers and struck up a stadium chant: *"Greg Amante...clap clap clap clap clap... Greg Amante...clap clap clap clap clap."* Pedro's role on the story was to find players to talk about Covid—most of us couldn't get them on the phone. Within a week or so he'd rounded up a dozen: Mike Trout...Max Scherzer...Jonathan Lucroy, all confiding to Pedro about their hopes and worst fears during a dangerous time. I sat in on his Zoom interview with Carlos Carrasco, who'd recently been diagnosed with leukemia. Carrasco had five kids and spent half his day training and shopping for groceries. But he was happy to accommodate Pedro. The interview was like watching two old friends catch up—except the camera was rolling and Pedro was painlessly extracting information from Carrasco's head:

Carrasco: "I'm the only one who goes out—my mom, my wife, my kids, they don't go out."

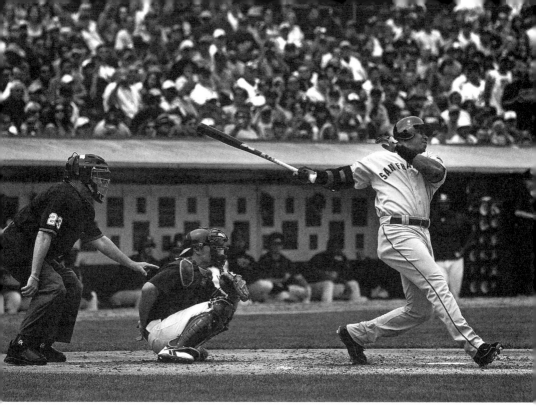

No. 714

Pedro: "But you're the one that's in danger because of your treatments!"

Carrasco: "Yeah, Pedro, it is what it is, man. I know this is gonna sound weird, but I need to take care of my family. Every time when I go home, I just get naked and spray Lysol."

I was with Pedro a lot during the joyless Barry Bonds home run chase in 2006. My brother Mark summed it up well: "There's a journalism master class to be taught simply by taking the breadth of Pedro's work on Bonds and unspooling it, day by day, report by report, question by question." The entire cross-country affair was pretty unpleasant, like covering a mobile toxic waste site. But what I remember most was how little it changed Pedro. The contrast between Bonds and the man trailing him for ESPN could not have been more stark—one isolated, dour and not infrequently, mean; the other inclusive, cheerful and always kind.

Bonds tied Babe Ruth at 714 during a day game in Oakland. That night, a bunch of us gathered at a house I was renting in Berkeley, having just separated from my wife. To put it mildly, this was not an uplifting period for my family. My brother and Lance Williams were facing prison for refusing to divulge their sources on the steroids story. In addition to my imploding marriage, I was feeling the effects of a year and a half in Iraq; my newspaper had parked me on Bonds to help me get my mind off of it. That night, surrounded by a stranger's furnishings, we ate and drank and listened to Pedro, his voice getting louder and louder as he leaned into some baseball argument I can no longer recall but it doesn't matter because everyone who knew Pedro will hear his voice for the rest of our lives.

Pedro happened to be standing near a gigantic television as he ranted. We had ESPN on, and suddenly there were *two* Pedros—the sober one on TV and the half-drunk one directly in front of us. We all stopped to watch his Bonds report, the signoff coming with a reassuring nod of the head: "Pedro Gomez... *ESPN*."

The room erupted.

"Pedro Gomez...*ESPN!*" we shouted gleefully, imitating him. "Pedro Gomez...*ESPN!*"

Maybe you had to be there, but we were all in tears. As I was, for other reasons, when Geracie, Jenkins and I remembered that moment the day Pedro died.

Pedro wrote his open letter to Clinton in 1999 after visiting Cuba for the first time to cover the Baltimore Orioles' historic game against the Cuban National Team. I so wish I could have been there with him. I couldn't because the Castro government had banned me from the country for associating with treasonous right-hander El Duque and writing several stories about human rights—despite a warning from the Cuban Embassy in Mexico City.

A little context about Pedro's courageous letter, which was first published in the *Arizona Republic*. Cuba at the time was in the last throes of the economic meltdown that followed the collapse of the Soviet Union. The level of deprivation was breathtaking: gasoline, eggs, cooking oil and other staples were all but impossible to find. In 1998, after flying from Havana to the city of Las Tunas, I went to catch a cab and instead encountered a line of horse-and-buggies outside the airport.

The government was in the middle of one of its periodic crackdowns on independent thought. This included El Duque. I had a front-row seat as the state tried to crush him. After his half-brother Livan defected, the government banned El Duque from "revolutionary baseball" and left him to starve in the national hellscape. He lived alone in a cinderblock shack. Sometimes, with a friend, he sold black-market gas and ice cream on the streets. "Hope," he told me one day. "That's what I have for breakfast every morning."

El Duque spent New Year's Day 1998 in a Nassau immigration cell after washing up in the Bahamas. Ten months later, he won Game 2 of the World Series.

Pedro could have had any number of reactions when he arrived in Havana five months later. He was thirty-six, and had grown up in the seething alternate universe of exile Miami. Baseball—his passion and one shared by both countries—was so politicized in Cuba that a Miami agent had been imprisoned for fifteen years for recruiting ballplayers. Rage—that might have been one reaction. Or resignation and disgust. That was not Pedro. Instead he took it all in and found empathy, while undergoing a profound personal transformation: "Even as I write this, I can barely contain myself, for now that I have met what I consider my countrymen, I can't help but feel an overwhelming sense of pride to say I am both Cuban and American. In a way, I feel I have been twice blessed."

Steve Kettmann has it right: By urging Clinton to end the obscene embargo (still, even now, firmly entrenched), Pedro was taking on the community that raised him, including his parents and many of his friends. For a man who so valued family, it was an act of bravery not unlike an excommunicated baseball player setting off on a fishing boat into the great unknown.

But what comes through more than anything is the man's humanity. To transcend decades of history, and conflict, and hatred, and strife, only to say: I am them, and they are me.

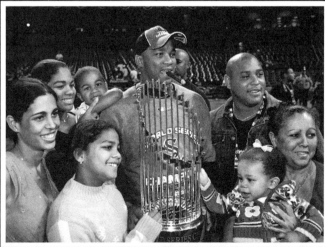

El Duque with his family after winning the 2005 World Series with the White Sox

YO SOY DE LA MISMA TIERRA

BY ORLANDO "EL DUQUE" HERNANDEZ

The first time I met Pedro—that's the day our friendship began. He came up to me at the stadium one day, very respectful as always, and when he introduced himself he said: "*Yo soy de la misma tierra*. I'm Cuban, just like you." It's a moment I'll never forget.

It was the beginning of my career, I had recently arrived in the United States and it was hard for me to communicate. From then on, we were friends. There were many times he stepped in and helped translate my conversations—with teammates and other players, or not even players but just people we'd meet. A lot of times he was my connection to the world.

When I was still playing I would see him a lot, especially around the ballpark. He was just a man and a gentleman in every respect. I loved him.

Later when I joined ESPN, we got to work together. Really it was more joy than work. And he really helped me. The advice he gave me I continue to follow today.

"Obviously, I can't teach you much about baseball," he said, "but what I can try to do is walk you through the world of journalism."

One time we did a tour together of interviews with maybe ten or twelve local television stations. It was fantastic and while we were on that tour he talked to me about everything about broadcasting: How to present yourself during an interview; how to ask the questions; how to deal with the players; how to deal with your colleagues. They were basically consultations—how to present myself as a broadcaster.

He always emphasized one thing: "Respect everyone, but don't *empalaga* (fawn or flatter excessively) to the point where you bother people or turn them off. Just be smooth and respectful." That was good advice.

I was at home in Miami when I heard the news from my son. I didn't really believe it. I thought it couldn't be right—a man so happy, so alive. But it was true. Imagine, he was just a huge figure in baseball, not just baseball but the whole sports world. It's an immense loss. In addition to the help he gave me, he was just a tremendous person. I miss him.

That's Dante standing on the far left with his Ahwatukee Cardinals teammates

DO RIGHT BY PEOPLE

BY DANTE GOMEZ

One time when I was ten or eleven my dad took me to an Anaheim Angels spring-training game at Tempe Diablo Stadium. We stopped off in the executive offices and he introduced me to everybody we saw. Then we were in the stands watching the game in the concourse behind home plate. My dad was telling me about different players, and different things to watch for, just bringing the whole game alive for me. It was fun to think along with him.

"What do you think is going to happen here?" I asked him at one point. He dove right into his answer.

"Well, the pitcher is struggling to throw strikes, and the batter is a pretty good fastball hitter," he said. "I think the pitcher is going to give him one here, and I think he might get ahold of it."

The very next pitch was a fastball and the batter cranked it for a home run. The ball flew right out of there. I was in amazement. So were the three people one row in front of us and three people in the row behind us, who all overheard the conversation. They kept talking about how my dad had called the home run.

"Oh my God!" they were all saying.

Finally my dad kind of smiled and told me: "I do this for a living. You shouldn't be so surprised."

I thought it was the coolest thing, knowing sports so well you could predict what was going to happen one minute later. I played baseball growing up and for four years my dad coached my team along with a couple other dads. It was awesome sharing so many moments over those four years, waking up at 5 a.m. to drive to a baseball tournament. He traveled a whole bunch for work, but I feel like he hardly ever missed a practice or a game. He had that crazy Cuban energy every day at practice too. He loved it. He'd be out there hitting fungoes, just as excited as any of us were. Obviously we were trying to get better and win games, but he was out there having a good time and wanted us to have a good time, too.

At times, I felt almost embarrassed that he was the coach, because especially at that age, you don't want the spotlight on you. He had that Cuban temper sometimes, where he'd be out there freaking out a little and I'd wish I could disappear. When I was eleven he was coaching our team when the other team tried a hidden-ball trick, but they did it wrong. My dad went out to talk to the teenager who was umpiring the game, and wasn't getting through to him, so he called up Laz Diaz, the major-league umpire. It was like it would never end. They had the whole thing out. I remember thinking: *Oh my God, I can't believe they're on the phone for five minutes and this eighteen-year-old umpire is talking to Laz Diaz trying to get this call right.*

Later when I was in community college I played one year of college baseball. I'd messed around pitching sidearm here and there, but one day I tried it during a scrimmage and ended up throwing really well. No one could believe it. My motion looked weird, but it felt so much more natural to me. I was throwing hard and I was throwing strikes. My dad was on the road, working, and I sent him a video of me pitching sidearm. One day later he just happened to be in Cleveland and talked to the sidearm reliever Joe Smith. Sure enough, my dad sent me a five-minute video of Joe Smith talking me through everything he could think of, from how he started throwing sidearm to what he envisions in his head trying to get a certain kind of arm action, not wanting to bend at the wrist. It was incredible. I'd thrown sidearm one day and my dad was already reaching out to big-leaguers to get advice for me. I ended up throwing sidearm that whole season.

Now I'm at that age where I'm still trying to figure out what I want to do with my future after I graduate from college. My older brother, Rio,

is a pitcher in the Red Sox organization. I never had that kind of talent or, to be honest, desire. My dad always told me I was more cerebral than the other players. Whatever I lacked in talent I made up in thinking the game. I wasn't throwing the hardest and I definitely wasn't running the fastest, but I definitely knew where the play was. When I was pitching, I was thinking ahead of the batter. I was able to do my thing and be successful even if I wasn't the most talented guy out there.

I love sports, and I keep thinking, maybe I'll end up working in sports somehow. I know it's tough to get a break, tons of candidates for any job that opens up, but if I ever had an opportunity, I'd like to be involved with sports talk radio.

I never put two and two together on this, but in recent weeks when I thought about it more, I realized I already feel like I've been a sports talk radio host for the last ten years of my life. All that time, I've been constantly talking sports with my buddies and with my dad and my family, breaking down all different kinds of angles on every sport. Every

day we'd watch a game and talk throughout, and even when there was no game we'd still be talking about all kinds of different stuff in the sports world. We'd talk about the choices of the team GM. We'd talk about the bullpen, the payroll, the farm system, everything. We got into all kinds of aspects, and I feel like that's what sports talk is—that and coming up with good one-liners. My dad always believed in me and my creativity and always wanted me to put it to good use.

The TV in the living room would be on to a game, and even from a young age, I feel like we were always discussing every aspect, and it wasn't just X's and O's. We'd get into deeper talks about so-and-so is going to be a free agent next year. How much money do you think he's going to get? Where do you think he's going to get this money? Years, that kind of stuff. Topics would come up, like the infield fly rule, and we would discuss that for five or ten minutes and move on. We watched a lot of Diamondbacks games, and their being a National League team, there was a little bit more strategy on the manager's side, and we'd be discussing that throughout the game.

One thing cool about this book for me is reading different perspectives on my dad and learning more about how people who worked with him saw him and how they see the business. It may not bring me any closer to actually getting a job in sports radio, but it may inspire me to go for it. Brian Murphy of KNBR in San Francisco wrote an essay about my dad showing him the ropes as a sportswriter, "Always Grab the Corks," and he's worked full time in sports talk radio since 2004.

"The No. 1 requirement for success in sports talk radio is a deep and abiding passion for three things—for sports, for conversation and for people," Brian says, offering me a little good-natured advice. "You need to have a passion for all three. You can't go two-for-three. You have to go Tony Gwynn three-for-three. Pedro had all three. He'd have been great on sports talk radio. Dante has the DNA handed down to light it up. He has the love of sports, conversation and people to never tire of any of it. People say to me, 'Don't you get tired of talking about sports all the time?' I say: 'No! It's the most fun I've ever had.' You have to look deep within yourself and be honest. If you don't love it, you're not going to be good at it."

The shows I like are smart and fast paced, like "Pardon the Interruption" on ESPN or "The Dan Patrick Show" or "The Rich Eisen Show." You can't talk about sports without talking about numbers, about statistics and the whole analytics piece, but my dad and I talked about how the people side of sports was getting left behind. He used to talk to me about Tito Francona and what a people guy he is. He goes gut feeling a lot. Some of those other guys still have that old school aspect to them. But my dad always thought the game was moving toward too much emphasis on numbers versus a little bit of a mix of the numbers with the people aspect.

We had our disagreements. Like: Should they kick the field goal here? Should they go for it on fourth down for the touchdown? Should a team play for overtime? Or in baseball a manager coming out to pull his guy or to leave him in. We'd disagree on that kind of stuff, and it was always funny because we'd give our take and then seconds later you'd have the announcers give their take. They'd agree with one of us, and we'd always take that as a kind of win.

My dad would tell us about how athletes were as people and how they were seen by others in the sport. If someone was a good guy, that was important to him. He had good morals and high integrity, and I feel like he and my mom did a good job of instilling that in me and Rio and Sierra. Do right by people. Do things the right way. That was something he took pretty seriously. It was like: *I want to be known as a good guy.*

The thing about my dad that stands out the most was how joyful he was and the love that he lived life with. He had that angry Cuban side to him, but at the same time he was just so joyful. He was excited to do his job every day. He was excited to fly off to the playoffs every October or to go cover a random Sunday night game in Philadelphia. He was just always so excited to do his job. And then he'd be excited to come home to us. He had this thing where, any time he was on the road, he took the earliest possible flight to fly home to Phoenix. I always used to give him shit for that too.

"Dad, you flew at 6 a.m. when you could have just slept in and flown at like 10?" I'd say to him, laughing. "Why would you do that to yourself?"

"I wanted to get home," he'd say.

He was just really present at all times, whether it was hanging around with friends in our backyard or on vacation or even at our family dinners, where using your phone was strictly prohibited. He was always in the moment and enjoying life. Always up and at 'em. I feel like he never had a bad day. It was inspiring to see.

Bud and Nick

Kit Stier, Bud, Wally Haas and Sandy Alderson

YOU SHOULD CALL
FRANK

BY BUD GERACIE

In my darker decades, I would turn the pages of self-help books in a frenzy, desperately searching for the secret to happiness. This was like that, except it wasn't a book I was searching, or happiness I was seeking. Pedro was gone.

I didn't know how he had left this world, so suddenly. But the "how" wasn't what sent me on a desperate search through the pages of Facebook and Twitter, and into the archives of my own correspondence with him. The "how" didn't matter much to me. Pedro was gone. Nothing was going to change that.

I had looked down at my phone in the third quarter of what forever will be the worst Super Bowl ever, and there it was: A tweet from Charles Robinson, retweeting the shocking news from ESPN.

"Sometimes people just choose to leave us," an acquaintance offered at one point during the night.

She had done the math we do in journalism: sudden death + no cause given = suicide. Clearly, she did not know Pedro. Nobody I've known ever loved life more than Pedro. Even allowing for the many years that had passed since I knew him well... no, no way.

As the hours passed and night became dawn and dawn became day, I got reacquainted with my friend. Given his profession and his personality, I wasn't surprised that Pedro knew so many people. But it was staggering how many of them paid tribute to him with a story about something he had done for them.

I shared this discovery with one of Pedro's closest friends, maybe his closest friend, his "brother" Steve Kettmann. Steve said he'd been struck by the vast number of people who shared that they'd been in touch with Pedro just that week. I had noticed that too and can bet with supreme confidence which party initiated the contact. *The last time I last talked to Pedro... six days ago... five days ago... four days ago... three days ago...*

Our shared discoveries were summarized in one sentence, the opening sentence of a Facebook tribute from another friend and baseball-writing colleague, Mark Gonzales: "My last conversation with Pedro Gomez on Thursday captured what he was all about - the welfare of others."

I don't know if Pedro set out to help so many people. Or just came by it naturally. Whatever the case, he did it. Equally remarkable, he didn't say much about it. That's how it is supposed to be done. But ego often wins that battle. Have I mentioned how I helped launch Pedro's career, how important I was to his success?

"Tocame los huevos."

That's the first piece of advice I remember getting from Pedro. It was almost thirty years ago. We were together at spring training. He was the A's beat writer. I was a columnist, his predecessor on the beat once removed. I was being courted by another newspaper. I was ready to go, had all but accepted the offer. But now the *Mercury News* was sending someone down to Arizona to talk some sense into me.

Pedro, what to do?

"Tell them, '*Tocame los huevos*,'" he said.

OK, but what does that mean?

"Touch my balls."

We burst into laughter. Those three words are part of our history.

Last August, out of nowhere, a text from Pedro. No words. Two photos. Me and my son, age two or three. He's twenty-eight now. Back then, we didn't have phones with cameras. We didn't take pictures of every damn thing we did or ate or saw. These were snapshots, taken the old-fashioned way, developed at the drugstore and shared.... twenty-five years later?

"Funny," I wrote back, "I was just talking about you *ayer* and was gonna reach out. I told Donna someone could *'tocame mis huevos'* and when she asked what that meant. I got to tell the story. Do u remember? Love u, Petey. Forever.'"

"Love that story," he replied, "and love you. Also forever."

It was that easy with him. That easy to say those words, or at least type them and share them. That easy to reconnect, to pick up wherever the relationship had been left however long ago.

"You watching Astros/Rays?" he asked to open an October 15 text exchange. "Did you see Springer's shot to lead off the game?"

"What sport is that, Petey?"

We hadn't been in touch often enough over the last few years for him to know that my love for baseball, and then my interest, had evaporated. He asked what I thought of this Astros pitcher named Scrubb, an obvious set-up line for the smartass Saturday column I used to write.

"With a name like Smuckers," I wrote, "you better be good."

"*Exactamente*," Pedro replied.

Me: "*Tremenda.*"

Him: "*Jugada*"

Me: "*Ayer*"

Tremenda jugada ayer.

In 1992, when the A's pulled Jose Canseco out of the on-deck circle and traded him to Texas for Rubén Sierra, the *Mercury News* sent both of us to New York for Canseco's first game with the Rangers. That night we were sitting in a hotel room watching Sierra's first game with the A's. They won in a walk-off on a smart base-running play by Sierra—no, really—that brought him sliding across home plate with the winning run.

Pedro, I said, we're going to meet Sierra tomorrow night. Give me an icebreaker.

Tremenda jugada ayer. (Tremendous play yesterday.)

Our text exchange in October 2020 went on for seven hours, intermittently. The conclusion breaks my heart.

"Hey," I wrote, "one thing. I want to be sure we get one loooong hang in sometime before it's too late. Ya know?"

Rubén Sierra

YOU SHOULD CALL FRANK • BUD GERACIE

"I do know," he wrote back. "Yes. I'm in for that."

The last sentence was pure Pedro, all Pedro. Absolutely "in" for anything.

I had found the first sentence of his reply curious, out of character. Again due to our lack of regular contact, in tandem with my dwindling interest in baseball, I did not know he'd been off the air for an extended period in 2018 because of a health problem.

I am very much aware that the clock is running, like sands through an hourglass, so are the days of our lives. (Macdonald Carey, a track from the soundtrack of my childhood.) I'm bent that way. Plus, I've reached an age where reminders of mortality seem to come almost daily.

My son says I'm the most morbid person he will ever know. My closest friends already have given me the title. It's a standing joke. Whenever we gather, one of them will ask, loudly enough for all to hear. *"How many of these do we have left, Bud?*

But it's not morbidity that drives me now. It's wanting to ensure that people will know how I felt about them, what they meant to me. That's why I'm so grateful for the exchange in which I told Pedro I loved him. And another I found after he'd sent belated birthday wishes. I broke out the Spanish for that one.

"Te amo."

"Igualmente, hermano."

Our last correspondence—January 24, two weeks before Super Bowl Sunday—came after an especially heavy week of those reminders about mortality. Don Sutton on Monday. Hank Aaron on Friday. Bud Lea in between. I had history with all three. A memorable breakfast with Aaron that started at a table for eight and ended with just us two. A number of years with Sutton, which ended badly over a Hall of Fame vote.

Bud Lea was a man I'd grown up reading, a columnist and sports editor for the *Milwaukee Sentinel,* no doubt one of the reasons this profession found me. When I was hired by the *Sentinel* in 1983, to cover the reigning American League champion Brewers—they got screwed in that World Series and, incredibly, have never been back—Bud Lea was there. He tipped me to my first scoop. (I blew it.) He had covered the Packers during the Lombardi years, and he regaled us with stories. He traded barbs with Bud Selig in the Milwaukee press box—possibly the last press box that will ever include three Buds.

Bud Lea was ninety-two years old when he died January 20. Pedro sent me a link to the news story. I had already heard and was too upset with myself to send him a reply. Two years ago, I'd gone to the trouble of getting Bud Lea's phone number. I wanted to thank him, to let him know how I felt about him, what he had meant to me. So his name and number went to the top of my To Do list for the following week.

And that's where it stayed—top of my list, week after week after week. I shared this with Pedro when I finally returned his text four days later. Bud Lea was ninety years old when I got his phone number. What was I thinking, that I had all the time in the world, that the clock wasn't running on a ninety-year-old man when it is running on us all?

I mentioned Don Sutton. Don Baylor, who had died in 2017. Gerry Fraley and Tom Flaherty, class of 2019. Mike Shalin, just a month earlier in December. I had something more to say to all of them.

"My regrets are piling up so deep, Petey."

"You should call Frank," Pedro replied.

Wait. What? His suggestion after all that I had just shared was for me to call someone I hadn't spoken to in twenty-five years, someone with whom I'd never been exceptionally close, someone with whom even Pedro had never been exceptionally close?

He gave me Frank's phone number.

"Let me know if you talk to him."

Of course I didn't call Frank. I probably would have eventually. But for nine days I let it sit.

On the seventh day, Pedro left us.

On the eighth day, I knew what I had to do.

On the ninth day, I did it.

It wasn't a difficult conversation, at least not in the way I had feared a week earlier. Pedro had provided a reason for this call out of the blue, this blast from the past. I was calling about Pedro, not about Frank's terminal diagnosis.

Pedro had given me the news in the same text exchange he had suggested I call Frank. But I had missed it. While I was texting him a flurry of questions—*Why should I call Frank? Is he not well? You're going to make me call him cold? Why would I do that? What will he think?*—Pedro had given me the answer. I found it the next morning and shot him a text.

"I somehow missed the one where you told me Frank has pancreatic cancer," I wrote. "That's the worst."

"It's definitely not one of the good ones," Pedro replied. "Horrible way to go."

That was our last exchange.

Frank and I talked for ninety minutes that Tuesday night. We talked about Pedro mostly, how amazing he was, how full of life, that he was one of a kind, all the things we say about people in the immediate aftermath of their final departure. Except there was nothing empty about these platitudes. They were full, completely full, to the brim, overflowing. And they will be said, forevermore, when the name Pedro Gomez is mentioned.

In that desperate search of Facebook and Twitter on the Sunday night that became Monday morning and then Monday afternoon, I read so many tributes to Pedro. From the young reporter he had stepped in to defend against a Hall of Fame manager's verbal assault. From the female reporter he had helped climb a fence after they'd been locked inside a stadium. (She was wearing a skirt; ever the gentleman, he promised her he would look away while she climbed). From the Cubs fan who told of him reaching into his backpack at the end of a conversation to give her a gift: a Champagne cork he'd retrieved from the clubhouse floor the night the Cubs celebrated winning the NLDS. Apparently, he'd made a practice of gathering corks during Champagne celebrations to give to fans.

For people he knew to people he'd just met, Pedro made the world a better place, a happier place. What he did for me began with a line of three words—*tocame los huevos*—and ended with a line of four.

You should call Frank.

I don't think about Bud Lea with regret anymore. I can't pay him back. I can only pay it forward. I call Frank once a week. I just now realized that I call him every Sunday, around the time that Pedro left us. Frank is mystified by these calls. *You do know you're not going to cheer up a dying man, right?* He expresses surprise every time. When we hang up, he always expects that will be the last time we talk, not because of his declining health but because.... *Who does this? Why would you do it?*

One of these times, I'm going to tell him why. It's WPWD.

What Pedro would do.

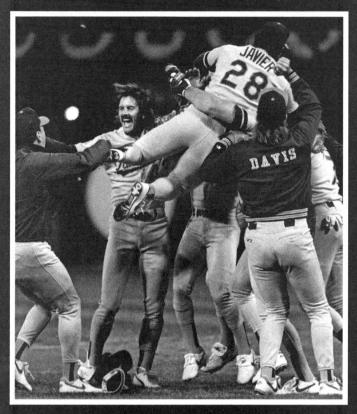

Eck and the A's celebrate winning the 1989 World Series

A BRIGHT LIGHT

BY DENNIS ECKERSLEY

I t's been almost thirty years since I first got to know Pedro. That was in spring 1992 when he started covering the A's as a young reporter for the *San Jose Mercury News*. He came on the beat after we'd been so successful, going to three straight World Series at the end of the '80s and winning the 1989 Earthquake Series. Those A's teams, Pedro later wrote, had been "the kings of baseball, averaging more than ninety-seven wins per season from 1988 to 1992 and reaching the postseason four times, the World Series three times and winning a championship in that span." We were "the kings of swagger," Pedro wrote.

That was a lot of powerful people to cover, right? It was not an easy thing for a reporter to walk into that, starting from scratch on that beat at age twenty-nine. That had to be intimidating, but you'd have never known it watching Pedro in that situation. He took to me that year and I took to him. It was just a feeling that he exuded, a kindness about him.

Pedro loved the way I talked about pitching. His favorite was "cookie," as in, I threw him a cookie. That was a mistake pitch, right down the middle. I'd talk about cheese and gas and hair, all ways of talking about fastballs, and salad, the way a guy had to pitch who didn't have much of a fastball. Pedro got it all right away. He loved talking about "cookies" after that.

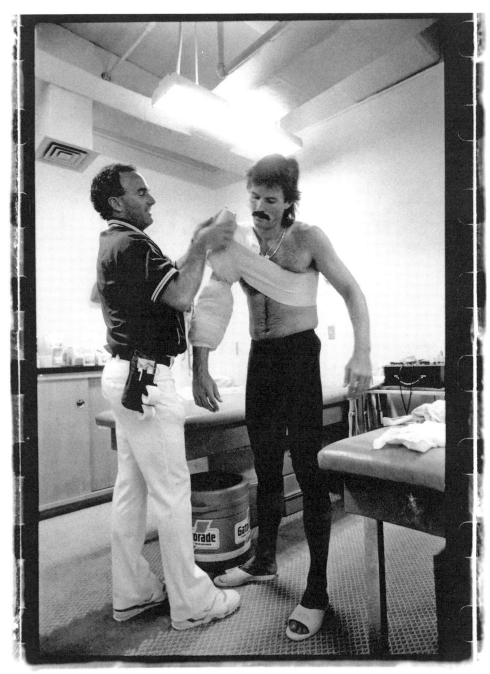

A's trainer Barry Weinberg working on Dennis in Oakland

I was thirty-seven that year and ended up winning the Cy Young Award as a relief pitcher. I had more than fifty saves. In July, Pedro did a feature just before the All-Star Game talking up my chances of making it to Cooperstown. "In his six seasons with the A's, Dennis Eckersley has gone from washed-up starter to strong Hall of Fame candidate," Pedro wrote. He quoted Tigers manager Sparky Anderson saying, "He's actually getting better with age. There are very few players who get better the closer they get to forty. He's kind of a freak, like Ryan or Rose, guys who are playing top-caliber baseball at a late age." Later, when I was inducted into the Hall of Fame in 2004, Pedro couldn't have been happier for me.

I've never met anybody like Pedro. There is nobody like him. He was different. He was so nice, but he could also be ballsy. To be a good reporter, you can't just be a nice, kind guy. You've got to get to the point, and that's not always pleasant. Pedro was brave, too.

I read about one time in Pedro's early years on the beat when he was part of a group of reporters interviewing Tony La Russa. Howard Bryant was a young reporter just starting out then, and Tony hammered him over a headline that had appeared in his paper (a story Howard touches on in essay #11, "Speechless"). Pedro wasn't friends with Howard yet, he barely knew him, but he rose to his defense.

"C'mon, Tony," Pedro said. "You know we don't write the headlines. Leave the kid alone. Why are you embarrassing him?"

That story really stuck with me. If you could stand up for somebody in a situation like that, it's very telling. That's character. Especially in a position like that with Tony, it was intimidating to say the least. We're talking about major character here. Isn't that the most important thing in life?

Pedro was just a bright light. You felt a friendship with Pedro, you just did. I saw him years later, there was a big gap of time, and when I saw him again it was like you picked up right where you left off. When I saw him, I felt like we were tight. It's hard to explain. That was the feeling.

Looking back, after the fact, I was envious of his disposition. He was always the way you want to be, maybe because he was grateful to be doing what he was doing. It wasn't a grind for him, like the daily grind can be for most. It gets to you, you know? It gets to all of us. I can imagine having an attitude as a player, let alone being a journalist on a daily basis. That's why you can appreciate somebody that has that type

A BRIGHT LIGHT • DENNIS ECKERSLEY

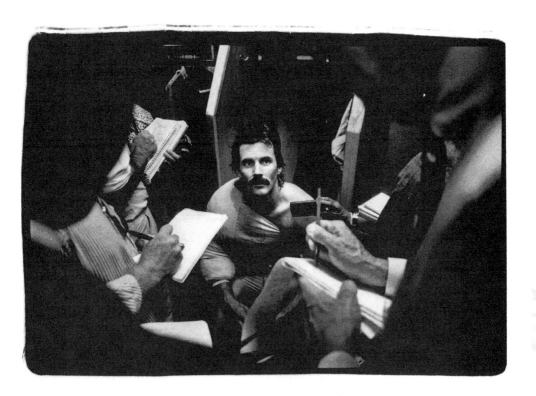

of disposition. It says a lot about somebody.

It stopped me in my tracks when I heard the news that Pedro had passed away. I was very moved. It's not like I knew him that well, but obviously he touched me. I'm trying to think of the last time I saw him. I can't even remember. Because he was with ESPN, he would just sort of pop up. He'd come out of nowhere. Poof, there he was.

Pedro always smiled. There was a sincerity that came across, which I never questioned, and that's what was unusual. You're always a little afraid or a little standoffish with reporters, you know what I mean? You think you've got to be careful. With Pedro there was just something about him that made you feel very comfortable. It was a gift. I guess it's a goodness about somebody, a human being in a difficult profession, that you walk away from suddenly, and that's what you're left with and it's all good. It's all good even though it's sad, because this was a really quality human being. That's what it is, yeah. Because I did like him so much, and it takes for somebody to pass to make you realize how much you did.

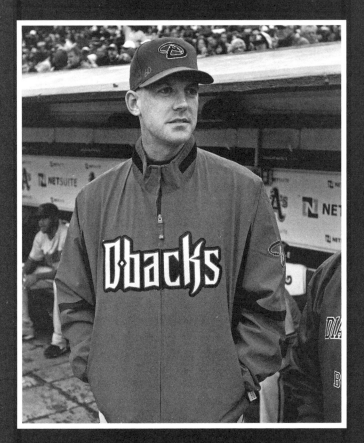

Al Kaline, 2013

DEEP DOWN
A TIGERS FAN

BY AJ HINCH

A few days before he died, Pedro called me up and we had a long talk about his love of the Tigers, his team growing up in Detroit in the 1960s. He was speaking from the heart, the way he always did, but it was his way of getting me even more excited about managing the Tigers and being back in baseball after losing my job in Houston under a cloud because of everything that happened with sign-stealing.

Little known fact about Pedro: His all-time favorite uniform in sports was Tigers home whites. As he put it in one interview, "You can take a look at Ty Cobb in the 1920s and compare it to today's version and there are so many similarities. I love the piping around the neck and especially the Old English D. It is such a gorgeous look. I am very glad they never messed with their home uniform."

I never realized until that last conversation how much of a Tigers fan Pedro was. He grew up going to Tigers games with his grandfather, who left Castro's Cuba in 1967. Pedro told me about how he obviously fell in love with Ernie Harwell, the Hall of Fame announcer for the Tigers. His parents were refugees, they left Havana three weeks before Pedro

Ernie Harwell

DEEP DOWN A TIGERS FAN • AJ HINCH

was born in August 1962, and there weren't jobs in Miami, so the family relocated to Detroit a year later. Both his parents found work in a Formica plant, so his grandparents would look after Pedro as a small child. His grandfather, born in Spain in 1899, had moved to Cuba as a teenager and worked as an umpire in Camaguey in the Cuban Winter League.

In that last conversation, Pedro told me all about how his grandfather, Isaac Gonzalez, would listen to Harwell calling the Tigers on the radio and even though he didn't speak English, he spoke baseball, and always knew just what was happening. When Ernie said, "He stood there like the house by the side of the road," his grandfather got the idea. He could even translate it into his own idiom: He was, in one of Pedro's all-time favorite expressions, *un out vestido de pelotero,* that is, an out dressed up as a ballplayer.

Pedro's favorite player was Al Kaline, except to him and his grandfather, it was pronounced Kah-LEEN-eh in Spanish. Hearing Pedro pronounce that one name, you could hear his love for his grandfather— and for baseball. As he told La Vida Baseball in one interview, "My grandfather was an enormous, enormous baseball fan. Every day I got indoctrinated into something different with baseball and it just got under my skin and into my blood, and hasn't left."

It was the 1968 World Series, the Tigers over the Cardinals in seven, that made Pedro a baseball fan for life. "I remember that the teachers at Sweetest Heart of Mary Catholic School, right in downtown Detroit, allowed us to listen on transistor radios," Pedro told FanGraphs. "The game was in the afternoon. The whole city was engulfed by Tigers. It was Tigers everything. I remember being swept up in the wave, and ever since then I've been a huge baseball fan."

Hearing Pedro talk about growing up a Tigers fan was fascinating. It brought in Ernie Harwell. It brought in old Tiger Stadium. I couldn't get enough of that, and I loved hearing about Pedro's grandfather because with Pedro, so often, he'd ask you about yourself before he ever shared his own personal stories, other than giving you the latest on how Rio was doing pitching in the Red Sox organization.

He always cared about you as a person. It wasn't enough for him just to cover the sport. He wanted to cover the human element of the sport. I think that's why we've seen such an outpouring of love and care for him after he died. All of us felt like we were in the trenches with him. He was

Kaline in 1955

on our side. He criticized me plenty, but it never felt like criticism, ever. Pedro really respected the difficulty of the managing job.

I first got to know Pedro when the Diamondbacks hired me as manager in May 2009. I was thirty-four at the time and had never managed at any level, so that opened the floodgates of second-guessing on the decision. So many people were asking me questions like "Why do you want to do this?" Everybody was trying to figure out the puzzle. Pedro, who still lived in the Phoenix area after ESPN hired him away from the *Arizona Republic* in 2003, had no time for any of that. He was less interested in theatrics and more focused on the people component. He was fascinated by details of my background, Stanford-educated, played in the Olympics, played in the big leagues, came to the front office, connected to the GM. He just had an uncanny way to capture my favorite human parts of the game.

I made an immediate connection with him, and we developed a friendship that I trusted. He could still cover the sport and cover games and ask baseball questions, but there was an underlying tone of a trusted friend that I really respected more and more as I got to know him better. Just before we signed Yuli Gurriel to a five-year deal in Houston in 2016, before it even went public, Pedro called to talk to me about the Gurriel family. He was thinking ahead for me: He knew for me that I was going to have a player whose dad, Lourdes Gurriel, was on the Cuban National Team I played against in Wichita, Kansas, in July 1993 with Team USA when he was thirty-six and I was nineteen. The pitcher for Cuba was El Duque, Orlando Hernandez, and he shut us out through four—then we broke through and ended up winning, 9-1. Pedro reminded me of that game and he and I talked for an hour about the Gurriel family and what they meant to Cuban baseball. He connected those dots before I had to. He saw through my eyes how managing Yuli was going to be unique. That goes a long way with me. It puts you on the right side of the line, because you truly are looking at it through my lens.

During the difficult time before and after I lost my job as Astros manager in January 2020 and was given a one-year suspension, I had to lay low. I wasn't answering a lot of calls, but when Pedro reached out I picked up the phone. That illustrates how much trust he developed with me. I shared a lot of details with him about how I was doing that I would never have done with anyone. I trusted him. I knew he had a genuine interest in me. He wasn't looking for gossip. He wasn't looking to break a story. He wasn't looking for the details of a huge investigation. We talked a lot about what my path would be. He was interested in ESPN getting the first interview and in doing his job. He was also interested in my family and in my well being. He was as much my advisor that day as he was a reporter calling to see about an interview.

He could simultaneously support me in what I was going through while also standing firm that sign-stealing had no place in the game. It bothered him that it stained the game, and it was a topic that too many people were investing a lot of time digging up ugliness within the game. He loved baseball so much, he hated what had happened, but I felt like he had empathy. He understood what I went through without even being in the clubhouse with me.

"How bad is it going to get?" I asked him. "How difficult a situation is this going to be?"

He was very straightforward with me, and I think emotionally that made me more attached to him. This was the hottest topic in the game, he warned me, and it was going to be super-emotional for a lot of people. He gave me one of the best pieces of advice I've had, which was that I needed to take responsibility. He told me: *AJ, the only way that people are going to forgive you is if you forgive yourself and then you show yourself to them.*

We'd just lost Game 7 of the World Series. The manager takes it the hardest, and bears the brunt of the criticism, which is fine. The heaviness of the sign-stealing situation just took a lot out of me. Pedro's empathy helped fill my tank back up. He was genuinely sad for me and that was a morale-booster, just a reminder that not everybody is rooting against you and celebrating your downfall. He kept telling me baseball needs me back in the game.

Then he followed up with an article for ESPN.com in December 2020 when I got the job in Detroit with the headline HOW AJ HINCH AND THE DETROIT TIGERS NEED EACH OTHER TO GET BACK ON TOP IN MLB. He talked to my boss, Al Avila, about the old-school connection he and I have.

"Within minutes of Hinch finishing his suspension on the night the Dodgers dispatched the Rays in the World Series, Avila had him on the phone, enticing him to fly to Detroit for an interview," Pedro wrote. "Hinch was on a flight the next morning. One day later, he agreed to become the Tigers' thirty-ninth manager." And he quoted me on Al saying: "I know he believes in me, and that was important to me."

After Pedro died, I read that story again, and it was hard. He was such a transformational person in the sports industry. If you polled all the managers in the game, they'd all tell you Pedro made a huge impact. I know for me he was the guy you wanted to see. When you came out on the field in the World Series, and you walked out of the tunnel, and you'd been pulled in every single direction, you'd gone and done this interview, talked to your team, had a coaches meeting, your GM has come down, maybe the commissioner's office people have come in, and you walked out on the field for BP with hundreds of people around the batting tunnel, on the warning track, if you saw Pedro Gomez, you stopped for that moment of normalcy amongst all the chaos to check in and say hello. He would squeeze in a story about Rio. He would ask about your family. Then he would ask if you were enjoying it all, flashing that smile, and you'd answer.

It hits you how certain people in your life and in the sport can have such impact, and then they're gone. It's made a lot of us take a deeper dive into how we can be a little bit better at some of the small things Pedro did that made us all feel really good.

Pedro and Charlie, 2007

ALL FRIENDS ARE BEST FRIENDS

BY KEITH OLBERMANN

The business of being a "best friend" implies an element of exclusivity.

Unless you do it right.

Unless you do it the way Pedro did it.

He always treated me as if I were his best friend, and as is testified to by the outpouring of grief at his passing, and by this book itself, I was anything but alone. There were certainly dozens of us. There were probably hundreds.

I also have no recollection of how our friendship built to that level. Because here, too, Pedro dispensed with unnecessary delays and forms. I thus have no historical milestones to even confirm *when* we met. My clear memory—and it is the clear memory of everybody I communicated with after he was taken from us—is that as soon as some beachhead of comity was established, he moved immediately to trusting you with his confidences, his uncertainties, his life. I imagine if you didn't live up to a certain standard (or if somehow he didn't) the beachhead was retreated from. I have yet to hear of that having happened with him.

It was a singular way to live a life. It really should be a model for— well, for the world.

I have eight years' worth of Pedro's texts in my phone and eleven years' worth of Pedro's emails in my laptop. They are all collegial, commiserative, even conspiratorial. Because he was emphatically dedicated to the truth rather than the scoop, he constantly sent me stuff he stumbled across that *he* couldn't report, but maybe I could. If I had attributed any of them to him—or even if I had lost my phone, or mistakenly forwarded his emails—it could have gotten him in trouble at ESPN. This not only didn't faze him, but he would follow up these secrets with texts to make sure I got the theoretically dangerous emails. He sent these when he worked for ESPN and I didn't. He sent them when we both worked there. He sent them after I left. He sent them after I got back.

Trust. Trust. Trust.

Then there was all the personal stuff. If somebody I didn't like, or he didn't like, or we didn't like, made a fool of himself, in would come the Pedro Gomez email with the cut-and-paste or the link. A good sidebar story that might have fit somewhere into my show on MSNBC or the one on ESPN2 or GQ or SportsCenter? In would come the Pedro Gomez text. A compliment about me? A text, an email, and another text.

I look at his messages and they describe most of my life for the last dozen years. Politics. Bad World Cup refereeing. Nominations for "Worst Person In The World." Nomination for "Worst Person In The *Sports* World." The passing of a sportswriting legend from New York. The passing of a sportswriting legend from Boston. An owner mocking a reporter who was being carried out of a stadium by EMTs. Why Mark McGwire was a historical comparison for Charles Van Doren. Fox News mistaking the NCAA for the NAACP. How his son was doing in the minors. More politics. How he noticed my name was written on the wall near the press elevator at Dodger Stadium. Fabulous typos on Twitter. Some off-the-record stuff from players that might improve the live shot he heard I was doing from Yankee Stadium that night. Me leaving MSNBC. Even more politics. Me rejoining ESPN. Me re-rejoining ESPN. Covid spikes. Shows we liked on ESPN. Shows we didn't like on ESPN. A book about the election I might want to write for...

For context, you must understand something: We only worked together for a total of five years. I don't think we were on the same broadcast more than ten times. I don't think we were in the same place at the same time more than a dozen times in our lives. Didn't matter. I doubt he conceived it this way, but to Pedro, all friends were best friends.

Gomez-Kettmann fiftieth birthday party in Santa Cruz:
Pedro with Bud, Lefty, Jenks, Z and Kristin

In February, 2019, I was anchoring SportsCenter the day Oakland A's spring training opened and their top minor-league prospect Kyler Murray was supposed to report. Instead, Murray bailed out, that day, to pursue his career as an NFL quarterback. You can't spell "Astonished" without "A's" and that they were such was underscored by a prop Pedro used in his report on the show I was anchoring. Murray was listed on the first official A's spring training roster handed out by the club that morning. The team made sure the stack of printouts then vanished as quickly as Murray did. As a memorabilia collector who has since 1967 walked the tightrope of becoming a hoarder, I answered Pedro on the air by telling him that even if they had all been shredded, he *had to* get me one of those roster sheets with Murray on it.

It arrived the next day by FedEx and, no, ESPN didn't pay for the shipping. He did.

Some men look at the world and ask what they can get out of it. I don't know if he planned it this way or it was something deep in his psyche or it just happened, but Pedro looked at the world and asked what he could do that day to help his best friends. And we were *all* his best friends.

"I know the '21' is for the year, but Pedro would have insisted it was for Clemente. These tributes have been wonderful. Nothing like the first week of the baseball season and the Godfather movies showing on a constant loop to remind me how badly I miss him."

—T.J. Quinn

ABOUT THE CONTRIBUTORS

STEVE KETTMANN, author of *One Day at Fenway* and *Baseball Maverick,* edited the Roger Angell collection *Game Time* and co-wrote the *NYT* bestsellers *Juiced* (Jose Canseco) and *Play Hungry* (Pete Rose).

FRANK MARTIN, head coach of the University of South Carolina men's basketball team, was the 2017 recipient of the Jim Phelan National Coach of the Year Award.

Washington Post sportswriter **DAVE SHEININ'S** many awards include the Dan Jenkins Medal for Excellence in Sportswriting. In 2018 he released *First Thing Tomorrow*, an album of original pop/rock songs.

ESPN Senior Writer **TIM KEOWN**, a former *San Francisco Chronicle* columnist, is the author of *Skyline* and the co-author of three *NYT* bestsellers, including *Bad As I Wanna Be* with Dennis Rodman.

BRUCE JENKINS has been a *San Francisco Chronicle* sports columnist since 1989. His books include *Goodbye: In Search of Gordon Jenkins* and *Shop Around: Growing Up With Motown in a Sinatra Household.*

Former *Washington Post* sportswriter **RACHEL NICHOLS**, described by *Sports Illustrated* as "the country's most impactful and prominent female sports journalist," is host of ESPN's *The Jump.*

MARK KREIDLER, a former sportswriter for the *San Diego Union*, the *Sacramento Bee* and ESPN, is the author of *The Voodoo Wave* and *Four Days to Glory.*

Washington Nationals pitcher **MAX SCHERZER** won the 2019 World Series with the Nationals. A seven-time All-Star, he has won the Cy Young Award three times and pitched two no-hitters.

Eight-time Emmy Award winner **BOB LEY**, a longtime SportsCenter anchor and host of "Outside the Lines," was with ESPN from 1979 to his retirement in 2019.

Before joining ESPN in 2003, **PEDRO GOMEZ** was a sportswriter for the *Miami News,* the *San Diego Union,* the *San Jose Mercury News,* the *Miami Herald,* the *Sacramento Bee* and the *Arizona Republic.*

Former *Boston Globe* columnist **PETER GAMMONS** was honored at the Baseball Hall of Fame as the 2004 recipient of the Spink Award, and was a baseball analyst on ESPN for twenty years.

ESPN Senior Writer **HOWARD BRYANT**, a regular on NPR's Weekend Edition, is the author of nine books and a two-time Casey Award winner for best baseball book of the year.

MIKE BARNICLE, an award-winning former columnist for the *Boston Globe*, *New York Daily News* and *Boston Herald*, is a regular contributor on MSNBC's "Morning Joe."

Former *San Francisco Chronicle* sportswriter **BRIAN MURPHY** has been a co-host of "The Murph and Mac Show" on KNBR-AM (680) in San Francisco since 2004.

CHELSEA JANES is the *Washington Post's* national baseball writer. She was Washington Nationals beat writer for the paper from 2014 to 2018, and covered the 2020 presidential campaign.

Houston Astros manager **DUSTY BAKER,** author of *Kiss the Sky: My Weekend in Monterey for the Greatest Rock Concert Ever,* is the only manager ever to lead five different teams to the playoffs.

ROB KING is ESPN's Senior Vice President and Editor-at-Large ESPN content. Before joining ESPN in 2004, he was deputy managing editor of the *Philadelphia Inquirer.*

RIO GOMEZ, a Boston Red Sox pick in the thirty-sixth round of the 2017 draft, is a left-handed pitcher. He is the oldest son of Pedro Gomez.

Former *Los Angeles Times* baseball writer **ROSS NEWHAN** was honored at the Baseball Hall of Fame as the 2004 recipient of the Spink Award.

JON DANIELS is the Texas Rangers' President of Baseball Operations. When the Rangers first hired him as general manager in 2005 at age twenty-eight, he was the youngest GM in baseball history.

KEN ROSENTHAL, a Fox Sports field reporter for Major League Baseball, is a Senior Baseball Writer for The Athletic.

BUSTER OLNEY, a former New York Yankees beat writer for *The New York Times*, is a regular analyst on ESPN's "Baseball Tonight" and hosts the Baseball Tonight daily podcast.

Emmy Award-winner **SHELLEY M. SMITH**, a former sportswriter for the *San Francisco Examiner* and *Sports Illustrated*, has been an ESPN correspondent since 1993.

T.J. QUINN, a former baseball beat writer for the *Daily Southtown* in Chicago and *The New York Daily News*, has been an investigative reporter for ESPN since 2007.

SCOTT BORAS, a former minor-league player in the St. Louis Cardinals and Chicago Cubs organizations, was dubbed by *Forbes* "the most powerful sports agent in the world."

SANDY ALDERSON is president of the New York Mets. He was general manager of the Oakland A's teams that reached the World Series three straight years and won in 1989.

DAN SHAUGHNESSY, a longtime *Boston Globe* baseball writer and columnist, was honored at the Baseball Hall of Fame as the 2016 recipient of the Spink Award.

MIKE SWANSON is the Kansas City Royals' Vice President of Communications and Broadcasting. He's worked in baseball forty-three years.

ROBIN CARR is a Senior PR Counselor at Landis Communications in San Francisco. Previously she worked for the San Francisco Giants, Nike, EA Sports, Gap Inc.

Chicago White Sox manager **TONY LA RUSSA** has led his teams to three World Series titles. Third all-time in wins by a manager, in 2014 he was inducted into the Baseball Hall of Fame.

JASON LA CANFORA is a former ball writer who has covered the NFL for CBS Sports the last ten years and talks Orioles year-round afternoons on 105.7 The Fan in Baltimore.

RAY RATTO, a staff writer for Defector, talks sports afternoons on 95.7 The Game in the San Francisco Bay Area. He's a former *San Francisco Chronicle* sports columnist.

RON WASHINGTON is third base coach for the Atlanta Braves. He managed the Texas Rangers to the World Series in 2010 and 2011.

CHUCK CULPEPPER is a *Washington Post* sportswriter. He is the author of *Bloody Confused: A Clueless American Sportswriter Seeks Solace in English Soccer*.

TRACY RINGOLSBY, a former president of the Baseball Writers' Association of America, was honored at the Baseball Hall of Fame as the 2005 recipient of the Spink Award.

BUD BLACK is the manager of the Colorado Rockies. Previously he managed the San Diego Padres from 2007 to 2015, and was 2010 National League Manager of the Year.

TIM KURKJIAN is a baseball analyst on ESPN's SportsCenter and "Baseball Tonight." His most recent book is *I'm Fascinated by Sacrifice Flies: Inside the Game We All Love*.

JACK CURRY, a former New York Yankees beat writer and national baseball writer for *The New York Times*, has worked as Yankees analyst on the YES Network since 2010.

MICHAEL ZAGARIS has been team photographer for the San Francisco 49ers since 1973 and for the Oakland A's since 1981. He made his name shooting rock and roll in the 1970s.

CNN contributor **PAUL BEGALA** served as Counselor to the President in the Clinton White House. His latest book (2020) is *You're Fired: The Perfect Guide to Beating Donald Trump*.

Sports photographer **BRAD MANGIN**'s clients include *Sports Illustrated*. Pedro Gomez wrote the foreword to his book *Instant Baseball: The Baseball Instagrams of Brad Mangin*.

Eleven-time Emmy Award winner **JEREMY SCHAAP** of ESPN authored the NYT bestseller *Cinderella Man: James J. Braddock, Max Baer, and the Greatest Upset in Boxing History.*

Former *Kansas City Star* baseball writer **JEFF PASSAN** is an ESPN baseball columnist and author of *The Arm: Inside the Billion-Dollar Mystery of the Most Valuable Commodity in Sports.*

BOB MELVIN has been Oakland A's manager since 2011, making him the longest-tenured manager in baseball. He previously managed the Seattle Mariners and Arizona Diamondbacks.

SCOTT OSTLER, a *San Francisco Chronicle* sports columnist since 1991, has been voted California Sportswriter of the Year thirteen times.

GEORGE A. KING III ("the King," to Pedro) was New York Yankees beat writer for the *New York Post* from 1997 to 2020.

TERRY FRANCONA is manager of the Cleveland Indians. In 2004 he managed the Boston Red Sox to their first World Series championship since 1918.

DERRICK GOOLD, a former president of the Baseball Writers' Association of America, covers the Cardinals for the *St. Louis Post-Dispatch.*

ALEX COFFEY covers the Oakland A's for The Athletic. Previously she covered the Seattle Storm for The Athletic. Her father is bestselling author Wayne Coffey.

SEAN MCADAM, a columnist for the Boston Sports Journal, has covered the Boston Red Sox for more than thirty years. His Delta Tau Chi name is ... he has no Delta Tau Chi name.

BRIAN SNITKER has been manager of the Atlanta Braves since 2016. Before that he spent fifteen years managing in the Braves' minor-league system.

BRETT KURLAND is the Director of Strategic Initiatives and Sports Programs and a Professor of Practice at the Walter Cronkite School of Journalism and Mass Communications at Arizona State University.

ALDEN GONZALEZ, previously a Los Angeles Angels beat writer for MLB.com, is a Los Angeles-based multimedia reporter for ESPN.

SARINA MORALES, a former SportsCenter anchor, covers the Los Angeles Rams as team reporter.

Sacramento Bee metro columnist **MARCOS BRETÓN**, a former baseball writer, is the author of *Away Games: The Life and Times of a Latin Baseball Player.*

JOHN D'ANNA is a senior reporter at the *Arizona Republic*, where his jobs over twenty-five years have included Page 1 editor, deputy managing editor and public editor.

STEVE FAINARU, a Senior Writer for ESPN, won the Pulitzer Prize for his reporting on the Iraq War as a *Washington Post* foreign correspondent. His books include *The Duke of Havana.*

ORLANDO "EL DUQUE" HERNANDEZ, a former pitcher for Industriales in Cuba, won World Series championships with the Yankees in 1998, 1999 and 2000 and with the White Sox in 2005.

DANTE GOMEZ is Pedro Gomez's second son. He'd love a chance to pursue a career in sports analysis and broadcasting.

BUD GERACIE, a former *San Jose Mercury News* A's beat writer and columnist, is Executive Sports Editor of the Bay Area News Group.

DENNIS ECKERSLEY, a Cy Young Award winner as Oakland A's closer, was inducted into the Hall of Fame in 2005. He's a NESN color commentator for Boston Red Sox games.

AJ HINCH is manager of the Detroit Tigers. He managed the Houston Astros to a World Series championship in 2017.

KEITH OLBERMANN, a regular host on ESPN's SportsCenter as recently as 2020, hosted "Countdown With Keith Olbermann" on MSNBC from 2003 to 2011.

PHOTO CREDITS

Brad Mangin: 12, 14 (bottom), 20 (2), 26 (bottom), 40 (2), 58 (top), 76, 78 (2), 84, 94 (2), 110 (bottom), 118 (2), 124 (top), 134 (bottom), 140 (bottom), 150 (bottom), 156 (bottom), 168 (2), 188 (top), 200 (top), 204 (2), 246 (bottom), 248, 249, 252, 254, 268 (top), 282 (top), 300 (bottom), 308 (2), 332, 334, 341, 346 (bottom), 349, 352 (2), 368, 372 (2), 378 (2), 389

Michael Zagaris: 6 (bottom), 26 (top), 64 (bottom), 68, 114 (bottom), 130 (bottom), 140 (top), 146 (top), 170, 172, 192 , 220, 227, 230 (2), 232, 236, 238, 239, 268 (bottom), 272 (bottom), 294 (bottom), 296, 314 (bottom), 364 (bottom), 374, 376, 377, 408

Osvaldo Salas/National Baseball Hall of Fame and Museum: 282 (bottom), 286; **Hy Peskin/National Baseball Hall of Fame and Museum:** 382; **National Baseball Hall of Fame and Museum:** 284, 380; **Kim Komenich:** 182 (2); **Dennis Desprois:** 234; **José Luis Villegas:** 330 (2), 390; **Peter DaSilva:** 405; **Scott Clarke/ESPN:** 54 (top), 58 (bottom), 70 (bottom), 124 (bottom), 188 (bottom), 240 (top); **Phil Ellsworth/ESPN:** XXX (bottom); **Joe Gosen:** 250; **Shmuel Thayer:** 403; **Charles Wenzelberg:** 276 (bottom); **Eric Risberg/AP:** 30, Back endpaper; **Rick Swig:** 54 (bottom); **Chis Gruener:** 246 (top); **Courtesy Sandi Gomez**: Front endpaper, IV (2), V, XXIII, XXIV, 104 (top), 146 (bottom), 171 (2), 194 (bottom), 216 (bottom), 221, 256 (bottom), 356 (top), 359, 386 (bottom); **Courtesy Rio Gomez:** 104 (bottom), 262 (bottom), 278; **Courtesy Dante Gomez:** 360; **Pedro Gomez:** IV (2), 288 (top), 364 (top); **Courtesy Pedro Gomez:** XXVI, 176 (bottom), 338 (bottom); **Dustin Morse:** 391; **Steve Kettmann:** VI (middle); **Courtesy Steve Kettmann:** VI (top), VI (bottom); **Courtesy Rob King:** 100 (2); **Courtesy Laura Ramos:** 356 (bottom); **Courtesy Bob Lee:** 46 (2); **Courtesy Chelsea Janes:** 86 (2); **Courtesy Scott Ostler:** 272 (top); **Courtesy Keith Olbermann:** 386 (top); **Courtesy Steve Fainaru:** 346 (top); **Courtesy John D' Anna:** 338 (top); **Courtesy Alden Gonzalez:** 320 (2); **Courtesy Sarina Morales:** 324 (2), 326, 327, 328; **Courtesy Brett Kurland:** 314 (top); **Courtesy Sean McAdam:** 300 (top); **Courtesy Alex Coffey:** 294 (top); **Derrick Goold:** 288 (bottom); **Courtesy Jack Curry:** 216 (top); **Courtesy Jeff Passan:** 262 (top); **Courtesy Mike Bauer:** 276 (top); **Courtesy Jeremy Schaap:** 256 (top); **Courtesy Tim Kurkjian:** 208 (2); **Courtesy Paul Begala:** 240 (bottom); **Courtesy Tracy Ringolsby:** 200 (bottom); **Courtesy Chuck Culpepper:** 194 (top); **Courtesy Robin Carr:** 162 (2); **Courtesy Jason La Canfora:** 176 (top); **Courtesy Ross Newhan:** 110 (top); **Courtesy Jon Daniels:** 114 (top); **Courtesy Mike Swanson:** 156 (top); **Courtesy Shelley M. Smith:** 130 (top); **Courtesy T.J. Quinn:** 134 (top); **Courtesy Dan Shaughnessy:** 150 (top); **Courtesy Frank Martin:** XXX (top); **Courtesy Dave Sheinin:** 6 (top), 32 (bottom); **Jeff Fisher:** 14 (top); **Courtesy Mark Kreidler:** 32 (top); **Courtesy Ryan Kreidler:** 38; **Courtesy Howard Bryant:** 64 (top); **Courtesy Mike Barnicle:** 70 (top); **Keith Rendel:** 222; **Courtesy Alexis Bernardireis:** 298, 299

PEDRO GOMEZ FOUNDATION

Profits from every purchase of this book will benefit the Pedro Gomez Foundation, which was created by Nikki Baloch and Micah Kinsler for the Gomez family to honor Pedro's legacy in sports journalism. Currently all donations are being directed to undergraduate students completing a degree in Sports Journalism at the Walter Cronkite School of Journalism and Mass Communication at Arizona State University. Donations, which are tax deductible, can be made directly: **https://tinyurl.com/pedrogomez**

Longer term, the Gomez Foundation looks to expand its scope and offer a range of programs and initiatives to further the Pedro Gomez legacy, reflecting his passions—for baseball and journalism and beyond.

To give directly to the Pedro Gomez Foundation, send checks to:

The Pedro Gomez Foundation
P.O. Box 93872
Phoenix, AZ 85070

ABOUT WELLSTONE BOOKS

Wellstone Books is the publishing arm of the Wellstone Center in the Redwoods—**www.wellstoneredwoods.org**—a small writers' retreat center in Northern California founded in 2012 by Sarah Ringler and Steve Kettmann. WCR offers writing residencies, fellowships and three-month resident internships for aspiring writers, and hosts periodic Author Talk events with writers like Mary Roach, Cara Black, Jonathan Franzen and Viet Thanh Nguyen. Wellstone Books does not accept unsolicited manuscripts, but we are always looking for writers who are familiar with our publishing philosophy and want to work with us to develop future projects. Interested writers, or journalists in search of review copies or author availability, write to: **steve@wellstoneredwoods.org.**

ACKNOWLEDGEMENTS

Thanks first of all to Sandi Gomez and the Gomez family for offering their immediate support for this project and helping us in countless ways, from their unflagging patience in digging up pictures at our request to having both Rio and Dante take part as contributors. For anyone who was there at the Salt River Fields stadium in Scottsdale six days after Pedro's death and heard Dante, Sierra, Rio and Sandi all standing up to speak about Pedro, the admiration and respect—and awe—for this family runs deep.

On behalf of Sandi and the family, warm gratitude to Nikki Baloch and Micah Kinsler for their invaluable help in quickly setting up the Pedro Gomez Foundation Fund to support students at the Walter Cronkite School of Journalism and Mass Communications at Arizona State University.

Brad Mangin, one of Pedro's favorite photographers, dove into the work of being picture editor for this book, as well as contributing an essay, and his incredible creativity and passion, working closely with crack designer Alicia Feltman (Lala Design), gives the book's interior its distinctive look. Alicia is an amazing combination of unflaggingly creative and talented, and

Brad Mangin and Michael Zagaris

easy to work with; every book she designs feels special. Thanks as well to artist Mark Ulriksen, whose work has often appeared on the cover of *The New Yorker*, for once again gracing a Wellstone Books cover with original art. Pedro loved Mark's covers for our Dusty Baker book *Kiss the Sky*, our Bruce Jenkins book *Shop Around* and our Ken Korach book *Holy Toledo!* Talking about Mark's combination of passion, wit and style would usually get Pedro reminiscing about nights spent at Elaine's in New York.

Also a special thanks to the Z-Man, Michael Zagaris, whose iconic rock-and-roll pictures (check out the Debbie Harry shot!) add so much to the book, and add so much to his essay on hanging with the Stones and how Pedro saw himself as a Stones guy. Pedro loved and respected Z, but most of all, he loved hanging with him. For Pedro, Z was on a certain high plane of exalted figures, along with heart-of-gold A's equipment manager Steve Vucinich, retiring after the 2021 season after one of the more remarkable lives in baseball ever recorded. So glad Alex Coffey was able to include quotes on Pedro from Vuc, along with a great Z shot.

For helping us line up pictures for the book, and giving us permission, we'd like to thank: ESPN photographers Scott Clarke and Phil Ellsworth, John Horne from the National Baseball Hall of Fame and Museum, Maxx Wolfson of Getty Images, Kim Komenich, Eric Risberg, Rick Swig, Shmuel Thaler and José Luis Villegas.

We can't thank every single contributor, and yet, yes: We thank every single contributor. Profoundly. With undying gratitude. So many, like Paul Begala, responded to a call by instantly declaring they were in. "It would be an honor—an *honor!*" Paul said emphatically. He was not alone. Some, like Howard Bryant, Bud Geracie and Keith Olbermann, were too hurt, too leveled, to get a handle on writing anything, and yet, write they did. Jason La Canfora and Ken Rosenthal were both amazing in writing beautifully and quickly and offering help whenever asked. Rachel Nichols, a friend going back to late nights in Nagano in '98, was modest and gracious—and nailed it. Bob Ley was a friend of the project in every sense; he flew out to Arizona for the private memorial at Salt River and offered sage advice—and timely one-liners—at every turn. Warm gratitude to Dennis Eckersley and Max Scherzer, of course, and especially to the seven active big-league managers who found a way to squeeze this project into busy schedules: Dusty Baker, Bud Black, Terry Francona, AJ Hinch, Bob Melvin, Tony La Russa, Brian Snitker. Also a shout-out to Scott Boras and his team, led by

Rachel Viglietta, for getting behind the project. And undying gratitude to Roy Eisenhardt for his friendship, counsel and support.

So many deserve thanks for advice and ideas on finding contributors, including the remarkable Glenn Stout. Paul Begala suggested Mike Barnicle, who in turn had other suggestions. Steve Fainaru and Ken Rosenthal helped in gathering material, and Bob Bradley and Philipp Abresch were, alas, left on the cutting-room floor. Heartfelt apologies to anyone whose contributions, in a time of foggy recall, go unacknowledged here.

Rob King has been with ESPN since 2004, but deep down he's a print guy, having worked his way up at the *Louisville Courier-Journal* and *Philadelphia Inquirer*. Thanks, Rob, for the bracing honesty that ended up giving the book its title—and its deeper inspiration—and thanks for your help in getting out the word on Pedro's legacy as conveyed in this book. Bob Ley was an incredible resource, and an inspiration. You, sir, are a Wilbury!

To everyone at Publishers Group West/Ingram Content Group,, from Angela Maclean and Gillie Collins to all the sales reps who jumped on this drop-in title like a loose fumble, our deep gratitude. Aaron Hobbs of Ingram lives in Denver and often heard Pedro on Sports Radio 104.3 The Fan Denver. He was literally the first person to hear the idea for this project, and he was effusive in his encouragement and support, polite enough not to bring up how insane a challenge it would be. Thanks, Aaron, for your heart, your passion. You truly are KGB.

So many people offered their support in a challenging time, but special thanks go to Kurt Aguilar, Pete Danko, David Davis, Bonnie Ford and Michael Shapiro for reading different versions of the manuscript. Their sharp eye and editorial guidance were invaluable. Robin Carr and Jay Alves came up huge in helping us reach out to people. Thanks to Joe Genovese of Goat Jerseys and the *San Jose Mercury News* library for research help. T.J. Quinn—Teaneck, in Pedro-speak—cast off post-Covid lethargy and brain fog to write an astonishing essay and lent vital support. This was a Teaneck-Berlin-Ahwatukee project from the get-go.

Finally, thanks to all those who have supported the Wellstone Center in the Redwoods as a small institution trying to inspire a few people, especially our resident interns, most recently Charlie Gleason and Alaina Joleen. It's Sarah Ringler who gives so much of herself to make this center possible and to support all-consuming projects like this book. Good thing she loved Pedro, too.

ALSO AVAILABLE FROM WELLSTONE BOOKS

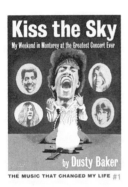

Kiss the Sky: My Weekend in Monterey at the Greatest Concert Ever

BY DUSTY BAKER

For his eighteenth birthday, Dusty Baker's mother gave him a great present: Two tickets to the Monterey Pop Festival of June 1967, a three-day event featuring more than thirty bands, and use of the family station wagon for the weekend so young Dusty could drive down from Sacramento to the Monterey Bay. He was another young person, trying to take it all in, sleeping on the beach with his buddy, having the time of his life soaking up the vibe and every different musical style represented there. Baker's lifelong love of music was set in motion, his wide-ranging, eclectic tastes, everything from country to hip-hop. He also caught the Jimi Hendrix Experience, who put on such a show that to this day Baker calls Hendrix the most exciting performer he's ever seen. He went on to years of friendship with musicians from B.B. King and John Lee Hooker to Elvin Bishop. This account grabs a reader from page one and never lets up.

"At its best, the book evokes not only the pleasure of music, but the connection between that experience and the joy of sports," NewYorker.com writes.

"Reading *Kiss the Sky* is like having a deep conversation with Dusty Baker—about baseball, fathers and sons, race, culture, family, religion, politics—and always music," says Joan Walsh of MSNBC. "He doesn't sugarcoat anything, but he makes you feel good about being alive nonetheless."

#1 in Wellstone Books' "Music That Changed My Life" series.